Strategic Communications Planning

For Effective Public Relations and Marketing
Fifth Edition

Laurie J. Wilson, APR, Fellow PRSA
Brigham Young University

Joseph D. Ogden
Brigham Young University

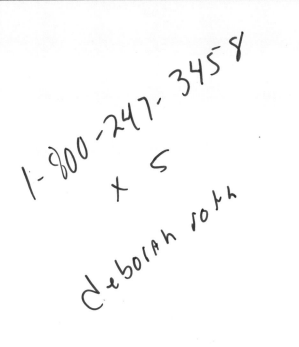

KENDALL/HUNT PUBLISHING COMPANY
4050 Westmark Drive   Dubuque, Iowa 52002

Book Team

Chairman and Chief Executive Officer   Mark C. Falb
President and Chief Operating Officer   Chad M. Chandlee
Vice President, Higher Education   David L. Tart
Director of National Book Program   Paul B. Carty
Editorial Development Manager   Georgia Botsford
Senior Developmental Editor   Tina Bower
Assistant Vice President, Production Services   Christine E. O'Brien
Senior Project Coordinator   Angela Puls
Permissions Editor   Colleen Zelinsky
Cover Designer   Jenifer Chapman

All Shutterstock images used under license from Shutterstock, Inc.

Contents

"Tips from the Pros"

Preface

The last edition of this text was prompted by "the staggering rate of technological innovation." If we were staggering then, we've now stumbled headlong. When I sat down to write this text to use in my classroom at BYU over a decade ago, I'd never even heard of "social media." If you had asked me to define it, I'd have probably said it was the music at the high school's Friday night dance. Now I am recommending students and graduates take seminars in measuring social media. And while most people still don't consider it truly credible, that hasn't slowed usage a bit. In fact, for many, this source of questionable credibility is now the only source of information they access.

At the time of the fourth edition, our business community was in crisis. For the first time since public relations was established as a corporate function, unprecedented numbers of corporate executives began to recognize the necessity of establishing and maintaining long-term relationships with key organizational publics. This crisis of trust and reputation finally demonstrated the direct bottom-line contribution of good public relations and marketing. With relationship building, all organizational publics became a key focus—communication began to be an integrated function, whether for the purpose of advertising and marketing, human resources, or public relations.

Now business has begun to emerge from the trust crisis and, hopefully, will retain the lessons learned. Research emphasizes the continual need of organizations to build trust and demonstrate social responsibility. Perhaps the growth of the Internet and social media will actually have a positive effect on organizational relationships. In an environment where we don't control access to information or even our message very well, the organization may be forced to be more authentic. That authenticity will mean better communication and stronger relationships. And it will certainly make our jobs a lot easier. Nevertheless, in this uncertain communications environment, we need all the help we can get. For this reason, we have included in this edition a new feature: Tips from the Professionals. Each chapter features advice from a recognized practitioner whose long experience can teach us how to deal with the issues we now face.

Strategic Communications Planning Matrix

While the communications environment has dramatically changed, the basic principles of public relations and communication upon which the Strategic Communications Planning Matrix was built have not changed. The planning process outlined in the matrix is as viable as ever and, in fact, has become an even more crucial tool. It provides the framework to integrate solid research to drive the establishment of objectives, the selection of key organizational publics, the design of messages to those publics, and the use of channels and tools to deliver those messages. The Strategic Communications Planning Matrix, developed nearly two decades ago by the faculty at BYU, is a systematic, analytical model expanding the four-step public relations process—research, action planning, communication, and evaluation (RACE)—to a step-by-step research-based communications planning and programming tool. It has been proven—in education and industry alike—to be a valuable analytical problem-solving tool enabling the integration of information and translation of knowledge into sound communications practice. One of the key advantages of the Strategic Communications Planning Matrix continues to be that it links research to problem-solving action.

Goal of the Text

As in the other editions of this text, it is assumed that the reader already has a basic foundation in, and understanding of, communication and persuasion principles. The goal of this text is not to present the principles, concepts, and skills taught elsewhere. For added detail on specific topics, readers are referred to supporting references at the end of each chapter. The goal of this text is to synthesize information and provide a methodology to successfully apply it in an integrated communications environment. The Strategic Communications Planning Matrix is that methodological tool.

This strategic approach to communication planning and implementation must be appropriately placed in the overall context of long-term, relationship-based communication.

Chapter 1 addresses building relationships of trust with our publics and presents some of the latest trends. It elevates relationship building to equal status with strategic planning and shows its application across all organizational communication.

Chapter 2 reviews the principles of public information, public opinion, and persuasion, and it discusses the ethical basis for an organization's communication within society. With this foundation laid, we can proceed to integrate the principles, concepts, and skills of communications using the Strategic Communications Planning Matrix.

Chapter 3 discusses the methodologies of communication research and the diverse sources of information.

Chapter 4 demonstrates how data gained through research is effectively used in planning and implementing communication.

Chapter 5 turns our attention to setting the goals and objectives to accomplish any task or challenge set before us.

Chapter 6 helps us understand and select those publics that are key to an organization's success and to develop the messages to build trust-based relationships with those publics necessary to our success.

Chapter 7 discusses the design of strategies and tactics to deliver messages and facilitate two-way communication with the organization's publics.

Chapter 8 demonstrates effective calendaring and budgeting.

Chapter 9 provides tips for effective implementation of our strategic communications plan.

Chapter 10 focuses on what has been the very elusive methodology of evaluation and measurement of the effect of communications.

Chapter 11 provides tips for executive summaries and for giving business presentations.

Chapter 12 addresses the importance of ethics and professionalism in effective communication.

The text concludes with a teaching case and sample campaign plan, found in Appendix A, that illustrates the effective use of the Strategic Communications Planning Matrix outlined throughout the text.

Appendix B provides copy outlines for various communications tools, including some new outlines for social media, and Appendix C contains the professional codes of ethics from the Public Relations Society of America, the American Marketing Association, and the American Advertising Federation.

Although not the only approach to systematic and analytical communications problem solving, the Strategic Communications Planning Matrix is a highly effective and proven tool. The matrix approach provides a sound methodology for students and professionals alike to ensure communications planning is driven by research and analysis to reach and build relationships of trust with critical publics. The matrix also ensures the use of effective messages and delivery channels to meet an organization's communications challenges and opportunities.

New to This Edition

The changing communication environment in our society requires some new and updated information and approaches to public relations and marketing. This new edition features:

- Updated and new data regarding trust in our society—who has it and how we get it—including the public's most trusted sources of information.
- New content on the rise of social media and its impact on communication and public relations in our society.
- Updated examples including a new teaching case that focuses on nonprofit fundraising.
- Tips in each chapter relating best practices from seasoned practitioners on the front lines.
- Revised and updated copy outlines including new outlines for social media.

Acknowledgments

In the 13 years since the first edition of this book was published, the Strategic Communications Planning Matrix has proven to be not only a valuable professional tool but also an invaluable teaching tool. The matrix provides a structure for effective communications that inherently teaches analytical skills that are too often missing from education today. For our success, we owe a great debt to those who first conceived "the matrix" as it has come to be known by students and practitioners across the country. And we owe thanks to many graduates of our program who have made suggestions and lent their skills in editing and designing past editions.

Still, we acknowledge that without the foresight of those original Brigham Young University (BYU) faculty members, the Strategic Communications Planning Matrix would not exist. Lacking an analytical tool for students to use in solving public relations problems within the RACE—research, action planning, communication, and evaluation—model, they collaborated on a process that specifically outlined the type of research needed and how that research and its subsequent analysis should direct the planning and communication steps. Bruce Olsen, APR, Fellow PRSA, came up with the original tool with input from Ray Beckham and Brad Hainsworth. Dr. Beckham then initiated the use of the copy outlines for specific communication products resulting from matrix planning. In the early 1990s, Larry Macfarlane and I refined and further developed the matrix and JoAnn Valenti refined the copy outlines.

For the last edition, Joseph and I streamlined the matrix and enhanced applicability across all communication functions. Joseph has further refined the copy outlines based on his use of them in his function at the Marriott School of Management. In serving this large school, any communication materials prepared by the school or outsource professionals begin with a copy outline. This process has resulted in highly effective and award-winning communications materials. We acknowledge the efforts of Will Jensen and Chad Little in helping develop new copy outlines for this edition.

For this edition, we gratefully acknowledge the contributions of senior practitioners from across the nation whose advice and counsel is found in every chapter. We appreciate their time and efforts to share their experience and wisdom about this dynamic and uncertain communications environment.

While the authors bear sole responsibility for the content and any inaccuracies, this book expounds a solid strategic planning approach which owes much to the contributions and suggestions of professionals, faculty, and students across the nation. Nevertheless, the matrix and copy outlines were born of a desire on the part of those original BYU professors to excel in preparing their students for successful careers in public relations. The publication of this new edition is a credit to their dedication to students and to the profession. I gratefully recognize their initial work and their continued support and mentorship.

As the Strategic Communications Planning Matrix evolves and moves into a new era of communication, we salute those who first had the vision to create the process.

Laurie J. Wilson
Sandy, Utah

About the Authors

Laurie J. Wilson is an award-winning professor of communications at Brigham Young University. In 2001, she was named the Public Relations Society of America Outstanding Educator. In 1990, she was recognized as the Public Relations Student Society of America Outstanding Faculty Advisor. Five years later, she was inducted into the PRSSA Hall of Fame. She also received the Karl G. Maeser Teaching Award and three Student Alumni Association Excellence in Teaching Awards from BYU.

Wilson received her Ph.D. from The American University in Washington, D.C. After working in public relations and marketing for several years, she joined the BYU faculty in 1989 where she has served as chair of the Communications Department and of the public relations program. She was recently reappointed to a second term as BYU's director of internships, a half-time administrative position for the university.

Wilson recently served as co-chair of a PRSA task force on internship standards. She has served as national chair for a number of education initiatives in PRSA, has served in the Public Relations Division of the Association for Education in Journalism and Mass Communication and served on the diversity task force of the Association of Schools of Journalism and Mass Communication. She serves on site teams accrediting communications programs for the Accrediting Council for Education in Journalism and Mass Communication and certifying schools in public relations education (CEPR) for PRSA. She is on the editorial board for the Journal of Public Relations Research and the Journal of Promotion Management.

Wilson's areas of expertise, research, and publication include strategic planning and issue management, corporate social responsibility, and building community partnerships. She consults regularly in those areas. In addition to this book, Wilson has co-authored two other communication books. She also serves as a member of the Executive Board of the United Way of Utah County.

Joseph D. Ogden is assistant dean at Brigham Young University's Marriott School of Management, an internationally ranked business school. His areas of expertise include persuasive writing, media relations, strategic planning, and marketing. Ogden has taught introduction to public relations, PR case studies, and advanced media writing courses for BYU's Department of Communications and served as a member of the department's national advisory board. He has also taught international business and directed the undergraduate management study abroad to Asia in 2007.

Before coming to BYU, Ogden worked as corporate communications director for a nearly $1 billion-a-year personal care and nutrition products company. He was the company's spokesperson, oversaw public relations and marketing in Asia, and managed investor communications for the publicly traded firm.

In 1996, he founded JDO Consulting, a strategic marketing and PR firm. The firm has worked with a wide range of clients including a candidate for U.S. Congress, a music retailer, and a New Jersey-based Chinese Internet service provider.

Ogden earned his MBA from the Marriott School and his BA in communications with a minor in music from Brigham Young University.

Trust and the Relationship-Building Approach to Communication

"Trust is the most basic element of social contact—the great intangible at the heart of truly long-term success."

—Al Golin

40-year veteran of the public relations industry and founder of Golin/Harris International

LEARNING IMPERATIVES

- **To understand that an organization's survival is dependent upon establishing trust among key publics**

- **To understand the characteristics of a relationship-building approach to organizational communications**

- **To be introduced to the Strategic Communications Planning Matrix as a tool for planning and implementing organizational communication**

TRUST IN CORPORATE AMERICA

As we turned a new century, corporate America discovered through sad experience that trust was the primary issue of concern. In fact, it had always been the primary issue. Now, nearly a decade into the new century, with aggressive relationship-building strategies, business seems to be recovering somewhat. But it took the events of the early part of this century—9/11 and its effect on the economy; the demise of Enron, Worldcom, Arthur Andersen, and others; the security brokers' scandal; mismanagement by mutual fund managers; and many other similar events—for all sectors of our economy to finally realize that trust among an organization's publics is the single most important factor in organizational survival.

In a crisis of trust, organizations looked to professional communicators for counsel on rebuilding relationships with the publics upon whom their survival depended. Finally, the top tier of executives in all kinds of organizations recognized the need for an integrated approach to communication to build—or rebuild—relationships key to the organization's success.

Al Golin, a respected senior public relations professional, writes about his decades-long career as a counselor to chief executive officers (CEOs) of major corporations intimately involved in building relationships with all organizational publics in his book *Trust or Consequences* (2004). He asserts that trust is the key element of strong relationships that ensure organizational success in the long run. Mr. Golin's success with CEOs has been mixed. Many, like Ray Kroc of McDonald's, have followed his advice, making regular deposits in the *trust bank* and reaping significant benefits over the long-term. Others have disregarded his counsel in favor of short-term gains, leaving them ill-prepared and at risk when crises hit.

Trust

An emotional judgment of one's credibility and performance on issues of importance.

Trust in Mass Media

Recent research shows trust in business is rebounding. For the last eight years, Edelman Worldwide has conducted an annual global survey of public trust in institutions, government, and information sources. The trend for growing trust in business is encouraging (Figure 1.1), but the decline in trust of media institutions paints a disappointing picture. While business magazines led the 2007 Edelman Trust Barometer as the most credible source of information about a company, the credibility of traditional mass media is dropping: newspapers at 37% (down from 44%), radio news at 39% (down from 48%), and television news at 35% (down from 38%).

Trust in CEOs

Further, only 22% of respondents trust CEOs. Employees are actually more trusted sources of information than CEOs. In fact, the most trusted source of information now is a peer, or *a person like me*. These data have huge implications for communicating with today's publics. It would seem formal and informal opinion leaders are more important than ever before. And while the

Tips from the Pros

Who Do You Trust?

Richard Edelman, CEO of Edelman Worldwide, which for the last eight years has published the Edelman Trust Barometer—an annual survey of more than 3,000 opinion leaders in 18 countries to measure trust in institutions, companies, and sources of information—tips you off on who's most trusted.

Knowing who people turn to for information is invaluable to you as a PR practitioner. Over the years, the Edelman Trust Barometer has recorded a dispersion of trust away from authority figures. Trust in employees is, for example, significantly higher than trust in CEOs. Here are some of the most significant trends from the 2007 Edelman Trust Barometer.

Business is more trusted than either government or media in every region of the globe. In the United States, 53% of respondents report trusting business, which marks an all-time high for the survey. This is a recovery from a low of 44% in 2002, which came in the wake of the Enron and WorldCom debacles. Business is seeing a rebound in trust because of strong economic growth, visible consequences for executive malfeasance, and success in solving problems facing society.

"A person like me" is the most trusted spokesperson across the European Union, North America, and Latin America. In Asia, it is second to physicians. For the second consecutive year, "a person like me" or a peer is the most trusted spokesperson in the United States at 51%. A peer is tied with doctors as the most trusted messenger across the big three economies of Europe, at 45%.

Trust in non-governmental organizations (NGOs) is rising while trust in government and media is falling. In the 2007 survey, NGOs are either the most credible institution or tied for the most credible institution in 10 of 18 countries. This puts NGOs even with business, which also leads or ties for most trusted in seven of 18 countries. Trust in government and the media continue to decline.

Traditional media is still stronger than new media. Mainstream media sources such as newspapers, TV, and radio remain more credible than new media sources such as a company's own Web site and blogs.

Social responsibility is more important than ever. Trailing only "providing quality products or services," undertaking "socially responsible activities" is seen as the most important action an organization can do to build trust. "Socially responsible activities" surpassed providing "a fair price for products or services," "attentiveness to customers," and "good labor relations" in most markets.

Figure 1.1—Top Annual Findings of the Edelman Trust Barometer

2001   Rising influence of NGOs and increased need for corporate social responsibility linked to business goals.

2002   NGOs approach parity in credibility with business and government; end of era of celebrity CEO as trust in business wanes.

2003   Stories in editorial media more credible than advertising by 8:1 margin.

2004   Trust in business and government regaining strength.

2005   Trust in established institutions and figure of authority shifting to peers.

2006   "A person like me" most credible spokesperson; trust in employees significantly higher than in CEOs.

2007   Business more trusted than media and government.

Note: CEO=chief executive officer; NGO=non-governmental organization. From Edelman Worldwide (2007). Edelman Trust Barometer, retrieved October 16, 2007, from http://www.edelman.com/trust/2007.

Internet still has low credibility among respondents, the explosion in use of social media, particularly in forming networks of *peers*, portends a transformation in the communications landscape. Make no mistake, effective communication with our publics is crucial to building and maintaining relationships. Trust is established only when it becomes an organizational value tied to honesty and openness—a value that permeates the entire organization from the highest paid top executives through the lowest paid support and service people. It is an effort that integrates all of the organization's communications functions—internal and external.

THE EVOLVING ROLE OF PUBLIC RELATIONS

Public Relations

An organization's efforts to establish and maintain mutually beneficial relationships in order to communicate and cooperate with the publics upon whom long-term success depends.

Fortunately, because we have been researching and preaching relationship building for years, public relations scholars and practitioners know how to integrate efforts to do what needs to be done. Rather than being fragmented by public as organizational functions have been in the past, we can integrate our approach to all of the publics for the organization to thrive over the long term. The roots of trust-based relationship building are in the literature and practice of public relations.

When public relations emerged from the journalism profession as press representation for corporations in the early 1900s, the public relations counselor was positioned as a key adviser to the CEO. Over time, we lost that status to attorneys and accountants because we were unable to demonstrate a concrete contribution to the bottom line. Even when business entered an era of keen market competition for products and services where communication played a primary role in sales, classic public relationship building was seen as unimportant.

Regaining a Strategic Role

In the last two decades, public relations professionals have been waging a battle to regain a strategic role. Part of that effort is a strong emphasis on research and evaluation to justify communication efforts in terms of their specific benefit to the organizational mission. Another emerging value to organizations is the ability of communicators to manage issues that have affected the organization's focus on its primary business. And corporate management is recognizing the ability of communicators to manage certain organizational issues that do not respond to traditional economic and business principles and practices (Wilson, 1996; Wilson, 1994a, 1994b). As a result of the crisis of trust, we have finally demonstrated the bottom-line contribution of building strong relationships with publics. And we have justified our argument that ultimate organizational survival may depend upon building relationships over the long term.

WHAT DOES IT MEAN TO BE A *STRATEGIC* FUNCTION?

In this chapter, we introduce the strategic planning process that drives the tactical decisions made by communications professionals. But first, we must understand what it means to be a strategic function.

Very simply, strategy is a well-coordinated approach to reaching an overall goal. It may be helpful to draw an analogy to military strategy. In a given battle, the overall goal may be to secure a certain piece of ground or a particular town. The strategy is the coordinated effort of all participants to achieve that goal. When an organization sets a particular goal in support of its mission, strategy serves to integrate the efforts of all departments to achieve the goal. Communications is strategic when it aids in formulating the organization's approach to accomplishing overall goals and then supports those efforts in a coordinated and consistent manner, working in concert with all other organizational entities.

Functioning effectively in that role requires solid research with results that drive decision making. It requires vision or a long-term rather than short-term mentality. Strategic functioning necessitates a broad perspective of the organizational environment and all contributing members. It demands incisive understanding of the organizational mission and the goals that directly support the accomplishment of that mission. Finally, strategic functioning means that the communications and marketing efforts are driven by an understanding of the organization and where communications fits and coordinates with all other organizational functions. Strategic managers are:

- Analytical
- Pragmatic
- Visionary
- Discerning

Strategic Function

One that contributes significantly to the accomplishment of an organization's mission and goals.

what does strategic function have to do w/ PR?

THE DEVELOPMENT OF COMMUNICATIONS AND PUBLIC RELATIONS FUNCTIONS IN BUSINESS ORGANIZATIONS

Business organizations began giving serious attention to communication with publics in the early 1900s. Journalists began serving as press agents and publicists for major corporations such as Ford Motors and AT&T. By mid-century, public relations practitioners were organizational counselors, who responded to traditional American business management practices by manipulating the organization's environment, often in ways that might now be considered ethically questionable. By the 1960s, conflicts over issues important to key organizational publics gave birth to crisis management as a function of the organization's communicators. Rather than just reacting to crises, good managers began to anticipate problems and mediate them before they could affect the organization's environment and profitability, and issue management was born as a long-term approach to identifying and resolving issues.

Issue Management

The very concept of issue management fit well into traditional American business management techniques which were based almost entirely on economic principles. Nevertheless, there was obvious conflict between the long-term nature of issue management and the short-term profit orientation of American business management. Further, there was a more critical conflict between the self-interested rather than public-interested approach of American business communications and the publics who were beginning to demand accountability.

Strategic Management

In spite of the conflict, issue management techniques became popular in business communications practice and gave birth to the role of communication in strategic management, which evaluates all proposed action through a focus on organizational goals, usually defined in short-term contributions to the bottom line. Even though issues must be identified years in advance to be effectively mediated, as depicted in Hainsworth's issue cycle (1990), the purpose is to save the organization future difficulty, not to address the needs of organizational publics because they are intrinsically valued. This focus in communication brought us squarely into the camp of purely economically based, rationalist business management.

Rationalist Management

It is not surprising that the organizational communications ended up here. Throughout its history, public relations and business communications have consistently moved away from a *relations* orientation. Even with all of our technological advances, we have been slow to recognize the limitations of mass communication and mass media. We resisted a shift from using mass media to more targeted media, which means we have not been accessing appropriate message channels to reach many of our publics. Some of us still tend to see

Crisis Management

The process of anticipating and mediating problems that could affect an organization's environment and profitability.

Issue Management

A long-term approach to identifying and resolving issues before they become problems or crises.

Strategic Management

The process of evaluating all proposed actions by focusing on organizational goals, usually defined in short-term contributions to the bottom line.

publics as an inert mass, hypnotized by mass media, mindlessly absorbing our messages, and acting on them. The latest research should finally disabuse us of these outdated notions, if we will pay attention to it.

Shift to Relationship Building

Partially as a reaction to the economic (bottom line) orientation of strategic management and partially as a result of international trends in business, some scholars in the 1990s attempted to shift our emphasis in public relations to relationship building, particularly those in the critical school (Creedon, 1991; Kruckeberg and Starck, 1988; Wilson, 1996, 2001; Ledingham and Bruning, 2000). They have returned to the roots of human communication and persuasion in devising approaches that build more personal relationships based on trust and cooperation, viewing segmented and personalized communication as more viable approaches to publics than mass communication.

Relationship Building

A return to the roots of human communication and persuasion that focuses on personal trust and mutual cooperation.

SOCIETAL TRENDS AFFECTING THE PRACTICE OF BUSINESS, COMMUNICATIONS, AND PUBLIC RELATIONS

Five trends in society should have led us to our roots in communication and relationships long ago.

1. Increasingly segmented publics require alternatives to traditional media channels for the dissemination of messages. In fact, our study of audience has indicated that even within the groups segmented by demographics and psychographics, we find smaller segments which have been labeled interpretive communities (Lindloff, 1988) because of differences among them in the ways they receive, interpret, and act upon messages. These shared interest groups are evidenced now in the user communities fostered through Internet channels, particularly social media.

2. Dramatically escalating social problems that no longer affect only fringe or marginalized groups in society. The productivity of the workforce of corporate America is seriously jeopardized by problems affecting families such as drug abuse, physical abuse, gangs, teen pregnancy, and the declining quality of education. When such problems begin to affect the workforce—as they do now—they threaten the profit potential of the organization and must be addressed.

3. An increased reliance on organizational communicators to establish relationships with publics to mediate issues. The business environment has become increasingly burdened with social issues and problems that corporations have failed to control using traditional management techniques. Companies are forming alliances with communities, government, and special interest groups to address societal problems. These actions are ostensibly in the name of

© John Keith, 2008.

social responsibility, but a more accurate justification of the establishment of cooperative efforts is probably that corporations have been unable to solve those problems unilaterally.

4. Business entities face a more knowledgeable and business-savvy public that demands corporate commitment of resources to solve the problems affecting the community, employees, and their families. In fact, some would say that the public understands just enough about the operation of business to be dangerous. They are aware of corporate profits (although not always cognizant of net profits versus gross revenues) and apply pressure for organizations to use their resources in socially responsible ways.

5. The public's control over access to information. Whereas more limited channels of mass media place control in the organization, today's consumer has more personal control over what information they receive. Withholding information in today's technological society is virtually impossible. Controlling information or the "spin" on information is also unlikely when publics have multiple sources from which to secure information. This makes misinformation and disinformation from external sources a significant concern for organizations. Building trust-based relationships with publics is the only approach that results in sustained credibility.

Essentially, then, we in communications and marketing must think of our publics in terms of strategic communities. Wilson (1996, 2001) contends we must approach our publics as strategic cooperative communities, focusing on relationship-based interaction among all members of a community to achieve individual and collective goals.

Misinformation

Information that is unintentionally inaccurate or misleading.

Disinformation

Information that is intentionally inaccurate or misleading.

Strategic Cooperative Communities

Relationship-based interaction among all members of a community to achieve individual and collective goals.

BUILDING RELATIONSHIPS WITH PUBLICS

From the synthesis of the business-based strategic management approach to public relations and the strategic cooperative communities model, five characteristics emerge to typify organizations operating within this style of management.

1. Long-range vision. Rather than selecting key publics and critical issues by their immediate effect on the organization, companies identify all potential organizational publics and systematically establish relationships. They are using their relationships to identify the issues that will be critical in the next century, not just the next decade. They have a respect for people and work toward a consensus for action.

2. Commitment to community, not just to profit. Companies involved in the community are often led by a CEO who is personally committed to charitable work. Commitment at this high level gives the organization's community involvement strength and integrity because it is based on a sincere desire to serve rather than to manipulate for the sake of profit alone. It is understood that what is good for or improves the community almost always benefits the company as well.

3. **Importance of people.** Underlying this community commitment is an organizational value orientation emphasizing the importance of people. Progressive policies and initiatives based on trust of and respect for employees are usually evidence of a people-first orientation. Human dignity is highly valued and policies and procedures are designed accordingly.

4. **Cooperative problem solving.** The company values employees who will work together to solve problems. Employees are given the latitude to design and implement solutions within their work areas, relying on management to provide an overall vision. In such an environment, employees are not afraid to make a mistake because management understands that mistakes are indicative of an effort to progressively solve problems.

5. **Relationships based on respect and trust.** Lastly, such organizations build relationships with all of their publics based on mutual respect, trust, and human dignity, not just on self-interested gain. These relationships engender an environment in which community members seek solutions where all participants win. The community begins to look out for the best interests of the organization because it is in the community's best interest for the organization to thrive.

Relationships with an organization's publics are based on critical values that have little to do with profit motivation. The values of service, respect, and concern for community are at the base of the relationships we establish with people. Whether we build a relationship with an individual, or with an individual representing an organization, does not change the fact that the strength of the association is determined by the salience of shared values that place a priority on people.

It is important to note that durable relationships are not created out of rationalist, bottom-line business management techniques. They are created and strengthened through mutual trust, respect, cooperation, and benefit. Trust of a community actor is based on honest communication and cooperation. Trust is a prerequisite of cooperative relationships as well as a tangible result.

How do you build relationships w/ your public

Planning Initiatives

Given this framework for approaching integrated organizational communications within an overarching scheme of relationships cultivated with all publics, we can now turn to planning initiatives to solve specific challenges or take advantage of emerging opportunities. Now that we have established a strategic role for communications in developing relationships, or cooperative communities, we are able to implement the strategic communications planning that will accomplish specific objectives and is targeted at publics immediately important to the organization. If we have worked to identify and assess our strategic relationships, the selection of key publics for any particular communication or marketing effort will be simplified and much more accurate. We have less chance of omitting a critical public and we know more about all of our publics so part of our research is already done. We are also better

Strategic Communications Planning

An approach to communications planning that focuses actions on the accomplishment of organizational goals.

prepared to send messages because our relationships with organizational publics have been maintained and strengthened in our overall approach to marketing and communication.

RACE Model

A strategic, analytical approach to an organization's communication is absolutely requisite. Public relations has used the four-step RACE model—research, action planning, communications, and evaluation—but making that a true analytical process, so that each step is determined by the information acquired and decisions made in previous steps, is a challenge. Incorporating feedback during implementation and making needed alterations to ensure success is even more difficult. We are finally doing the kinds of research and measurement that can help us make wise decisions. But doing so requires a framework for applying what we have learned in the research.

It is not enough to discover the attitudes, values, and beliefs of a segmented demographic public; we must interpret those in terms of the issue or problem at hand and predict behavior. Determining that a public's self-interest regarding a certain issue is the health and welfare of its children is of no use unless we then formulate messages that emphasize the health and welfare of the public's children. Identifying certain targeted media as the best channels to deliver messages to a segmented public does us no good if we then shotgun the message through mass media anyway.

The Strategic Communications Planning Matrix

The Strategic Communications Planning Matrix (Figure 1.2) was developed by the faculty at Brigham Young University. It was designed to direct problem solving analytically, making research-based decisions in each step of communication planning and implementation. The matrix is the tool we use throughout this book to support the strategic communications planning process. The process begins with the identification of a problem or opportunity that sets the stage for background research and a situation analysis based on the research. It outlines additional research necessary for decision making that will take place in the planning and implementation processes.

The planning process then starts with setting a goal that directly resolves the identified challenge. This goal may or may not be a tangible measurable outcome. You next move forward to determine objectives—specific and measurable outcomes—that will ensure the accomplishment of the goal. Based on research, key publics are selected, messages determined, and strategies and tactics designed to send those messages. Calendaring, budgeting, and evaluation are also addressed in a strategic way, using research as the foundation for decisions in each step.

The Strategic Communications Planning Matrix enables professionals in communication and marketing to address problems and issues of concern to organizations in a strategic way, in concert with the overall organizational goals and objectives. It is enhanced by the understanding of how

Analytical Process

A process in which action in each step is determined by the information acquired and decisions made in previous steps.

Research-based

Decision making in the planning and implementation process that is based on the acquisition, interpretation, and application of relevant facts.

each organizational public forms a strategic relationship. Planning is simplified because of the nature and direction of the cooperative relationships already established. Implementation is made easier because of established channels of interaction and publics' predisposition within cooperative communities to give heed to the organization's messages.

Summary

The world business community is just beginning to rebound from a crisis of trust. The crisis was precipitated by neglecting the relationships that are key to our success. We neglected those relationships because we were so focused on short-term profit measures that we were unable to see the necessity of strong, trust-based relationships as crucial to long-term survival.

In the past few years, public relations scholars and communication professionals have been struggling to return the practice of the organization's communication to its strategic role and function. Recognizing that we evolved away from, rather than toward, the strategic counseling role we should be serving, we have examined our roots in communication as well as current trends in business, society, and technology.

Essentially, we are now in a better position than ever in terms of functioning in our role as builders of relationships strategic to the organization. We must systematically track the status of those relationships to ensure appropriate allocation of resources over the long term. Within the context of those relationships, we can more effectively use traditional analytical and strategic planning to solve organizational problems. The Strategic Communications Planning Matrix provides the tool to approach all communications problems, challenges, and opportunities within the trust-based relationship framework of today's successful organizations.

Exercises

1. Discuss the corporations in your community and the national and international issues they have become active in resolving. Why do you think they selected those particular issues to address?

2. Select one or two corporations actively doing business in your locality. Imagine yourself in the position of the corporate communications counselor and identify the strategic relationships of those organizations and assess the status of those relationships.

Figure 1.2 10-Step Strategic Communications

Research

Steps One, Two, and Three—Background, Situation Analysis, Core Problem/Opportunity

1. Background

Planning begins with a synthesis of primary and secondary research providing background information on the industry, external environment, product or program, market situation, and current trends in opinions and attitudes. The background section also uses demographic and psychographic data to identify and profile potential publics that may be affected by the problem/opportunity, or could aid in its resolution/accomplishment. Intervening publics and available resources are also identified.

2. Situation Analysis

The situation analysis consists of two paragraphs. The first paragraph is a statement of the current situation and a description of the challenge or opportunity based on research. The second paragraph identifies potential difficulties and related problems.

3. Core Problem/Opportunity

The core problem/opportunity is a one-sentence statement of the main difficulty or prospect—including potential consequences if not resolved or realized.

Action Planning

Step Four—Goals and Objectives

Goal

The goal is a one-sentence statement of the end to be achieved to resolve the core problem or seize a significant opportunity. The goal does not have to be stated in quantifiable terms.

Objectives

Objectives are numbered or bulleted statements of specific results that will lead to the achievement of the goal. Objectives must be specific, measurable, attainable, time-bound, and mission-driven.

Step Five—Key Publics and Messages

Key Publics

Key publics include a description of each audience that must be reached to achieve the goal and objectives. Five elements should be identified for each public or audience:

1. Demographic and psychographic profile
2. Motivating self-interests
3. Status of current relationship with the organization and issue
4. Third party influentials and other opinion leaders
5. What objectives each public will help you accomplish

Messages

Messages are public-specific and appeal to the public's self-interests. They are designed as primary and secondary. Primary messages are one- or two-sentence summary statements similar to sound bites. Secondary messages are bulleted details that add credibility to and support the primary messages with facts, testimonials, examples, and other information and persuasive arguments.

Planning Matrix

Step Six—Strategies and Tactics

Strategies
: Strategies identify approaches to send messages to each public through specific channels in order to motivate action. Multiple strategies may be required for each public.

Tactics
: Tactics are communications tools and tasks required to support each strategy. Each strategy is supported by a number of tactics designed to convey key messages to a specific public through the communications channel outlined in the strategy.

Steps Seven and Eight—Calendar and Budget

7. Calendar
: Calendaring should be done with a time-task matrix (such as a Gantt chart) used to plan and strategically time implementation. The calendar should be organized by public and strategy with scheduling for each tactic.

8. Budget
: Budgets should also be organized by public and strategy. The budget projects the specific cost of each tactic. It should also indicate where costs will be offset by donations or sponsorships. Subtotals should be provided for each strategy and public.

Communication

Step Nine—Communication Confirmation

9. Communication Confirmation
: The communication confirmation table confirms the logic of the plan by converting it into short statements for each public in tabular form. This format (see below) aids in checking strategies and tactics to make sure they are appropriate to reach the public, that messages appeal to the public's self-interest, and that the planning for each public meets the objectives.

Key Public	Self-Interests	Primary Messages	Influentials	Objectives	Strategies	Tactics

Evaluation

Step Ten—Evaluation Criteria and Tools

10. Evaluation Criteria and Tools
: Evaluation criteria are the specific measures used to determine the success of each objective. Evaluation tools are the specific methods used to gather the data identified by each criterion. The evaluation tools should be included in the calendar and budget.

References and Additional Readings

Creedon, P. J. (1991). Public relations and 'women's work:' Toward a feminist analysis of public relations roles. *Public Relations Research Annual, 3*, 67–84. Hillsdale, NJ: Lawrence Erlbaum Associates.

Cutlip, S., Center, A., & Broom, G. (2006). *Effective public relations* (9th ed.). Englewood Cliffs, NJ: Prentice-Hall, Inc.

Edelman Worldwide. (2006). Edelman Trust Barometer. Retrieved October 16, 2007, from http://www.edelman.com/trust/2007/prior/2006/full supplement-final.pdf.

Edelman Worldwide. (2007). Edelman Trust Barometer. Retrieved October 16, 2007, from http://www.edelman.com/trust/2007/.

Golin, A. (2004). *Trust or consequences: Build trust today or lose your market tomorrow.* New York: AMACOM.

Grunig, J. E., & Hunt, T. (1984). *Managing public relations.* Fort Worth, Texas: Holt Rinehart & Winston.

Grunig, J. E., & Repper, F. (1992). Strategic management, publics, and issues. In J. E. Grunig (ed.), *Excellence in public relations and communication management* (pp. 117–158). Hillsdale, NJ: Lawrence Erlbaum Associates.

Hainsworth, B. E. (1990). The distribution of advantages and disadvantages. *Public Relations Review, 16:1*, 33–39.

Hainsworth, B. E. & Wilson, L. J. (1992). Strategic program planning. *Public Relations Review, 18:1*, 9–15.

Heath, R. L., & Cousino, K. R. (1990). Issues management: End of first decade progress report. *Public Relations Review, 16:1*, 6–18.

Kruckeberg, D., & Starck, K. (1988). *Public relations and community: A reconstructed theory.* New York: Praeger.

Ledingham, J., & Bruning, S. (2000). *Public relations as relationship management: A relational approach to the study and practice of public relations.* Mahwah, NJ: Lawrence Erlbaum Associates.

Lindloff, T. R. (1988). Media audiences as interpretive communities. In N.J. Anderson (ed.), *Communication Yearbook, 11*, 81–107. Newbury Park, CA: Sage Publications.

Lukaszewski, J. E., & Serie, T. L. (1993). Relationships built on understanding core values. *Waste Age*, March, 83–94.

Newsom, D., Turk, J. V., & Kruckeberg, D. (2007). *This is PR: The realities of public relations* (9th ed.). Belmont, CA: Wadsworth Publishing Company.

Wilcox, D. L., Ault, P. H., & Agee, W. K. (2006). *Public relations: Strategies and tactics* (8th ed.). New York: Harper and Row.

Wilson, L. J. (1994a). Excellent companies and coalition-building among the Fortune 500: A value- and relationship-based theory. *Public Relations Review, 20*, 4.

Wilson, L. J. (1994b). The return to gemeinschaft: Toward a theory of public relations and corporate community relations as relationship-building. In A. F. Alkhafaji (ed.), *Business research yearbook: Global business perspectives,* Vol. I (pp. 135–141). Lanham, MD: International Academy of Business Disciplines and University Press of America.

Wilson, L. J. (1996). Strategic cooperative communities: A synthesis of strategic, issue management, and relationship-building approaches in public relations. In H. M. Culbertson and N. Chen (eds.), *International public relations: A comparative analysis.* Hillsdale, NJ: Lawrence Erlbaum Associates.

Wilson, L. J. (2001). Relationships within communities: Public relations for the next century. In R. Heath (ed.), *Handbook of public relations* (pp. 521–526). Newbury Park, CA: Sage Publications.

Public Information and Persuasive Communication

"Public sentiment is everything. With public sentiment, nothing can fail; without it, nothing can succeed."

—Abraham Lincoln
16th President of the United States

LEARNING IMPERATIVES

- To understand the role of public opinion and its impact on successful communication with an organization's publics

- To understand the principles underlying persuasion and how to use them to change behavior

- To understand the legitimate role of advocacy in a free market economy and the ethical standards that apply to persuasive communication

As communications professionals, we are in the public information and persuasion business. The ethical basis of marketing and public relations is in advocacy. We play a critical role in a democratic society with a free marketplace of ideas and a free market economy as we provide information and advocate products, services, or issues honestly, responsibly, and in accordance with public and consumer interest. That advocacy is a crucial public service that allows people to make informed decisions for their lives.

Because we are engaged in public information and persuasion, what we do is inextricably tied to public opinion. What publics think and believe directly affects how they behave. As we established in Chapter 1, an organization that ignores public opinion simply will not build sufficient trust to survive in today's society. Although this text is not designed to be a comprehensive treatment of the theories and models of public opinion and persuasion, understanding some of the basic principles identified in that literature is necessary for effective advocacy. Here we mention and synthesize relevant ideas. Nevertheless, because our circumstances and our actions are so shaped by the force of this phenomenon, we should understand what public opinion is, how it is formed, who influences it, and how we deal with it.

Public Opinion

What most people in a particular public express about an issue that affects them.

PUBLIC OPINION

Behavior: The Ultimate Objective

As important as public opinion is, the savvy communications professional will always remember that behavior is the final evaluation. According to practitioner Larry Newman, in public relations we are ultimately trying to get people to:

* Do something we want them to do.
* Not do something we don't want them to do.
* Let us do something we want to do.

© 2008 JupiterImages Corporation

Figure 2.1—Pat Jackson's Behavioral Public Relations Model

Awareness → Latent Readiness to Act → Triggering Event → Behavior

Knowing what our publics think is only useful insofar as it leads us to accurately predict what they will do. Even when we simply disseminate information in the public interest, we do so with some behavioral expectation in mind. We must determine what behavior we are trying to influence and then lay the groundwork to get there. Pat Jackson (1990) developed the Behavioral Public Relations Model (Figure 2.1) that is equally applicable to all motivational communication efforts.

The awareness stage is the communication process itself. Publicity, advertising, publications, and other communication tools help to create awareness and reinforcement. They should be designed to tie the message into people's existing perceptions and attitudes, or to adjust those attitudes if necessary. Awareness efforts must be based on quality research to determine the attitudes and perceptions that are the foundation for a certain public's behavior or potential behavior. From this awareness, people begin to formulate a readiness to act according to their attitudes and the influence of the communication. Action itself requires some kind of triggering event such as an election in a political campaign or a sale at a clothing store. The event thus transforms readiness into actual behavior.

Studies done by James Grunig in the early 1980s concluded that publics can be identified by similarities in their communication behavior, but that the behavioral characteristics that segment them are unrelated to demographics. In his research, he consistently identified four types of situational behavioral publics:

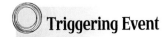

Triggering Event

An event that transforms readiness to act into actual behavior.

1. **all-issue** publics (active on any and all issues)
2. **apathetic** publics (inactive and disinterested)
3. **single-issue** publics (active on one or a few issues)
4. **hot-issue** publics (bandwagon jumpers)

The notion that publics coalesce and emerge from situations is an important one, particularly as we deal with crisis communication and management. Psychographics may be of more help in profiling publics than demographics, but even psychographics may be of limited worth when segmenting publics by issue.

As we will see in the next several chapters, behavior is the ultimate objective. The Strategic Communications Planning Matrix leads us through the steps to motivate behavior. It helps to determine which publics we need to

What do you need to know about Public opinion + behavior

target and what messages will shape their latent readiness to act. It also aids in designing the specific strategies and tactics to deliver those messages and to provide the triggering event. And, it helps us use opinion leaders or a public's *influentials* in the persuasion process.

What Is Public Opinion?

Before we address motivating behavior, let's first investigate the communication process beginning with what people think and how opinions and attitudes translate to behavior. Extensive psychological and sociological studies have been done on the phenomenon of public opinion. Its measurement in an attempt to predict behavior has become not only a science but also a highly profitable career track. Most of the descriptions of the phenomenon contain similar elements and can be synthesized into a straightforward definition: Public opinion is the collection of beliefs, attitudes, and opinions expressed by the majority of individuals within a particular group or public about an issue or topic of interest to them.

Let's examine the elements of this definition.

- Public opinion is collective. It is not what just one individual thinks, it is the collection of what several people think.
- Beliefs and ideas must be expressed to be public opinion. Public discussion usually crystallizes opinion into something that can be expressed.
- The opinion must be held by the majority of individuals within the group.
- The opinion is identified with a certain group or public, not the mass or "whoever" is out there. The particular public holding the opinion is identifiable from the mass.
- The opinion is focused on a particular issue or topic.
- The masses are segmented into publics differently from topic to topic. The issue of embryonic stem cell research will create within the mass audience certain public segmentations that will be different than those created by the issue of Palestinian sovereignty in Israel.
- The topic must hold a particular interest to the individuals within the group, or it must involve their self-interest.
- Interest is typically aroused and sustained by events relating to the topic or issue. The stem cell debate heats up as we begin to lose scientists to other nations that have advanced such research. At some point other news takes precedence and attention wanes. But the debate is again fueled when someone famous contracts a disease that could potentially be cured through stem cell research.

Opinion Formation

Because public opinion is a collection of individual opinions, the logical place for us to begin in determining how public opinion is formed is with the individual. A review of the basic models and principles of human communication will aid us in determining how individuals form opinions.

Opinion is basically a thought process. We attach meaning to the world around us based on a collection of our past experience, knowledge, culture, and environment. This collection is often referred to as our frame of reference. It is within this frame of reference that we establish our own personal beliefs, values, and attitudes. All of our thoughts, ideas, and communicative acts are processed through our frame of reference, and no two individual frames of reference are identical. Our frame of reference determines how we perceive or sense our world, and the communication of others directed toward us.

In the mid-1940s, Hadley Cantril proposed 15 laws of public opinion that are still relevant today. Those laws can be synthesized into a few basic observations that serve as guidelines in persuasive communication aimed at shaping public opinion.

- Opinions are more easily influenced by events than words, but opinion changed by events requires subsequent reinforcement.

- Opinion is basically determined by self-interest and persuasion is only effective if it maintains a consistent appeal to self-interest over time. Opinion rooted in self-interest is extremely difficult to change.

- Information is most effective when opinion is in formative stages.

- If people already trust their leaders, they will allow them the opportunity to handle sensitive situations. People trust their leaders' decision making more when they feel they (the people) have had a part in shaping the decision.

- Public opinion is focused more on expected results than in methods to achieve those results. People care more about an outcome than the process to reach the outcome.

Elisabeth Noelle-Neumann (1984) has identified another phenomenon of public opinion we characterize here as the *sleeper effect*. An individual's fear of social rejection or isolation may cause them not to verbalize opinions they perceive to be in the minority. In other words, vocal groups may suppress mainstream or majority opinions because the majority believes itself to be in the minority and, therefore, remains silent. This *spiral of silence* as Noelle-Neumann termed it, or the *silent majority* as former president Richard Nixon called it, is a sleeper factor usually unaccounted for in our research unless we dig for it. Noelle-Neumann identified mass media as an accomplice in the spiral of silence because their own voice may often reflect the minority opinion, but it has become one of the loudest and most dominant voices in the free marketplace of ideas. Once the spiral of silence is broken, however, the silenced opinion flows forth like water from a breached dam. Once people discover that others think as they do, they are no longer silent.

Measuring Public Opinion

Saturday Review/World columnist Charles Frankel said, "Majority opinion is a curious and elusive thing." It is certainly not stable. It changes from moment to moment as circumstances are constantly changing. For that reason alone, any measure of public opinion is never absolutely accurate. The moment the

Frame of Reference

The collection of experiences, knowledge, culture, and environment that forms our perceptual screen.

How do you measure public opinion?

Tips from the Pros

Public Information and Public Opinion

Phil Bussey, Senior Vice President of Corporate Affairs for Puget Sound Energy and the former president of the Washington Roundtable (a group of CEOs from major corporations dedicated to advocacy of business priorities in the public arena) tips you off on informing your publics.

With three decades in the public affairs and public relations business I've learned that within the phrase, "there's a sucker born every minute," lies the temptation and ultimate undoing of all who enter the public information arena with the intent to unethically persuade or mislead publics. Practitioners have a crucial and valued responsibility to inform the public on behalf of the organization. Disseminating factual information in a timely and persuasive manner helps the public make more informed decisions. Our job is not to take advantage of the uninformed, it is to educate them.

Three principles have brought me success in the world of public information and public opinion.

Honesty really is the best policy. The public will tolerate a fool, but not a liar. Don't say it if you can't back it up with evidence or facts. The only thing worse than inaccurate or misleading statements are the retractions or confessions published when they are discovered. You lose not only momentum, but far worse, you lose your credibility.

Speed kills. Getting your message out first "kills" the competition. Most important, it puts you in control. Even with bad news it limits the damage and keeps communication lines open. Remember, bad news doesn't get better with time. To be effective: be first, be fast, and be factual.

Know thy customer. A major problem in dealing with public opinion is that "you don't know what you don't know." Successful practitioners work hard to understand their publics' desires, concerns, and opinions and then to craft their message accordingly. Use every tool available to know your audience and be sure to focus on the grass roots level. Know your customer and you'll know what to say, how to say it, and when to say it.

What is Public Info? [handwritten marginal note]

survey is completed, the interview is concluded or the focus groups are dismissed, the results are dated material.

James Stimson (1991), a well-known scholar in the field of public opinion measurement, contends that most measures are not accurate predictors of behavior because they measure attitudes and opinions in isolation from other members of the social group. He points out that individuals may formulate opinions on issues when approached, but those opinions are altered, refined, and crystallized through discussion and interaction with others. Additionally, people do not behave in isolation; they are part of social systems that strongly influence behavior.

The Coca-Cola Company learned this lesson the hard way when they introduced "New" Coke in 1985 (Schindler, 1992). Taste tests demonstrated a taste preference for the new formula. In opinion surveys, people expressed the belief that if the majority preferred the new formula then Coke should change to it. But a curious phenomenon occurred in the focus groups. When the groups began discussion, participants favored a formula change as they did in the opinion surveys. Then, as some members of the groups began to voice their preference for the old formula, the overriding value of personal choice caused individuals within the focus groups to change their attitudes to support the rights of those who preferred the old formula (either because of taste or out of habit) to purchase it.

Because quantitative opinion surveys were judged to provide more credible data than qualitative research, Coca-Cola trusted them instead of the focus groups, changed the formula and scheduled a phasing out of the old. For the first couple of weeks people accepted the new formula; then the outcry of the masses for the rights of the old Coke loyalists forced the company not only to create "Classic Coke" to leave the old formula on the market but also to eventually scale back its production of New Coke. That is exactly what should have been predicted from observing the focus groups. Opinion surveys that measure opinion and predict behavior in isolation from the group may be inherently flawed. Coke found out that Americans value the right of personal choice more than they value the majority's rule.

Further, the opinion expressed by individuals in a public may reflect a number of realities other than the opinion on that particular issue. The expression may be indicative of party or organizational loyalty, peer group pressure to conform, or a reflection of the opinion of an influential whose judgment the respondent may trust more than his/her own. And, the combination of beliefs and attitudes that are the basis for behavior are far more complex and multidimensional than a singular opinion on a particular topic. Opinions do not necessarily directly lead to behavior; too many other factors, events, and attitudes intervene. Unless the measuring device is carefully designed and implemented, it may not measure the most salient opinion and resultant behavior. The results will be misleading, causing costly strategic errors.

In spite of the difficulties, we must still do our best to measure public attitudes and opinions as a foundation for persuasive efforts. Measurement problems are identified to aid us in designing research that corrects for and minimizes the difficulties, to help us understand and better interpret results, and to design programs that are flexible enough to respond to changing opinion ascertained either through feedback or continuing research. The methods for measuring public attitudes and opinion are described more fully in the next chapter. The most typical are survey research, which yields statistical results, and personal interviews and focus group research, which provide qualitative results.

THE PHENOMENON OF PERCEPTION

Perception is an unpredictable phenomenon, largely because it is so individually determined. Unless you have a solid understanding of an individual's frame of reference, it is impossible to predict how they will perceive an event, experience, or message. In communication we sometimes forget that meaning is in people. Our words and messages do not transfer meaning; they can only invoke images that we hope will carry similar meaning in the minds of others.

In addition to being very individual, perception also carries with it the power of truth. What is perceived by an individual is what they believe to be true. We express this in clichés such as "seeing is believing," but the impact of perception is far greater than we usually realize. Whether or not a perception is accurate has no bearing on its power as truth to the perceiver. When police question witnesses to an event, they get as many different stories as there are observers—each absolutely certain their version is the truth.

Sometimes perception is so intimately tied to an individual's belief and value system that it is difficult, if not impossible, to alter even when it is flawed. Norris calls these *cast-iron* perceptions. Such perceptions are almost impossible to change.

Some perceptions are shared with others in a group and are "preformed." We have already decided how certain things should be and that is the way we perceive them. We call these stereotypes. We often stereotype people (i.e., dumb blondes or computer geeks), but other phenomena can be stereotyped as well (i.e., government is wasteful or political revolution is bad). Stereotypes are often useful in helping us deal with the world around us, but they become dangerous when they prevent us from perceiving things as they really are, and when they create an environment in which people are denied the opportunity to reach their potential.

As public relations professionals, we should also be aware of Klapper's concepts of selective exposure, selective perception, and selective retention. Because of the barrage of stimuli we receive from our environment, including increasing numbers of messages from people trying to persuade us to do something, our perceptual mechanism also works as a screen or a filter to keep us from experiencing overload. We choose the media we pay attention to and those stimuli we want to perceive as well as those we want to retain. This is a critical principle in marketing, advertising, and public relations. Our professions depend on channels to get messages to key publics, but if those publics are electing not to perceive or retain our messages, our efforts are useless.

For example, think about how you read a newspaper. Few people read a newspaper word for word, first page to last. As you flip through the pages, you read headlines or look at pictures to decide which stories you want to read. You do the same with e-mail. You check the sender and the subject and often delete without opening. Individuals selectively perceive far fewer messages than are targeted at them in a given day, and they actually retain even less of the content once those messages have been filtered through the perceptual screen to determine whether or not they are useful. In fact, studies of selective perception in advertising demonstrated that people actually pay more attention to ads and

Selective Perception

The inherent human function of selecting from the millions of daily stimuli only those messages one chooses to perceive.

Selective Retention

The inherent human function of selecting from the hundreds of stimuli perceived only those messages one chooses to retain.

consume more information about a product after they have purchased it than before. Just as agenda setting theory predicts, they are looking for reinforcement of their purchase decision.

Selective perception becomes an even more poignant phenomenon when we consider how new technologies have given the consumer, or public, control over how and if they receive information. As people seek information less from mass media and more from increasingly specialized and segmented sources, we must become more sophisticated in appealing to their self-interests. The uses and gratifications theory identifies three motives for media use:

1. environmental surveillance,
2. environmental diversion, and
3. environmental interaction.

A basic assumption of the theory is that people choose how media will serve them and use media for those purposes.

A problem with this user-driven access to information, and with the Internet in general, is the variable reliability of the information. Now, more than ever, misinformation abounds. Anyone with a story to tell, accurate or not, can post it on the Internet. Blogs, YouTube, Facebook, MySpace—all provide the masses a soapbox for expression. Most people know all online information should be verified for accuracy, but how many actually do that? Just like we typically believe what we read in newspapers, so also do we believe what's online. Except online information is much more suspect than information compiled and fact-checked by journalists.

What all this means for communications professionals is that we must make a greater effort to understand the frames of reference of our key publics, use good research to try to predict how messages and events will be perceived by those publics, and design messages that those publics will select, retain, and act upon. But we must also constantly monitor cyberspace as well as media to find out the information and misinformation reaching our publics and respond accordingly.

© Tan Kian Khoon, 2008.

ATTITUDES, VALUES, AND BELIEFS

Integral to our frame of reference is the value and belief system upon which attitudes are based. One of the best explanations of human behavior and possibly the finest theory on attitude and attitude change was developed by Milton Rokeach. In this theory, beliefs are the fundamental building blocks of attitudes. Rokeach asserted that some beliefs are more central to an individual's cognitive system than others. These core beliefs, or values, are typically well-established and relatively stable. They are very difficult to change because they are most salient to the individual and his/her belief system. They function as "life guides," determining both our daily behavior and our life goals.

Beliefs

Inferences we make about ourselves and the world around us.

Values

Core beliefs or beliefs central to our cognitive system.

Attitudes

Collections of beliefs organized around an issue or event that predispose behavior.

According to Rokeach, collections of beliefs organized around a focal point (like an issue, an event, or a person) constitute an attitude. He identifies two kinds:

1. attitudes toward **objects** and
2. attitudes toward **situations**.

The combination of these two kinds of attitudes will determine an individual's behavior in any given situation. Rokeach uses gardening as an example. The collection of an individual's beliefs—that gardening is fun, that it saves money, that it releases tension, and that it produces beautiful flowers—will result in a favorable attitude toward gardening. Given the absence of intervening attitudes, a person's collection of beliefs and resultant attitudes will motivate their gardening behavior.

For communications professionals to motivate behavior then, requires that they understand and tap into core beliefs and values that shape attitudes. In some cases, we may need to change beliefs and attitudes. Remembering that core beliefs are difficult to change, we may try to tap into a value and base the alteration of peripheral beliefs on that central belief. We may also need to motivate people to change the depth of a belief or value to help us build a foundation for attitude change. At any rate, it is important for us to recognize that people do not do something just because we want them to do it or because we think they should consider it in their self-interest. They behave in their own self-interest according to their own beliefs and attitudes. Changing behavior requires addressing those beliefs and attitudes.

Another set of theories that aids us in understanding how to change attitudes are the balance or cognitive consistency theories. This body of research has found that people are comfortable when their beliefs, attitudes, knowledge, and behaviors are consistent. The presence of conflict among those cognitive elements creates discomfort or dissonance. Leon Festinger contends that when the cognitive elements are in conflict, people tend to reduce or eliminate the dissonance by changing the elements or introducing new elements (like new information).

The classic example is that of a smoker. In today's environment with today's information, smoking behavior potentially causes great dissonance or conflict in the cognitive processes. The smoker will try to reduce the dissonance. One way would be to change one or more of the cognitive elements (like behavior) by stopping smoking. Another way would be to add a new element, like switching to a pipe which is perceived to be less harmful. A third way is to see the cognitive elements as less important than they used to be (i.e., longer life isn't such a desirable belief if I have to give up pleasure to achieve it). A fourth method would be to seek consonant information such as evidence contradicting the health hazard studies. Fifth, you might reduce the conflict among cognitive elements by distorting or misinterpreting (misperceiving) the information available on the ill effects of smoking. Finally, you have the option to flee the situation, or simply refuse to contemplate the conflict thereby avoiding the dissonance.

If we understand these cognitive processes, we are better able to work with people to bring about cognitive consonance. The process of changing the cognitive elements is the process of persuasion. We may conclude that the art of persuasion, to be effective in motivating behavior, must be implemented at the most basic level of public opinion: at the level of individual beliefs and attitudes.

METHODS OF PERSUASION

More often than not in today's environment, public relations engages in disseminating information rather than in persuasion. Knowledge and information are key cognitive elements that help shape attitudes and opinion. Further, public information provides the awareness foundation necessary for persuasion to effectively motivate publics. Nevertheless, sometimes even objective information of benefit to a public must be designed and delivered in such a way as to draw the attention of publics accustomed to filtering out messages to prevent overload. The message itself may not be designed to persuade, but the targeted publics may need to be persuaded to pay attention to the message.

Newsom, Turk, and Kruckeberg (2007) contend that people are motivated to action in three ways:

- **Power** may be legitimate authority, peer group pressure, or informal status.
- **Patronage** is simply paying for the desired behavior either monetarily, in-kind, or by favor.
- **Persuasion** is the method most used by public relations and typically involves information dissemination and appeals to change attitudes and opinions to achieve the desired behavior.

Methods and approaches to persuading typically focus on getting a public to pay attention to a message, accept it, and retain it. Yet persuasive attempts fall short if they do not address motivating behavior. Carl Hovland's Yale Approach suffers from just such a shortfall. His four-step approach addresses persuading people to a particular opinion first through gaining attention; designing the message for comprehension (understanding); creating acceptance through appeal to self-interest; and, finally, ensuring retention through well-organized and presented arguments. Hovland believed attitudes change if you change opinion. But, as we have seen, merely changing opinions is insufficient. Unless attitudes and opinions are changed in such a way that they motivate the behavior we are seeking, we have expended valuable resources (time

Persuasion

Using information and other appeals to motivate a change in attitudes, opinions, and/or behavior.

How to Persuade? methods

© Viktor Pryymachuk, 2008.

and money) to no avail. Behavior change is not only the ultimate measure of success; it provides the reinforcement necessary to retain an attitude change.

The Powerful Influence of Conformity

The group dynamics approach recognizes the powerful influence of conformity. The pressure to be accepted into certain social groups is often a motivator even when attitudes and opinions have not been altered through persuasive communication. The power of opinion leaders and other influentials is a manifestation of this approach.

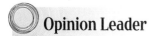

Opinion Leader

A trusted individual to whom one turns for advice because of his/her greater knowledge or experience regarding the issue at hand.

An **opinion leader** is someone we turn to for advice and counsel, typically because he/she has more knowledge or information about the issue in question. We all have a number of opinion leaders in our lives. They may be authority figures of some kind, or they may be our next door neighbors. When you get ready to buy a car, who do you talk to about the best value? Before voting on a local referendum, who do you usually call for information? All of these people are opinion leaders for those particular issues or decisions. Whether their knowledge and information comes from personal experience, special training, extensive reading, or any other source, you trust their judgment.

Studies of opinion leaders show that they are usually heavy consumers of media. In the 1940s, Katz and Lazarsfeld conducted studies of voting behavior that led to their seminal two-step flow theory of opinion leadership. They found that certain individuals within a community search out information from the mass media and other channels and pass it on to their peers. (Subsequent research has altered this hypothesis to a multiple-step flow, finding that the number of relays between the media and the final receiver is variable.) Reaching opinion leaders with media messages is one of the most effective persuasive methods used in public relations today.

As noted in Chapter 1, the most effective opinion leaders now are peers, and the Internet is the great equalizer for peer-to-peer communication. Viral campaigns are a new reality because people trust others who are "just like" them. While the ethics of such campaigns are not yet sorted out, they are already being used with notable success.

However, we still must consider the effect of mass media in persuasion. Agenda-setting theory contends that mass media do not tell people what to think, rather they tell people what to think about. Media set the agenda or determine what is important and, as Lazarsfeld reiterates, they serve to reinforce existing attitudes and opinions. Uses and gratifications theory affirms that people choose the media they pay attention to based on their own purposes. Agenda-setting studies have also shown that people select what they pay attention to for the purpose of reinforcing the decisions they have already made. People who had already purchased a car were the heaviest consumers of car ads. The same phenomenon is true across the board. People choose news channels that project their same political and social opinions. The vast majority of TV and talk radio personality Sean Hannity's listeners are people who agree with his political, social, and economic attitudes. For all of these reasons, media have not traditionally been considered to be capable of changing opinion.

Nevertheless, we live in a changing world where some media personalities seem to have transcended the role of information-giver and agenda-setter; certain commentators and newscasters have obtained a celebrity status and seem to be influential in shaping public opinion. The riots in Los Angeles following the verdict in the Rodney King case in the 1990s are a poignant warning that media (and the 30-second sound bite) may have more power than previously thought in shaping opinion. Although a jury in a trusted judicial system weighed all the available evidence and rendered its conclusion, most of America had already determined guilt based on more limited information provided by newscasters, news magazines, and talk show hosts. As advancing technology exacerbates the isolation of individuals in our publics, media celebrities like Oprah Winfrey, Matt Lauer, and Katie Couric have become increasingly influential.

Successful techniques for influencing opinions are shown in Figure 2.2.

Figure 2.2—Guidelines for Changing Attitudes and Opinions

- When opposite views are presented one after another, the one presented last will probably be more effective.
- Desired opinion change is more likely if you explicitly state your conclusions rather than letting the audience draw its own.
- Analysis of your key public and the message to be sent should determine the persuasive appeal or combination of appeals used.
- A strong threat may be less effective than a mild threat in inducing the desired attitude change.
- Opinions and attitudes are strongly influenced by groups to which a person belongs or wants to belong.
- A person is typically rewarded for conforming to the standards of the group and punished for deviating from them.
- People with the strongest ties to a group are probably the least influenced by messages which conflict with group standards.
- Opinions expressed or shared with others are typically harder to change than opinions held privately.
- Audience participation helps overcome resistance.
- Over time, the effects of a persuasive communication tend to wear off, but repeating a message tends to prolong its influence.
- The people you most want to reach in your target audience are the least likely to be present or to elect to perceive your communication.
- Successful persuasion considers the beliefs and values underlying attitudes as well as attitudes and opinions themselves.
- A highly credible communicator is more likely to persuade opinion change than someone with low credibility; nevertheless, the communicator's credibility is less of a factor over time since people tend to remember ideas longer than they remember sources.
- The communicator's motives affect his/her ability to persuade and motivate.
- A communicator is more effective if he/she expresses some views shared by the audience.
- The audience's opinion of the persuader is often directly influenced by its attitude toward the message.
- The more extreme the opinion change requested the more actual change is likely to result.

Persuasive Appeals

Perhaps the most effective persuasive appeals date back more than two millennia to the philosopher and rhetorician Aristotle. His classic logos (logical argument), pathos (emotional appeal), and ethos (source credibility) are as salient today as they were in ancient Greece. These three appeals constitute the majority of persuasive appeals used in communications, either singly or in combination. To Aristotle's three appeals we should add the appeal to self-interest. One of the most important keys to motivating people is convincing them the desired behavior is in their best interest.

The message itself is a key element of persuasive appeal. It should appeal to an individual's self-interest and use other appropriate appeals based on key public research. Equally as important, the medium or channel for delivery must be carefully selected. The medium must be credible and believable, capable of reaching the target public, and technologically suited to the message itself. For example, television has high credibility and mass viewership, but it is suitable only for short, simple messages. Detailed messages are better conveyed through print and online media.

Robert Cialdini has developed an intriguing persuasion strategy he calls self-persuasion. He identifies five key elements.

1. **Consistency.** Once committed to an opinion, people behave accordingly. And those commitments are reinforced through behavior. Studies show that volunteers serving a cause are much more likely to donate to that cause than those who are not involved.

2. **Reciprocity.** People will actively support something if they feel they owe something to the person or organization inviting their support.

3. **Social validation.** This is the bandwagon effect. People are influenced by others' beliefs and behaviors. Get a lot of people to use a product and everyone thinks they have to have it.

4. **Authority (influentials or opinion leaders).** People follow the advice of someone they trust who has knowledge on the subject.

5. **Scarcity.** People rush to support or obtain something that is disappearing. If the availability is limited, people want to get it before it is gone.

THE ETHICS OF PERSUASION

At the heart of much of the conflict between journalists and marketing, advertising, and public relations professionals is the question of ethical practice. Whereas ethical codes for journalists are based in objectivity, the ethical basis for our communication efforts is in advocacy. That foundation does not make the practice of persuasive communication less ethical. In fact, advocacy is key to the effective functioning of a democratic society and a free market economy.

Because of the influence of marketing, advertising, and public relations in our society, it is of primary importance that persuasive appeals be used in an honest and ethical manner. The Institute for Propaganda Analysis has formulated a list of persuasive appeals designed to mislead (Figure 2.3). Sometimes

Figure 2.3—Persuasive Appeals or Propaganda Devices

Name calling	Giving an idea a label, either good or bad, to encourage the public to accept and praise or reject and condemn the idea without examining evidence.
Glittering generality	Associating something with a *virtue word* that is designed to encourage the public to accept and approve the idea without examining the evidence.
Transfer	Transferring the aura of authority and prestige of a celebrity or opinion leader to a less well-known product, person, or idea to persuade the public to accept or reject it.
Testimonial	Endorsement of a product by someone who actually uses it.
Plain folks	Attempting to convince the public that a speaker's (often a politician's) ideas are good because they are "of the people" or that they are "one of us."
Card stacking	Selective use of facts to tell only one side of the story, often obscuring the other side.
Bandwagon	An appeal to conformity with the majority, this method tries to persuade by encouraging the public to join their friends and neighbors because "everybody's doing it."
Emotional stereotypes	Designed to evoke an emotional image like the "ugly American" or a "PR flack."
Illicit silence	Withholding information that would clarify a situation or correct an incorrect impression or assumption.
Subversive rhetoric	A device frequently used in political campaigns, this appeal involves attacking the spokesperson rather than the idea.

From The Institute for Propaganda Analysis

called *propaganda devices,* these appeals raise the question of the difference between persuasion and propaganda. Some consider persuasion ethical and propaganda unethical because of its attempt to distort or mislead. Others contend they are the same, the judgment of propriety being a matter of perception.

Whereas some of the propaganda devices in Figure 2.3 are clearly unethical, others are used quite ethically in persuasive campaigns. For example, name calling is widely used as labeling an issue or event for ease in reference. A short label reference is selected based on the perception or image it conveys. The same revolutionaries in a Third World nation are alternately considered both terrorists and freedom fighters, depending upon your point of view. The label is consistent with the labeler's perception, not necessarily intended to mislead. To detractors, such a label is considered "propaganda;" to supporters it is an accurate depiction of reality.

In fact, persuasion actually began as propaganda and was not considered "evil" until World War II when Nazi Germany engaged in the practice. In the 17th century, Pope Gregory XV established the College of Propaganda to train priests to proselyte. The United States itself engaged in propaganda efforts in both World Wars, not only directed at the populations of Europe but also at Americans. Perhaps the most reasonable approach to evaluating persuasive methods and appeals is to avoid the persuasion versus propaganda debate and to simply follow ethical standards that prevent us from manipulating information and publics. Appendix C contains the codes of ethics from three advocacy-based professional associations—the American Marketing Association (AMA), the American Advertising Federation (AAF), and the Public Relations Society of America (PRSA). Following those ethical codes will help us engage in ethical persuasive communication.

According to retired television commentator Bill Moyers, the challenge for communications professionals engaged in persuasion is to do so ethically. Although many practitioners are held to ethical codes of conduct either through their employers or professions, anyone using persuasive devices should meticulously examine the integrity of their methods. In his book, *Persuasion: Reception and Responsibility* (1983), Charles Larson identifies a number of ethical criteria that can guide the communications professional. They can basically be reduced to the following guidelines:

- Do not use false, distorted, or irrelevant evidence or reasoning, or diversionary tactics.
- Do not deceive or mislead your audience or conceal your purpose.
- Do not oversimplify complex issues or minimize detrimental effects.
- Do not engage in advocacy for something or someone you do not trust or believe in personally.

Ethical decision making is critical to our reputation as professionals. Although ethical codes and behavior are addressed more fully in Chapter 12, it should be noted here that all decisions we make as communications professionals affect the profession itself as well as our own status and professionalism. No decisions are free from ethical considerations; every decision we make as practitioners has ethical consequences. Being aware of those consequences and carefully examining our proposed plans and behaviors according to sound ethical principles will help us avoid the ethical land mines that some of our colleagues unwittingly encounter.

Persuasion in and of itself is not unethical. Advocacy has a strong history and important role in our free society. Nevertheless, it must be conducted according to principles that support not only the public interest but also the public's right to know and choose.

Summary

Marketing and public relations is the business of disseminating information, persuading opinion change, and motivating behavior. Since behavior is based on values, beliefs, and attitudes, it is imperative we understand how to influence those cognitive elements or we will not meet with success. Sometimes providing public information is enough; often it is not. Persuasive methods, used ethically and responsibly, are inextricable elements of advocacy communication.

Exercises

1. Examine a local fundraising effort for persuasive appeals. What types of appeals are being used? How effective are they in this instance? What recommendations would you make for improving the effectiveness of the persuasive appeals?

2. Describe your own personal frame of reference in terms of basic beliefs, values, and attitudes that motivate your behavior.

3. Identify an issue of importance in your community. Identify three publics directly affected by that issue and the opinion leaders for those publics.

References and Additional Readings

Baran, S. J., & Davis, D. K. (1995). *Mass communication theory: Foundations, ferment, and future*. Belmont, CA: Wadsworth Publishing Company.

Cantril, H. (1944). *Gauging public opinion*. Princeton, NJ: Princeton University Press.

Cialdini, R. (1993). In Newsom, D., Turk, J. V., & Kruckeberg, D. (2004). *This is PR: The realities of public relations* (5th ed., pp. 205–206). Belmont, CA: Wadsworth Publishing Company.

Cutlip, S., Center, A., & Broom, G. (2000). *Effective public relations* (8th ed.). Englewood Cliffs, NJ: Prentice-Hall, Inc.

Grunig, J. E. (1993). Communication behaviors and attitudes of environmental publics: Two studies. *Journalism Monographs, 81* (March), 40–41.

Jackson, P. (1990). Behavioral public relations model. *PR Reporter, 33(30)*, 1–2.

Larson, C. (1983). *Persuasion: Reception and responsibility*. Belmont, CA: Wadsworth Publishing Company.

Littlejohn, S. W. (1992). *Theories of human communication* (4th ed.). Belmont, CA: Wadsworth Publishing Company.

Newsom, D., Turk, J. V., & Kruckeberg, D. (2007). *This is PR: The realities of public relations* (9th ed.). Belmont, CA: Wadsworth Publishing Company.

Noelle-Neumann, E. (1984). *The spiral of silence*. Chicago: University of Chicago Press.

Norris, J. S. (1984). *Public relations*. Englewood Cliffs, NJ: Prentice Hall, Inc.

Schindler, R. M. (1992). The real lesson of New Coke: The value of focus groups for predicting the effects of social influence. *Marketing Research, December*, 22–27.

Stimson, J. A. (1991). *Public opinion in America: Moods, cycles, and swings*. Boulder, CO: Westview Press.

Wilcox, D. L., Ault, P. H., & Agee, W. K. (2002). *Public relations: Strategies and tactics* (7th ed.). New York: Harper and Row.

Communications Research Methods

"... *digital media collectively provide searchable access to a wealth of experiences and insights, the quantity and diversity of which seems likely to increase substantially.*"

—Jonathan M. Levitt
Contributor to the *Journal of Digital Information*

LEARNING IMPERATIVES

- **To understand the necessity of research as a foundation for decision making**
- **To recognize the variety of information available**
- **To understand the basic research methodologies for effective communication research**

Research

Gathering information to
clarify an issue and solve a
problem.

For years in the communications field, research has been an unaffordable luxury seldom engaged. Not so in the field of marketing. Market research has been fairly common for the last several decades. But in one of the most critical functions of the organization—the function that builds the relationships and creates the environment within which all other organizational functions thrive—there has been little money for research. For years, public relations practitioners had to find their way in the dark.

Finally, somebody turned on the lights. Not only do most successful organizations now do research, there are a plethora of specialized consultants and research firms which have taken market, environmental, communications, and organizational research to levels of sophistication never before dreamed. Whereas, in the past, communications practitioners found themselves begging for a pittance to find out what their publics thought, they now have executives whose first question is, "What does the research tell us?"

As a result, our challenge here is no longer to convince the reader to do research and then painstakingly examine all the different methods and kinds of information available. At this point in your education or career, you have learned the value of research and how to do it or how to buy it. Further, there are dozens of texts and handbooks on conducting research now in publication. The challenge here is to provide the basic framework for thinking about and organizing research and analysis and then in Chapter 4, to apply it in the strategic planning process.

THE ROLE OF RESEARCH IN COMMUNICATION

Research is only as good as its application to the problem-solving process. To be research-oriented means gathering information is a natural part of your daily routine. Continually gathering and analyzing information means your decisions will be research-based. To be effective in communicating with an organization's publics we must be constantly listening, scanning the environment for information. We should establish good communication channels so information is constantly flowing to us—resulting in adjustments and refinements of our efforts as plans proceed. Research helps us to:

- Save time and money
- Understand our publics
- Make sound decisions
- Avoid mistakes
- Discover new ideas
- Identify potential publics
- Justify plans
- Connect with communities

Knowing what we know about how people perceive and misperceive, as professional communicators we should be wary of "gut reactions." Always test the information that leads to conclusions and especially to key decisions. The next chapter provides a checklist of the information you need to meet the various challenges of an organization and to plan strategically to seize opportunities. In this chapter, we identify some of the best sources of information and the methodologies used to obtain it.

RESEARCH METHODS AND THE DIVERSITY OF TOOLS

Research methods are often categorized as formal and informal, quantitative and qualitative, and primary and secondary. Nevertheless, these categorizations are not parallel. For example, formal research is not necessarily quantitative research, nor is it always primary research. A few definitions regarding research will help to avoid confusion.

Formal and informal research. Formal research implies a structured study. It is governed by rules of research that include previously identifying what you hope to learn, how, and from whom. Informal research is less structured and more exploratory. It does not follow specific rules.

Quantitative and qualitative research. Quantitative research gathers statistical data for analysis. Qualitative research is focused on individual cases or groups not statistically representative of a given population. While qualitative research may be supported by some statistical data analysis, it is not governed by laws of probability. It may, however, be governed by rules of research. Focus groups, for example, are a qualitative tool. They used to be considered informal research. Now that focus group methodology has actually become a dominant method of research, the rules of research governing this methodology are meticulously followed to ensure the most reliable results. Although the method is classified as formal research because it follows rules and structure, it is still a qualitative approach.

Primary and secondary research. Primary research implies gathering the information firsthand, for a specifically identified purpose. It does not necessarily refer to survey research. Personal interviews as well as mail and telephone analysis also yield primary information. Survey research that you implement yourself or contract out for a particular purpose is primary research. Secondary research is primary research data originally collected by someone else for a different purpose that is now being drawn upon for a new use. Typically, it is cheaper and faster to use secondary research. You should exhaust secondary sources before embarking on any costly primary research efforts.

Given these definitions, the research tools become more difficult to categorize. Focus groups may be formal or informal. They are typically qualitative, but if enough groups are conducted some data analysis may be done on the results. They are primary research when you organize and conduct them for the immediate purpose, but reviewing transcripts and analysis of focus groups conducted for other purposes is secondary research that may shed light on the problem you are trying to solve.

Similarly, personal interviews may be informal and qualitative research. They may be one of your "listening" techniques. Or, given more structure and

Formal Research
Data gathering structured according to accepted rules of research.

Informal Research
Data gathering that does not follow standard rules.

Quantitative Research
Gathers statistical data for analysis.

Qualitative Research
Focuses on individual cases or groups that are not statistically representative of a given population.

Focus Group
Moderator-led discussions with fewer than 15 participants providing in-depth information on attitudes and behaviors.

Primary Research
First-hand information gathered specifically for your current purpose.

Secondary Research
Information previously gathered for other purposes that can be adapted to your needs.

an appropriate design, they may be formal and quantitative, allowing statistical analysis with a high degree of confidence. They would be a primary research tool if conducted for the project at hand, yet may be useful as secondary data in subsequent programs.

Whether the research you do is formal or informal, quantitative or qualitative, primary or secondary depends largely on what you need and how you structure it. You should determine your purpose (what you are hoping to accomplish with the research) and what you are trying to find out from whom, before you decide on the best tools to use and how to structure the effort.

Secondary Research

Organizational Research

The first place to begin in gathering information is within the organization itself. Many primary and secondary research tools are available to help gather and assess the information available to you. A communication audit examines all of the organization's communication to see if it is on mission and message. Environmental scanning within an organization monitors the mood and feelings that exist among workers, customers, investors, suppliers, and many other publics of the organization. Mail and telephone analysis, including e-mail, helps you track what issues cause concern among your publics. Certainly customer service and complaint lines help you track opinion trends and potential problems.

Important background information about your company or your client is found in the publications of the organization. Employee publications, annual reports, brochures and marketing material, policies and procedures manuals, organizational charts, sales and accounting records, histories, and any other material available from the organization in hard copy or electronically can be valuable research. Keep in mind that such material usually possesses an inherent bias, and you need to look outside the organization as well as inside to make sure you have the complete picture. Organizations do not often open their closets to display the skeletons through their own printed and electronic material. You will get rich information about the organization through its material, but you will not often get the bad news. And not knowing the bad news may sabotage your communication efforts.

The organization may also have data from past surveys or research. You may need some primary research to determine the mood and opinion of employees. Most organizations would benefit by taking a searching look inside before focusing research efforts externally.

Internet and Library Research

Information technology and the computer revolution have given us access to incredible resources for research. Information that would take weeks or months to find from original sources is now readily available at our fingertips. The communication professional of today and of the future must understand how to get good data from the Internet to compete in this new environment.

© Bobby Deal/RealDealPhoto, 2008.

Online research has, in most cases, replaced a personal visit to the library. It gives the researcher access to the collections held by thousands of libraries and to databases full of information and references. Nevertheless, much is available in library documents that may be difficult to find or expensive to secure elsewhere. Most of us underestimate the value of the data available in our local college and public libraries. And unless you actually take the time to investigate, to talk to a resource librarian, or just to explore the collection, you will not appreciate the vast amount of information at your fingertips.

Remember the latest census? That demographic data is available on the Internet. In that census, some people received a more in-depth questionnaire than the rest of us and the psychographic data are accessible as well. Further, the census is continually updated with interim studies. Also accessible is a host of government documents and studies published every year, and many private research studies. You can find national and local newspapers and magazines that date back years, sometimes to the beginning of publication. Often the results of opinion polls can be found in addition to rich economic data on local, state, national, and international markets.

Some universities have separate libraries for their business schools. In that case, the business library probably contains detailed market analysis and other such valuable information as well. While most of this information may be available electronically, there are volumes of information that can only be accessed by visiting a library in person. The more current the information, the more likely you will be able to get it via the Internet. Nevertheless, there may be significant risks in ignoring the deeper background that older documents contain.

Organizational information is also readily available on the Internet. And increasingly, you will find many independent Web sites, blogs, and other Internet sites that contain valuable information. Be careful of the source of the information and seek secondary confirmation when possible. The information may be credible, such as that from an industry analyst with a professional responsibility to provide such information, or it may be a site constructed by a disgruntled customer or employee containing extremely biased, if not inaccurate, information, rumor, and innuendo.

External Organizations

Our tax dollars support local, state, and national government offices which have a charge to operate in the public interest. Providing public information is often an integral part of that responsibility. Much of the information is now available over the Internet, but some of the valuable information you seek may only be available upon request, or by digging through studies and papers. Sometimes the bureaucracy can be difficult and getting information can take weeks or even months. Nevertheless, the information available is often critical.

Most cities and states have economic development offices of some kind that collect invaluable information on industries and markets. State, and sometimes local, governments have information on population, wages, education, unemployment, health, and just about everything else you can imagine. Be persistent; the information you want may be part of something else. You will have to do most of the searching, so start specific but be ready to broaden your search until you find documents and reports that will provide the

Demographic Data

Information used to segment publics according to tangible characteristics such as age, gender, and socioeconomic status.

Psychographic Data

Information used to segment publics according to values, attitudes, and lifestyles.

information you need. Environmental data is readily available from area Chambers of Commerce and Travel Councils.

Inherent in the missions of associations, pressure groups, or professional societies is gathering and disseminating information. One of the most valuable benefits of membership may be access to the research they gather. You may be able to access the information you want from them through their publications or resource libraries. You may have to pay a search or use fee to access the material. In some cases, you may need to get the material through an association member. But the data available is generally very rich, current, and valuable.

A word of caution is appropriate here. When you receive data from these kinds of organizations, especially from activist groups, check the sources and methodologies used. Be aware that any information published by an interest group of any kind will be inherently biased to some degree. Make sure you understand and allow for that bias, and seek confirming and/or disputing information from other sources or carefully examine the research methodology used and adjust for distortion.

Media Research

A number of professional media analysis firms produce Internet-accessible media guides that provide current and valuable information about media throughout the nation by category: newspapers, magazines, radio stations, television stations, cable stations, and so on. Online media guides such as Bacon's Media Map (mediamap.com) and Burrells (burrells.com) list editors and reporters by assignment, how to submit pieces, and what is typically accepted. The guides also indicate readership, viewership, or listenership and will sometimes provide additional demographic information that may be of help in profiling key publics. They at least provide a way to contact the media organization to request more detailed information. Most media organizations can provide detailed viewer, listener, or reader profiles because they sell advertising. And, advertisers want to know to whom they are buying access.

Media and Internet analysis and clips are a critical part of communications research and evaluation. Whether in-house or a contracted service, tracking such coverage is essential. Nevertheless, because of the time it takes to be thorough, you will usually get more comprehensive and cost-effective clipping and analysis if you contract to a clipping service. Clipping services may do as little as simply clip anything (print, broadcast and other electronic media) that mentions the company or an issue of interest to the company. At the other end of the spectrum they may engage in extensive analysis and evaluate the positive or negative impact of the pieces that discuss the organization and its competitors or any of the issues faced by the industry. You can specify the level of service you want and pay accordingly.

Primary Research

Focus Groups

Focus group research has become one of the most important and reliable sources of data to understand publics. A focus group is a moderator-led discussion with 4 to 15 participants. The moderator asks open-ended questions to garner qualitative responses on attitudes and behavior. The moderator must be careful not to bias the discussion by injecting personal opinion or information into the group. They should encourage participation from all members of the group and probe for in-depth understanding. The moderator must also create an atmosphere of openness, honesty, safety, and confidentiality in order to engender free and open discussion. With the permission and knowledge of the participants the session is usually recorded by electronic means (audio or video), and the discussion transcribed for further evaluation and data tabulation.

The increasing popularity of focus group research is partially because it is generally easier to conduct than survey research, because it can provide more rapid results, and because it provides more depth of opinion and attitudes within the group where discussion shapes, refines, and crystallizes opinions and attitudes (see Figure 3.1). Further, while not always less expensive than other kinds of research it is often more cost effective. Focus groups used to be conducted in communications and marketing research primarily as discussion forums for advisory committees or idea panels to supplement quantitative research. The information was often used as a precursor to survey research to assist in developing a questionnaire that adequately probed attitudes and opinions. In today's research-oriented marketplace, many practitioners recognize that, while survey research is becoming less credible as an accurate representation of publics, focus groups provide the kind of information needed to immediately address and resolve problems.

As discussed in Chapter 2, people do not behave in isolation. The discussion and refinement of opinions and attitudes which occur in focus groups often provide problem-solving behavioral information that surveys cannot. The example cited in Chapter 2 of the New Coke formula introduction is a case in point. Both research techniques were used, yielding opposite results. Yet because of the reputation for validity of survey research over focus group responses, the company chose to rely on predictions of behavior based on attitudes expressed in isolation. They should have more carefully considered the group behavior that emerged from the focus groups.

Further, focus group research can demonstrate the process of opinion formation. While not representative, the group is a social microcosm of a larger public. The analysis of attitude and opinion changes based on the flow of the discussion can help us know what information people need to make sound decisions and what appeals will be most effective in the larger arena. Innovations in focus group research now allow quantification of results if certain conditions are met. Conducting large numbers of groups and employing content analysis techniques can make the data statistically reliable.

The Internet provides an interesting new resource to traditional focus group research. Scheduled online chats can produce similar results without the geographic restrictions. Nevertheless, care must be taken that participants are invited and known. Otherwise, the data may be inappropriate for the researcher's purpose. Face-to-face group discussion is still preferable, because it allows researchers to capture non-verbal communication and facilitates better interaction.

Figure 3.1—Uses and Abuses of Focus Group Research

USES

- Immediate results. Focus group research is relatively easy to organize, implement, and analyze. That often makes it much less costly as well.

- Comfort in numbers. A group is usually less intimidating than a personal interview. People feel more comfortable expressing opinions.

- Flexible and response-oriented. Because the structure is less rigid, the group takes the discussion where it wants to go and a broader investigation of the topic is possible. The focus is on responses (attitudes and opinions), not on the questions, so information emerges on salient topics through the natural flow of discussion.

- Gauge of group behavior. Rather than researching individual behavior or potential behavior, focus groups explore attitudes and behavior influenced by the group or society, a far more reliable measure and predictor.

- Issues explored and opinion crystallized. Because the group is discovering and examining attitudes and behaviors they may not have thought about before, it allows time for discussion and rumination to discover motivations.

- Sensitive issues addressed. When members of the group can empathize with one another because of similar experiences, they are more open in the discussion of sensitive, value-laden issues like stem cell research or spouse/child abuse.

- Attitudes of activists included. A focus group provides a cooperative atmosphere which may encourage the participation of activists and organizational detractors not willing to participate in other types of research.

- Issues and jargon identified. The responses from a focus group identify the issues of most concern to the group as well as the language they use in discussing those topics. Such a foundation provides solid ground for subsequent research and message development.

ABUSES

- Weak or dominant moderator. If the moderator is weak, he/she may allow some members of the group to dominate and others may be intimidated or refrain from offering opinions. The group result will be biased and probably useless. If the moderator dominates the group, he/she will impose opinions and attitudes rather than probing the attitudes of the group.

- Not homogenous. A focus group should be homogenous or the members will be intimidated and uncomfortable with sharing their attitudes. Broad representation is achieved by conducting focus groups among several homogenous publics, rather than mixing representation within a single group.

- Too few groups. For the research to be valid, a number of groups must be conducted among various homogenous publics. Then the information can be consolidated to provide a more comprehensive look.

- Generalizing to a population. Focus group research is qualitative, not statistical. You cannot generalize your conclusions to any "general public." Your conclusions are very much issue- and group-specific. The results may lead you in problem solving or in designing quantitative research, but they do not represent public opinion.

Copy and Product Testing

One classic use of focus groups is for copy and/or product testing. But this is not the only method by which to test. Copy testing simply selects individuals within your target publics and requests their review of copy, whether survey copy or communication copy (brochures, advertising, and the like). In product testing, individuals are asked to examine and use a product—providing feedback on everything from packaging and sales methods to product quality. Product tests may be done individually by personal interview, by mail, in focus groups, or online.

Honest responses in copy and product testing help avoid costly mistakes. Survey research instruments should always be tested before being implemented. Testing copy helps ensure that the messages are coming across in such a way as to produce the desired result. Marketers test promotional campaigns or products in areas representative of the overall market. Sometimes, two or three different versions of a product or a campaign will be tested in similar areas to determine which is most effective. Copy and product testing is one of the most valuable kinds of research available to the practitioner. Their greatest value lies in their ability to prevent mistakes—saving money, effort, and time.

Psychographic Studies

Values and Lifestyles Segmenting (VALS), developed by SRI International in the mid-1970s, is research methodology that classifies publics by psychographics or attitudes, beliefs, and lifestyles. Found to be far more effective in segmenting publics than demographics alone, psychographic studies help us to know what motivates individuals within a particular public. The VALS categories—achievers, survivors and sustainers, belongers, and so on—have been used extensively in advertising and marketing to segment and tailor messages to specific target publics. They provide the same valuable segmentation for communication with all the organization's publics. Communicators should know the VALS categories, both the original and the most recently revised segmentations, and understand the motivations tied to the differences in attitudes and lifestyles.

Often, local media and other similar organizations will have segmented and profiled their own target audiences using a combination of demographic and psychographic information. Whereas some will be unwilling to disclose the information, which is quite costly to compile, others may be persuaded to share the data—especially if the request comes from a nonprofit organization or is for a charitable purpose.

Another valuable tool for understanding key publics is Values in Strategy Assessment (VISTA), a process developed by Wirthlin Worldwide, recently purchased by Harris Interactive. This tool's premise is that values are the fundamental determinant of an individual's behavior and decisions. Understanding the fundamental values of a public provides the strategy to motivate action.

Survey Research and Opinion Sampling

A popular quantitative research method is survey research, although its credibility has declined somewhat in recent years. Several events have affected the

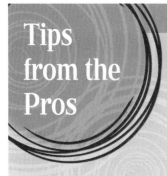

Beyond Sampling Error

Dee Allsop, Ph.D., President of Harris Interactive Solutions Research Groups—producers of the Harris Poll—tips you off on understanding key factors in survey accuracy. Knowing what to pay attention to is your key to confidence and success.

With increasing use of surveys and polling for entertainment and news as well as critical business decision making, it is important to understand that survey and sampling science are all about accurately measuring a small number of people to understand the attitudes and predict the behavior of an entire group. Accuracy in survey research is the direct result of identifying, eliminating, or correcting for *all* types of error or bias that can enter into research. While sampling error is the most visible indicator of survey accuracy reported in the media, your success depends upon understanding both sampling and nonsampling errors.

Sampling Error

Sampling error is the statistical estimate of variation that will occur when using a small number of people (a sample) to approximate a result from a much larger population. One way to think of sampling error is the range of results that would occur if you were to repeat your survey hundreds of times. For example, many surveys in the media report a sampling error of ±3% at the 95% confidence interval. This simply means that if you were to repeat this study 100 times with a similar sample, 95% of the time your results would fall within a range of six percentage points.

Nonsampling Error

While sampling error is inherent in all surveys, we understand it well and can predict it accurately. Other sources of error are much more elusive, yet far more important to judging the accuracy and utility of survey results.

Sample frame. One of the first things I do is make sure the sample was taken from the group of people that matter. For example, if the survey is about who will be elected president, the sample should come from people who can actually vote for president—registered voters.

Non-response error. Several factors influence a respondent's likelihood to respond (i.e., mode effects, interviewer effects, and sensitivity effects). Rather than sampling error, I would much prefer to know the response rate for a survey. A low response rate indicates the survey is less likely to reflect the population in question.

Construct validity. Questions can be worded or constructed to generate just about any result desired. Always read the questions that were asked before interpreting the results. Biased wording will produce biased results.

Institutional reputation. Always check to see who conducted the survey and who paid for it. Reputable companies invest significant time and resources into eliminating nonsampling errors to produce objective findings and do not allow the agenda of a client to shape their results.

Take a lesson from marketing and survey research companies. Instead of worrying about sampling error, focus on understanding what steps are taken to reduce nonsampling error through good survey design, questionnaire construction, interviewing execution, and data processing and correction.

ability of researchers to secure truly random and representative samples. Mail surveys have always been extremely unreliable not only because of low response rates but also because of skewing. Only certain kinds of people will take the time to respond to a mail survey, making it anything but representative.

Telephone surveys have also declined in credibility for the same reason. And the National Do Not Call Registry has made telephone surveying more difficult than ever. Although telephone surveys are not prohibited by the registry, the very existence of a do not call list seems to have given people the courage to refuse calls they would have previously endured.

Nevertheless, survey research has been a popular research technique in communications and will probably continue to be in some form or another. For example, researchers may find the personal drop-off method to still be effective because of the personal contact involved in dropping off and/or picking up a survey. It is not as easy to turn down someone face-to-face as it is to say no over the telephone.

Survey research is a difficult and exacting approach. It requires meticulous attention to detail at every step of the process—questionnaire design, sample selection, survey implementation, data processing, and data analysis. A mistake or misjudgment at any point will skew the results, often without the researcher knowing the data is skewed.

To be valid and reliable, survey research must follow strict rules of research. The idea behind survey research is to take a sample from a population, or universe. If good statistical procedures are followed, we should be able to make that sample relatively representative of the universe, although we can never be absolutely sure of our accuracy unless we survey every individual in the population (a census). The total number of individuals surveyed in the population and the way they are selected will determine how accurately the results reflect the universe.

Statistical research on very critical issues, or in close political campaigns, needs to have a high level of confidence and a low margin of error. The confidence level reflects the researcher's percentage of certainty that the results would be the same (within the margin of error) upon replication of the survey. The margin of error reflects the percentage points that the sample results, on any given question, may vary from the population as a whole. Increasing the sample size increases the confidence level and decreases the margin of error. The only way to be 100% confident and eliminate the margin of error would be to survey the entire population. Research regarding an organization's publics generally requires at least a 95% confidence level, and a margin of error of +/– 5% or less. Further, the more important or controversial the issue the greater the need for a lower margin of error.

There are two basic kinds of survey sampling:

1. Probability sampling is scientifically random; every individual in the population has an equal chance of being selected.
2. Nonprobability samples survey whoever is available; for example, intercepting students during the lunch hour as they enter the student center or interviewing people at a grocery store on Saturday afternoon.

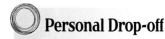

Personal Drop-off

Personally delivering a survey for later pick-up or mailing.

Confidence Level

The percentage of certainty that the results of a survey would be the same if replicated.

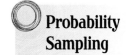

Probability Sampling

Every individual in the population has an equal chance of being selected.

Nonprobability Sampling

Surveying whoever is available.

Sampling Error

Measured as margin of error, it indicates the possible percentage variation of the sample data from the whole population.

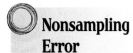

Nonsampling Error

Human error in selecting the sample and designing and implementing the questionnaire.

Purposive Sampling

Identifying and surveying opinion leaders to determine attitudes and behaviors.

Stratified Sampling

Selecting the sample to ensure proportionate representation of segments within the universe.

There are also two kinds of errors:

1. Sampling error is inherent because we are surveying a portion of the population and not the entire population. It is the percentage of possible variance in the sample's answers from the population. We decrease sampling error by increasing sample size; the closer we get to surveying the whole population, the smaller the sampling error. Sampling error is unavoidable in survey research (unless we take a census) and is measured as margin of error.

2. Nonsampling error is all other kinds of error introduced into the process. Mistakes made in questionnaire construction, sample selection, survey implementation, data entry, and tabulation are all nonsampling error. Great care must be taken in selecting the sample and designing and implementing the questionnaire. Questions and answer categories must be designed to avoid the introduction of bias so that answers accurately reflect the information the researcher needs.

Bias can also be introduced in implementing the survey. Ensuring strict confidentiality of responses can lessen courtesy bias. Training interviewers to ask questions without injecting value inflection or personal comments, explanation, or other bias is also critical. Further, care must be taken in coding the surveys and entering the data. Data processing converts the observations and responses into statistics for interpretation. Data analysis manipulates the data to make logical inferences. For the inferences to be reliable, the data must be accurately entered and processed.

Finally, the inferences made must be fully supportable by the data set. A few years ago, a ballot measure in Utah proposed a light rail transportation system to be funded by a small tax increase. When the measure was soundly defeated, many analysts concluded it was a vote against light rail. In reality, it was more probably a vote against the funding method, not the light rail system itself. When we deal with statistics and make inferences from data, we must be very careful that the data support the conclusions. Otherwise, we have established a faulty foundation for decision making.

In addition to the types of survey research discussed above, other variations have specific purposes and benefits. The following short descriptions will provide a basis upon which to investigate the techniques for any given research situation.

Purposive sampling. Based on Katz and Lazarsfeld's two-step flow theory, purposive sampling identifies and surveys opinion leaders to determine attitudes and behaviors. The researcher must devise a procedure that selects out the target public's influentials (or causes them to self-select), and then surveys opinion and behavior. It is also helpful to know a little bit about the influentials, such as where they get their information about certain issues.

Stratified sampling. Truly random sampling should yield a cross section of the population representative of the characteristics within the population (i.e., proportionate numbers of women and men and so on). Whenever we skew the randomness of the sample by using techniques that make it easier for us to complete the research, like surveying every nth number in the local telephone directory, we risk jeopardizing the representativeness of our sample. If obtaining a truly proportionate representation is critical, the research sample should be stratified so that it includes appropriate proportions of the key segments of the overall population.

Internet surveys. A growing area of survey research is conducting surveys over the Internet. While there is inherent bias because of the nature of accessible respondents, this data can be extremely valuable if the purpose is consistent with the population sample. Increasingly, organizations use this method to survey their members, employees or customers. Commercial firms with access to e-mail lists may further facilitate this method.

Personal interviews. Very sensitive issues and research that require deep probing for attitudes and behaviors are best addressed through personal interviews. The personal interview ensures greater control over the sample and the data, but not only is this method costly, it requires a lot of time and well-trained interviewers. Nevertheless, in certain circumstances, it is the only viable method to secure reliable and useful information.

Benchmark surveys. This type of survey is simply a periodic reexamination of attitudes and opinions within the population. An initial survey is done to set a benchmark against which subsequent survey results are compared. Benchmark surveys are good tools for measuring change and evaluating the success of a program.

Panel studies. Sometimes you will want to study attitudes and opinions on a variety of issues over a period of time. Panel studies select respondents who will be available for follow-up surveys at least once and often several times. For example, a newspaper will select individuals from its readership to follow a specific issue or election and respond to queries at specific points in the campaign. Behavioral studies are also sometimes conducted by panel to assess whether or not a change in behavior is temporary and what motivates permanent change.

Survey tag-ons. One of the easiest and least expensive methods of obtaining survey data is to add two or three questions to a questionnaire being prepared for another purpose or by someone else. Charitable community organizations often tag on a couple of questions to routine survey research done by corporations in their area. Frequently, the corporation will even pay for the data tabulation as a service or donation to the nonprofit organization. Even if the nonprofit has to pay a fee for tag-on questions, it is still significantly less costly than implementing a stand alone questionnaire.

Panel Study

A group of respondents who agree to be surveyed repeatedly to track opinion and attitude change over time.

Summary

To secure a constant flow of the information you need to make decisions, meet challenges, and plan strategic action, you must find the right combination of research techniques. The purpose of the research and the information desired drive the selection of methodology. Otherwise your research will sit on the shelf unused because it is inaccurate or because it does not provide the information you need to design campaigns that reach the publics you must target within the resources you have to meet the challenges you face.

Exercises

1. Volunteer to conduct focus groups for a nonprofit organization. Subsequently, design and implement a short survey to gather opinion, attitudes, and demographics on some of its key publics.

2. Visit the local library and talk with the reference librarian to discover the range of resources, databases, search engines, and other references available. Search through some of the material to discover the kinds of information accessible, not just online, but in the library itself. Try to find resources in every category mentioned in this chapter.

References and Additional Readings

Babbie, E. (1992). *The practice of social research* (6th ed.). Belmont, CA: Wadsworth Publishing Company.

Converse, J. M., & Presser, S. (1986). *Survey questions: Handcrafting the standardized questionnaire.* Beverly Hills, CA: Sage Publications.

Fink, A. (2002). *The survey kit* (2nd ed.). Newbury Park, CA: Sage Publications.

Greenbaum, T. L. (1997). *The handbook for focus group research.* Newbury Park, CA: Sage Publications.

Stacks, D. W. (2002). *Primer of public relations research.* New York: Guilford Publications, Inc.

Using Research for Effective Communications Planning

"I find that a great part of the information I have was acquired by looking up something and finding something else on the way."

—Franklin P. Adams (1881–1960)
American Journalist

LEARNING IMPERATIVES

- **To understand how to organize research and draw inferences that support strategic planning**

- **To learn how to organize information about publics into profiles to facilitate communication and relationship building**

- **To learn how to determine publics' self-interests, influentials and relationship status**

- **To understand how to use information to determine strengths, weaknesses, opportunities, and threats**

- **To learn how to synthesize broad information into a concise situation analysis and core challenge or opportunity**

Research should be an established and ongoing process in any organization. Successful organizations are always scanning the internal and external environment, gathering data and feedback from key publics, and measuring the effectiveness of their communication in moving toward established goals. At some point the key information is pulled together to support planning, but that does not signal an end to research. The savvy professional is always looking for new information that may adjust plans at any point or reconfirm the validity of current efforts. Measurement that we call *evaluation* may focus on measuring our success rather than gathering information to chart a course. Nevertheless, what we find out from evaluation integrates with the constant flow of other information to become the foundation of new efforts, programs, and campaigns.

Research provides the information that helps us find solutions that work. It also demonstrates our credibility to our clients or to management. If the research process can be said to have a beginning, it starts when someone first states a problem or discovers an opportunity. Someone—a client, a customer, a colleague, a supervisor, or you—identifies an issue or an opportunity. Then we start to organize what we know around that issue or opportunity. We also reach out to gather what we don't know but need to know.

That's when the real work begins. Facts and information are gathered from all sources and organized to be sorted and evaluated. Figure 4.1 indicates the depth of detail and the breadth of perspective necessary in this process. Although the research checklist in that figure has a commercial product orientation, the same principles apply to the nonprofit industry and to solving corporate issues as well as marketing challenges. When the checklist discusses sales and pricing and profitability, substituting words like participation and cost and success make the checklist applicable to any project or program.

If you are designing the first-ever communications effort or strategic communications plan for your client or company, the research section of your plan may take a significant amount of time to complete. It may require an exhaustive search and synthesis of new data. If, however, ongoing communications functions have systematically gathered and organized research data into easily accessible and usable information, your research task will be more of an update. Always take the time to record and file pieces of information you come across in your daily routine. Continually gathering information will make the research task for any given effort or issue much easier.

The next several chapters in this book are designed to take you through the 10-Step Strategic Communications Planning Matrix step-by-step. The teaching case example introduced at the end of this chapter provides practical application of that process. As we progress through each step of the planning matrix in this and subsequent chapters, the teaching case will illustrate each step as it is discussed in the text.

This chapter is designed to help you pull together information and analysis into a succinct document focused on a specific purpose. That purpose might be a complete strategic plan, a budget request for a new communications effort, a solution to a problem or challenge, a response to a perceived threat, or a proposal to take advantage of an emergent opportunity. For our purposes here, we call this part of a plan or proposal the research section to facilitate parallelism with the Research, Action Planning, Communication,

Figure 4.1—A Checklist for Communications and Marketing Research

1. **The External Environment**
   - Economic, political, and social environment within which the organization operates and the problem or challenge has occurred including underlying issues
   - Pressures on the organization and the impact of current events on its operation and the maintenance of key relationships

2. **The Industry**
   - Organizations, companies, sales figures, strengths, challenges
   - Industry growth patterns, primary demand curve, per capita consumption, growth potential
   - History, technological advances, trends
   - Characteristics, distribution patterns, control and regulation, promotional activity, geographic characteristics, profit patterns

3. **The Client**
   - History, size, growth, profitability, scope of business, competence, reputation, strengths, weaknesses, structure, personnel

4. **The Product, Service, or Issue**
   - The product, service, or issue story, development, quality, design, packaging, pricing policies and structure, sales and profit history, trends, distribution, reputation
   - Product, service, or issue sales features (exclusive, nonexclusive, differentiating qualities, competitive position in consumer's mind)
   - Sales force (size, scope, ability, cost/sale)
   - Product research and planned improvements

5. **Promotions**
   - Successes and failures of past policy, sales force, advertising, publicity
   - Expenditures, budget emphasis, relation to trends
   - Ad/PR/marketing strategies, themes, campaigns
   - Promotions of competitors and like organizations

6. **Market Share**
   - Sales history industry-wide and share of market in dollars and/or units
   - Market potential, industry trends, company trends, demand trends

7. **Competition**
   - Who and where the market is; how it is segmented; consumer needs, attitudes, and characteristics; how, why, when, and where consumers buy
   - Customers past and future, what they have in common, what they like/dislike about product or issue, how they are reached
   - Competitors and their potential, competing ideas and attitudes

8. **Resources**
   - Intervening publics and current relationship, influentials
   - Public's attitudes and opinions toward product, issue, or organization
   - Physical facilities and personnel

9. **SWOT Analysis**
   - Internal and external strengths and weaknesses including publics, resources, attitudes, organization, structure, sales force, ideas, allies, and enemies
   - Emergent or possible opportunities
   - Threats to the organization and to success

10. **Public Profiles**
    - Demographic and psychographic data
    - Current relationship to product, service, or issue
    - Motivating self-interests and influentials
    - Information sources and media use

Figure 4.2

10-Step Strategic Communications Planning Matrix   Matrix

Matrix: Research

Steps One, Two, and Three—Background, Situation Analysis, Core Problem/Opportunity

1. Background

Planning begins with a synthesis of primary and secondary research providing background information on the industry, external environment, product or program, market situation, and current trends in opinions and attitudes. The background section also uses demographic and psychographic data to identify and profile potential publics that may be affected by the problem/opportunity or could aid in its resolution/accomplishment. Intervening publics and available resources are also identified.

2. Situation Analysis

The situation analysis consists of two paragraphs. The first paragraph is a statement of the current situation and a description of the challenge or opportunity based on research. The second paragraph identifies potential difficulties and related problems.

3. Core Problem/Opportunity

The core problem/opportunity is a one-sentence statement of the main difficulty or prospect—including potential consequences if not resolved or realized.

---

and Evaluation (RACE) model. As depicted in the Strategic Communications Planning Matrix (Figure 4.2) and the teaching case, the research section consists of the background, situation analysis, and core problem or opportunity.

BACKGROUND

The background is a summary of pertinent facts and information drawn from primary and secondary research. It must be comprehensive, but written concisely. It does not contain everything you discovered in research, only the information necessary to establish credibility with your client or manager and build the foundation for your plan. A good background will often depict data and more detailed information in the form of figures and graphs. Data is more easily understood in graphic form. The checklist in Figure 4.1 represents the development of content that may be appropriate for the background. At the very least, it represents how comprehensive your understanding of organizations, issues, and publics should be.

The background sets the stage for understanding the situation at hand. It contains information about the industry and the client specifically: past efforts and events affecting organizational success and where the client currently stands in the marketplace or in relationship to the issue. Remember that it selects and highlights only those bits of information that build the foundation for the solution or plan you will propose. Although you have not yet fully defined the problem or begun the planning process, some obvious alternatives will have emerged as your team gathered and evaluated the research. The background should organize the information and present it in a way that will lead your client or manager to the solutions you propose.

SWOT Analysis

As you have organized and synthesized your data and information according to the first eight steps of the checklist in Figure 4.1, you have probably begun to make some inferences and drawn some conclusions relative to the issue or opportunity you are addressing. At this point, take some time to do a SWOT analysis—strengths, weaknesses, opportunities, threats. According to Stacy Collett (1999), a SWOT analysis is:

> A way to analyze a company's or a department's position in the market in relation to its competitors. The goal is to identify all the major factors affecting competitiveness before crafting a business strategy.

Although typically designed to support development of marketing strategy, a SWOT analysis is useful in supporting all the relationships of the organization, not just those developed with customers. It is equally valuable to analyze the internal and external factors affecting issues and the entire environment within which the organization exists. When conducting a SWOT analysis, remember that your organization's relationships with key publics as well as the key publics' opinions and values can also be considered strengths or weaknesses.

This analysis is a great way to sum up your research and focus your knowledge on the opportunity you face and the barriers to be overcome. It tends to take pages of information and focus them into a few key factors that will generate success.

Market and Public Profiles

The last step on the checklist is to use the information you have gathered to profile the publics you may potentially need to reach to solve the difficulty or take advantage of the opportunity. Remember that you cannot select *key* publics at this point because you have not set objectives. You have to decide what you need to do to meet the challenge (objectives) before you decide who you need to reach and motivate to do that. But while you are compiling and analyzing research, take time to profile potential publics so you will be armed with the knowledge and understanding you need to select the best combination of key publics when the time comes.

Conduct a brainstorming session to generate a comprehensive list of potential publics. Carefully follow the rules of brainstorming to ensure no potential publics are left out and everyone has a chance to contribute. Good group interaction should generate dozens of potential publics. More information on brainstorming is available in Chapter 7 of this text. We recommend you review Figure 7.2, Rules of Brainstorming, to help you develop a solid list of potential publics. Once the list has been generated, divide the potential publics into three categories:

1. **Probable.** You should have between 10 and 15 different probable publics, those that have a direct link to the problem or its possible solutions.

2. **Possible.** These publics are those that might be linked in some way to the issue, but based on research are an outside possibility.

3. **Unlikely.** Drop these publics as you probably won't be involving them.

Use your research to extensively profile your 10 to 15 probable publics. The profiles should contain both demographic and psychographic information (gained through primary and secondary research) as well as any information that will help you reach them (like media preferences and habits). We call these profiles because when you have completed the task, you should have a portrait in your mind's eye of the John or Jane Q. Individual who is a member of that particular public. You should know them intimately, because you may be appealing to them to act in a way that will help you meet your challenge. You should know their ideas, attitudes, values, opinions, behaviors, lifestyles, purchasing preferences, recreation habits, media use, and much more. Some of the information in the profile will come from hard data such as census or opinion research. Other information may be from focus groups, secondary research, personal observation, and informed stereotypes.

Once you have compiled your research into a profile of a public, you need to determine that public's motivating self-interests in connection with the issue at hand and their opinion leaders or influentials. Later you will be using these profiles to help you decide which publics you will need to reach and motivate once you have established your goal and objectives. You will also use the profiles and self-interests to devise the messages that will motivate the individuals within the public. Preparing extensive, thoughtful, in-depth profiles now will make the planning step of the matrix flow more quickly and easily to the best solution.

Self-interest

The fundamental motivation for an individual's behavior.

Influential

A formal or informal opinion leader that can serve as an intervening public to carry the message to your public or can influence your public to act.

Identifying Self-Interests

After using research to profile a public, focus attention on the tasks the public could help you accomplish or the roles it might play in a solution to the problem. Some publics may even be intervening publics to help you reach other targeted publics. (See Chapter 6 for a discussion of intervening publics.) Honestly and candidly assess the self-interests that will motivate the public to do what you need done. Remember that people don't do what you want them to do just because you want them to do it. They act in their own self-interests and unless you can plainly identify those self-interests and appeal to them, the public will not do what you want. Further, don't confuse self-interest with selfishness. The measure of success in our society has very much become position (power and fame) and money (and the material goods money buys). Yet human resource literature in the business field and studies of persuasive communication show that people are more often motivated to act from intrinsic values like care and concern, community improvement, quality of life, welfare of family and friends, and because it is the "right thing to do."

Clearly, it is in our self-interest to feel good about ourselves, to take care of our families and friends, to improve the quality of our community and living situation. That doesn't mean money and power are not motivators, but relying upon them as the primary or overriding self-interests for our publics will probably limit our success. Refer back to the Chapter 1 discussion of the critical values underlying trust and relationships. You will note that material property is much lower in priority than the people-oriented values.

As you will see in the following chapters, appealing to the self-interest of a public is necessary at two levels. You already know you must use a self-interest appeal to move a public to action. But with the clutter of messages and information bombarding everyone today, we must also appeal to self-interest just to get a public to pay attention to our message. People choose to perceive a message only when they believe it is in their self-interest to do so, otherwise they just tune out. Regardless of the channel used, you have to get over the perception hurdle before you can complete your primary task of informing or motivating.

© Rick Lord, 2008.

Identifying Opinion Leaders and Influentials

The profile of each public should also consider who influences them. Who are their opinion leaders regarding the particular issue or challenge to be addressed? A public's influentials or opinion leaders are individuals (either by personal acquaintance or reputation) who have the credibility to effectively give advice, affect opinion, or call for action. Influentials are typically heavy consumers of media and possess significant information and expertise. Most importantly, they are trusted.

Influentials and opinion leaders may be formal or informal. A formal opinion leader is one whose influence results from status or position, either elected or appointed in some way. Political officials, public figures, civic and religious leaders are good examples of formal opinion leaders. Informal or personal influentials may include family and friends, coworkers, teachers, and peers. If the issue is health-related, influentials may include the family doctor. If it regards the maintenance of your car, you may be influenced by the mechanic across the street. You would probably not ask the doctor how to fix your car or the mechanic about maintaining your child's health.

Influentials do not have to be personally known to us to be opinion leaders, and formal opinion leaders are seldom personally known. Role models and celebrities often become opinion leaders. If children idolize a professional sports figure, they are likely to take the advice of that figure regarding certain behaviors. You may not personally know the governor of your state, but you would probably accept his/her judgment on certain issues of importance to the state.

Tips from the Pros

Discovering Self-Interest

Cathy Chamberlain, market research expert and President and CEO of CTC, Inc., tips you off on getting to what is personally relevant.

Does a mother pay an extra $50 to buy her teenage daughter a pair of name brand jeans because they are more durable and double stitched? Obviously not. What she's really attempting to do is buy her daughter self-esteem. In-depth research that allows you to probe into people's subconscious minds and tap into their emotions and values can be the key to understanding their self-interests and creating messages that change behavior. Here are five tips to help you get to what makes people tick.

Look beyond just numbers. Numbers alone often don't tell the whole story.

Understand your key audience. What really matters to them in their every day lives? Ask yourself, "How does this issue affect them?" Look for ways to tie the issue or opportunity to your target audience's self-interests.

Ask a few open-ended questions. "What do you worry about when you can't sleep at night?" When looking at a specific issue, ask: "What are the benefits or consequences? How does it make you feel? Why is it so important to you?"

Find the themes that show up over and over. People will describe things differently but look for commonalities that can be used to group responses into themes.

Pick two or three dominant themes. Develop your key messages around the most salient themes that show up. Don't try to cover every point.

Similarly, marketers carefully select celebrities to push their products. Usually these actors, singers, and sports figures are selected because they represent talents or a lifestyle to which people are drawn. Brad Pitt, for example, received $4 million to appear in a Heineken beer ad that aired only once during the Super Bowl. But sometimes endorsements don't always result in higher sales or changes in public opinion. And a failed campaign can be expensive. Chrysler paid singer Celine Dion $14 million over three years for a campaign that largely failed.

In today's ever-changing media society, media figures may sometimes take the role of an opinion leader. According to agenda-setting theory, we understand that media typically do not have the power to change opinion (McCombs & Shaw, 1972). Media do not tell us what to think, but set the agenda for what we think about. They further reinforce decisions we have already made. Combining that theory with the theory of selective perception (Klapper, 1960) and with uses and gratification theory (McQuail, 1987) it becomes apparent that people choose the media they pay attention to—both channels and genre—based on what they already believe. The vast number of listeners and viewers who tune in to talk show hosts like Rush Limbaugh and

Sean Hannity already agree with what they expect will be the positions of those hosts. They select the media that will strengthen and reinforce their beliefs and lifestyles.

Nevertheless, as people have become more isolated and insular in their personal lives, certain media personalities have become influential. It cannot be denied that some media figures like Oprah Winfrey and Diane Sawyer clearly have influence on opinion and behavior. Their respectability and their ubiquitous presence have truly given them the status of opinion leaders on certain issues. Nevertheless, don't make the mistake of thinking media changes opinion. Opinion is shaped and changed by influentials, not by messages you place in mass media.

How do you identify who a public's opinion leaders are? Formal opinion leaders are relatively easy to determine. We see them every day (like political officials) or know who they are by the issue or influence involved (like religious leaders). Nevertheless, just because someone may hold a position of authority does not mean they can actually sway the opinion of our public. Identifying informal opinion leaders presents another difficulty. So how do we find out who actually influences a public? The answer is deceptively simple: we ask them. Part of research is asking people who influences their opinions and who they trust to help them make decisions. Focus groups and surveys are particularly useful in this process.

In using opinion leaders and influentials as a channel in communication efforts with key publics, keep in mind they are best used to persuade and motivate. You would not typically use an opinion leader to disseminate information because that would be wasting their influence unless it was particularly difficult to draw attention to the specific information you are trying to disseminate. It is usually fairly easy to disseminate information. It is more difficult to persuade or to move a public to action. Opinion leaders and influentials are particularly valuable in the motivation effort.

We all have a diverse circle of influentials and opinion leaders. We trust their judgment. We take their advice. They are typically better informed on the particular topic and trusted because of past performance. They have great influence on our attitudes and behaviors. Nevertheless, their credibility is based upon our assessment of their character and judgment. Influentials lose influence if they are perceived to be manipulated or manipulative. Using them in that manner is unethical and will ultimately lead to a decline in their influence.

Assessing Relationships

In the profile, it is also important to assess the current state of the relationship the client or organization has with each public. Assessment of a relationship with a public may use a formal methodology like establishing a scale of strength indicators of the relationship, or the assessment may be more informal. Nevertheless, research (Bruning & Ledingham, 2000) has shown the key factors or dimensions to be considered include levels of:

- Loyalty
- Trust

- Openness
- Involvement
- Community investment
- Commitment

Significant research has been conducted within the relationship building and the relationship management schools of thought in public relations. While that discipline has been advocating a relationship building approach to dealing with all organizational publics since the mid-1980s, it is only recently that research has led to the methodology to measure the strength of those relationships. The six factors identified above are those most often identified and measured. Loyalty and trust are arguably two-way factors, the strength of which is measured both from the perspectives of the organization and the publics. The other four primarily measure the public's perception of the organization's performance. The openness, involvement, community investment, and commitment of the organization to publics and issues are typically seen as responsibilities only on the part of the organization.

The purpose of your communication, particularly long term, is to strengthen the relationships with publics and move them to mutually beneficial action. Communication that highlights the organization's performance on these six factors will help you do that.

As you review the profiles of potential publics in the teaching case at the end of the chapter, you will see profiles of many publics that we would initially identify as probable participants in the solution to the problem. Because a vast majority of those served by the free clinic will be Hispanics and blue-collar workers, we profiled them as probable publics. But through our analysis of the problem and the publics, we find they can't really help us raise a large sum of money quickly. So we would typically then turn to those people in the community who already give to community efforts through the clinic partnership organizations like the United Way. But if we tap those donors, they may shift their support from current causes rather than give additional funds. Health care workers would be another obvious public close to the issue and likely to give. But because many already support community causes, and many will be involved in volunteering to staff the clinic, we don't want to overwhelm them.

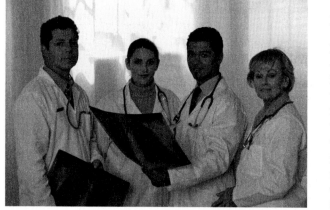

© dasilva, 2008.

We wouldn't have been able to make sound decisions about key publics without the profiles created from the research. Publics that may seem obvious targets turn out to be not such good choices once we have completed our analysis and profiles and set our objectives. Some of your profiled publics may turn out to be intervening publics (or third party publics) that will be resources to you as influentials or opinion leaders. They intervene to assist in getting your message to your key publics, or to motivate key publics to action. In a state immunization campaign for example, health care professionals and the PTA may be two very influential intervening publics.

Although intervening publics are resources, they should also be profiled because you may be requesting their cooperation. You gain their cooperation in the same way you motivate action in key publics: by making it in their self-interest. For this reason, you need to know about them, to understand their self-interests as they relate to your problem, know who influences them, and understand the status of your relationship with them.

SITUATION ANALYSIS

Although the problem or challenge was identified for us initially as we began the research process, it is important to redefine the situation after we have synthesized all available and pertinent information. The client's or organization's initial perception of the problem or opportunity may be quite unlike the actual situation. You may have initially believed people didn't donate to a cause because they didn't see the need. Research may have discovered the real reason was that they didn't know how. Based on the background, assess and describe in one paragraph the situation as it appears after the data has been organized and analyzed.

In a second paragraph, identify any related issues, problems, or difficulties. Honestly assess potential barriers to success that must be overcome, but use your research as a confidence builder so your client or manager will be certain that the difficulties can be overcome. Identifying a difficulty and then suggesting a reasonable way to neutralize it may be the best approach.

CORE PROBLEM OR OPPORTUNITY

Based on the synthesis of research in the background, you have narrowed the issue or challenge to a short assessment of the situation and any related difficulties. Now cut to the heart of the problem in one sentence. For example, "Because key publics are not getting adequate and timely information about mobile blood drives, blood donations have declined, threatening the local hospital's immediate access to needed lifesaving units." The statement gets right to the central core of the problem and translates it to a tangible consequence if the problem is not solved. Be careful not to mistake symptoms of a problem for the problem itself. Like an onion, problems are made up of many layers. The layers surrounding the problem often take the form of symptoms and effects. In order to identify the core problem you need to peel back the symptoms and effects to find out what is really causing the difficulty.

The Case of the Warehouse Welfare Health Care

Chapter 4 Teaching Case

A description of the case problem is given here along with the first three completed steps of the matrix. Subsequent completed steps accompany appropriate chapters of the text. Through this teaching case you will learn how to build a complete campaign for any marketing or communications opportunity or problem as you compare each step of the matrix with the example illustrated in this case.

Case Description

Navajo Flats and its suburbs is a mid-sized community nestled in a valley among the peaks of the Mystic Mountains in northern Arizona. With approximately 400,000 residents, Navajo Flats' economy is based on a variety of industries; the largest among them are four food packing and packaging plants owned by major corporations, a golf cart manufacturer, and several large and mid-sized technology companies. Smaller companies supplement and support the economic base and provide the range of services necessary in a community this size including health care, financial services, and other kinds of retail and service businesses. The valley is also home to a large private university and two state community colleges as well as a number of other technical schools supporting the high-tech and medical industries.

These robust businesses coexist with varying degrees of civility with the remnants of family farming and ranching operations that have shrunk with the demand for land for housing and industry but still retain much of the outlying land in the valley and other smaller mountain valleys nearby. Much of the produce from the farms is sold locally in retail stores or to the food processing operations in the packing and packaging plants. Some of the meat from the ranches is also sold locally, but most is shipped to other markets. The farming and ranching draw migrant workers and Navajo

Flats' immigrant community has grown significantly over the years.

One of the pressing needs in Navajo Flats is health care for underprivileged children, low-income families and the migrant community. These populations do not have insurance and cannot pay for health care. While the local health care facilities do provide as much charity care as possible, it is insufficient for the growing need. Local health care providers, local churches, and social service nonprofits recognize the need for a free clinic staffed by volunteers (retired medical people who want to give back to the community) to serve this population. And opportunity is knocking.

The local Wal-Mart has vacated its big box store on the west side of town in favor of a new Super Center the company has constructed on the other side of town. The local Community Action Services (CAS), the nonprofit that operates the food bank and housing and employment services for those in need, has sufficient reserves and loans to buy the vacated building at a concessionary rate offered by Wal-Mart. CAS will use 70% of the facility as a warehouse and processing center for the food bank and related services, but it will need to lease the remaining 30% of the space to service the loans and maintain the facility.

Working with CAS, the local United Way has leveraged partnerships in the community—health care providers and churches—to operate and maintain a free medical clinic in the remaining 30% of the warehouse facility, including the lease, a full-time administrator and assistant, and the necessary insurance coverage on volunteer medical personnel. Some of the equipment and furnishings will be donated by local health care providers as they upgrade and replace equipment, and an annual contribution from the United Way will provide renewable medical supplies. Local builders have volunteered their construction crews. But the partnership lacks the estimated $500,000 that is required for materials to build out the space and initially equip it as a free clinic. It has been determined that, for the goal of a free medical clinic to be realized, the clinic partnership will need to raise $500,000 from the community.

Sample Campaign

Matrix: Research
Step One—Background

Note: For the purposes of this teaching case, the background is abbreviated. Your investigation of the issues and the market may need to be much more extensive depending upon the challenge. Figure 4.1 in Chapter 4 is a guideline to follow for the information you may need to resolve a problem.

The case description provides an overview of the Navajo Flats community, but much more information is required. Our research shows that Navajo Flats has a very active nonprofit social service sector that is already well supported by community members. The local United Way runs successful workplace campaigns in all the major companies in town and in about 50% of companies with 500 or fewer employees. The average employee participation in workplace campaigns is 65%. Corporate donations are also substantial. Further, CAS and other local nonprofits are led by boards of directors drawn from respected business, civic, and religious leaders in the community. Navajo Flats is a community that contributes both time and money to good causes. Nevertheless, local nonprofits are anxious that the money to be raised does not deplete the annual giving to

their organizations. Approximately 90 nonprofit agencies provide for the social service needs in this community, services like improving literacy, drug rehabilitation, hospice, disaster relief, job training, and related needs. These agencies depend upon stable annual donations to meet current community needs.

The economic base of Navajo Flats is somewhat diverse. As mentioned previously, it includes four food packing and packaging plants owned by major corporations, a golf cart manufacturer, and several large and mid-sized technology companies. The economy is also supported by several smaller companies (250–500 employees) that have spun off or been inspired by the anchor businesses. Several small, high-tech companies do well in this environment and employ anywhere from 10 to 100 people each. The packaging plants and the golf cart manufacturer both count other businesses in the community as suppliers to their production. And, of course, the community hosts the retail and service businesses that build up to support any community of this size. Some, like several of the banks and a health care company, have grown quite large and expanded to other markets in the region, maintaining headquarters in Navajo Flats. The large private university, two state community colleges, and the technical schools provide part- and full-time employees for the high-tech and medical companies. Of course, typical businesses have grown to support the student population. The post-high school student population is estimated at about 50,000 full- and part-time students.

Because of the diversity of industry, the workforce is equally diverse. The high-tech, financial services, and health care industries employ mostly well-educated white-collar workers. The packing and packaging plants and golf cart manufacturer employ blue-collar labor (including students as part-time workers), some of which is unionized. There is also a substantial migrant population—both legal and illegal immigrants—built up initially to support the farming and ranching operations but now extending to other service industries in town requiring manual labor. It is estimated that 15% of the population of the greater Navajo Flats area is Hispanic.

Chapter 4 Teaching Case Continued...

The health care community in Navajo Flats consists of two major hospitals each owned by separate nonprofit health care corporations. Southwest Health Care (SWHC) is headquartered locally and has spread to other communities in the region. The other provider does not have local roots, but is a strong competitor to SWHC. Both have networks of local clinics and doctors, but SWHC is the provider that has partnered with the local United Way, the churches, and CAS on this project. With roots in this community, it has typically been more community-involved, but both corporations provide some charity care at their facilities. Dr. Bill Tucker, retired from SWHC, and his wife Eleanor Tucker, a retired SWHC nurse, are leading the team of retired health care workers who have volunteered to staff the clinic. The Tuckers are well respected members of the community who are known by many civic and community leaders because of their active support of social service causes over the years.

Those most affected by the rising cost of health care are blue-collar families or hourly workers and immigrants. Within that underserved population is approximately 15,000 children who potentially have no access to health care. Students are also affected by unaffordable health care. When people have no insurance coverage, they have few options when faced with the astronomical cost of the simplest of medical procedures and medications. They simply go without. The consequences are usually more complicated health care issues, the spread of illness and disease, an increase in demand on other social services, and exacerbation of other social problems. The lack of affordable health care has a ripple effect on a community.

Navajo Flats is served by two television stations and several radio stations with a variety of formats from talk to pop and country music. There is a daily metro newspaper and a few localized weeklies focused on local high school and college sports, local business, and arts and crafts. The migrant community is served by a Spanish-language radio station and a weekly newspaper.

SWOT Analysis

Strengths	Weaknesses
Generous community Supportive community leaders Strong economic base Viable project/trusted partners	Already giving substantially Limited experience with the issue Low awareness of the need
Opportunities	**Threats**
Engage people not engaged before Unite community Relieve suffering	Six-month deadline Depletion of support to other efforts

Profiles of Potential Publics

Partnership Boards: These are the members of the boards of directors or advisory councils for the organizations involved in the free clinic partnership. The United Way, CAS, and SWHC all have boards of directors that meet monthly to direct the affairs of those organizations. The involvement of local churches is coordinated through the Interfaith Council of Navajo Flats (ICNF), which includes a leader (either the religious leader or an influential member) from each of the participating churches. All of these individuals are well respected within their circles of influence and operation. They are looked up to by their professional colleagues, friends, neighbors, and fellow citizens. They are visible community servants within their spheres. Most are in their board positions because they have achieved professional success either because of expertise in a particular area or sufficient success, affluence, and influence to be invited to participate. By their nature, they are generous donors to community causes, both in time and money. They recognize that the invitation to serve on boards of organizations like these comes with an expectation of continued generous donation and a responsibility to use their position to sway others in support of the organization. Fully two-thirds are male, 70% are married with families, 80% are regular church-goers. Median annual income is in excess of $125,000. They are all very busy with many commitments professionally, socially, and in the community. They are willing to lend their names to the cause but have little time to dedicate above their current board commitments.

Probably most importantly, these individuals have been involved in the negotiations for the establishment of the free clinic. They are intimately acquainted with the issues, efforts, and commitments that have finally brought the clinic to the brink of realization. They recognize the need and have hammered out the solution. They have ownership in the effort and passion for the cause. We have established channels of personal communication with each board member.

Current relationship: Exceptionally positive. These board members not only support this effort, they have been involved in bringing it to fruition and are passionate about its success.

Influentials: Peers on the boards, board chairs, partnership executives, colleagues, religious leaders, and families.

Self-interests: Tend to be more altruistic because of their community commitment. Conserving time and energy for their professional responsibilities is crucial. Peer esteem and their opinion leadership is important to them.

Corporate Executives: The local business community has a handful of major corporations, each with 2,500 to 6,000 employees. Dozens of companies, predominantly high-tech, have between 1,000 and 2,500 employees. The executives of the large corporations are mostly imported to the valley and have been here for an average of about four years. Most of the companies in the technology sector are local entrepreneurial start-ups that have done well in the Navajo Flats community, particularly drawing on employees who are prod-

ucts of the excellent educational institutions. Hundreds of smaller companies also do business in the valley. Corporate executives recognize the health care problem in Navajo Flats, particularly among blue-collar workers and the migrant population. For a few of them, the problem is their own, as they rely upon those very populations for labor. The entrepreneurs among the corporate executives are less likely to believe it is an issue that concerns them. Nevertheless, a good portion of the mid- to large-size companies are partners with the local United Way and can be counted upon for support. Most executives see their community involvement as a significant element in their success as individuals and as companies. Only 25% of them are female. Their demographics are very like those of the members of the partnership boards, because those boards draw significantly from this public.

Current relationship: We have worked closely with many of these executives to address community problems in the past. Many are members of the partnership boards and most will be supportive with some kind of donation, even if small. They know us and trust us to know what is good for the community.

Influentials: Peers, partnership board members, United Way, and social service leaders in the community.

Self-interests: Their companies' reputations as community supporters, the success of their companies, their employees, the welfare of the community.

Employees of Local Business: This is a broad and diverse group ranging from white-collar salaried managers to blue-collar hourly workers. Their demographics would mirror the aggregate census, rather than segments. They would have to be further segmented either by some workforce demographics or by the kinds of employers. A significant number of this public already gives annually to local causes, many through workplace campaigns. The blue-collar workers are in a position to see the effects of the lack of affordable health care, whereas for the white-collar workers, it is just another social issue. The channels to reach this public are through their workplace, but the threat

Chapter 4 Teaching Case Continued...

is that they are more likely than other publics to shift their annual giving to this cause rather than giving additional money. This would result in the annual support of local social service organizations being threatened.

Current relationship: Varied relationships from none at all to a strong relationship with those who donate or serve annually with the local social service agencies. Some would empathize with the issue, others are distant enough from it that they would probably not be easy to commit.

Influentials: Peers, coworkers, employers, families.

Self-interests: Making a living, supporting self and families, quality of life, peer acceptance, job advancement.

Blue-collar Workers: Approximately 75,000 people in the workforce locally are blue-collar workers. They range in age from 16 to 65 and work for hourly wages. Annual income ranges from $18,000 a year to $60,000 for the more skilled and experienced workers. Division of male and female is equal, but a higher percentage is unmarried (60%). The majority of the Hispanic population falls in this category. About 65% of this public belong to unions that negotiate wages and benefits for them. The older they are, the more likely they are to be union members and working for one of the major corporations in town. About 35% of those in this public do not intend to work for hourly wages for their entire lives. They are taking advantage of educational opportunities for advancement or job training to improve their employment situation. Many attend local colleges and technical schools. This public tends to be more giving and empathetic than the white-collar worker because they are personally acquainted with people who need assistance of one kind or another. Many already give time and money through their workplaces to support local causes.

Current relationship: Very positive. They support social causes and understand the need for health care. Nevertheless, many already give to local agencies and we don't want to upset that relationship.

Influentials: Peers, families, friends and neighbors, unions.

Self-interests: Surviving, adequately supporting family and getting education to get a better job, helping one another.

Retirees and Senior Citizens: These individuals are at least 55 years of age, most between 65 and 75. Most have had successful careers which have given them the financial security to retire. About 25% live less affluently on social security, sometimes supplemented by a small pension. Nearly 90% are of local origin, or retired from employment locally. They are familiar with the culture and issues of Navajo Flats. Many have been involved in charitable organizations or causes locally both as donors and as volunteers. About 30% require some kind of care beyond family, either through home health care or in care centers or retirement communities. While many have limited ability to give, some are quite affluent and many of those already give generously. About half are married but the other half is either unmarried or widowed. Nearly 65% have children and grandchildren living locally.

Current relationship: Most in this group know of our partnership agencies and trust them. They would be supportive of the free clinic as a compassionate and caring service in the community.

Influentials: Spouse and family, doctors/health care workers, long-time friends, and former coworkers.

Self-interests: Although probably the most altruistic, especially if self-supporting, members in this group also have concern for their long-term ability to support themselves financially, particularly with the rising cost of health care. While some may have the capacity to give, they would be better targeted as community leaders than as retirees.

Small Business Leaders: Hundreds of business leaders in Navajo Flats fall into this category. Almost all are entrepreneurs who have started their own business. Some businesses have stayed small with a few employees, others have grown to companies of anywhere from 50 to 1,000 employees. A very small number of these leaders have hired from among the Hispanic community, but most have hired students or trained professionals. These individuals have initiative and an ability to confront problems head on and solve them. Many are members of the professional community as doctors, lawyers, accountants, or other professionals. Many are members of professional associations or of the local Chamber of Commerce or civic clubs. Some are leaders in the community but most are somewhat isolated from the community service mainstream unless they have taken the initiative to become involved. Nevertheless, it is a public that local nonprofits would like to get involved in the community because they are opinion leaders with the power to motivate their friends and neighbors, and with the ability to support community efforts. They range in age from about 30 to 65. About 65% are male. Among this group, women and those who are over 50 tend to be those most community involved. About 73% of this public is married with families.

Current relationship: Unless they are involved in community efforts already, this public has low awareness of the issue or the agencies involved in the partnership. They would be aware of SWHC and possibly of the Interfaith Council but would not have a strong affinity to help or support the partnership or the project unless they are among those few in this public who are community involved.

Influentials: Peers, customers, families.

Self-interests: Business success, profitability, financial security, family welfare.

Local Area Professionals: These individuals are in professions typified by private practice, like doctors, dentists, attorneys, and accountants. Many are members of business and professional associations in Navajo Flats. They are typically prosperous, with annual incomes in excess of $200,000. Most are approximately 35–55 years old and 70% are male. Nearly 90% are married and raising families in Navajo Flats. Hence, they are active in the local schools, sports, and cultural activities. All are somewhat entrepreneurial, some as small business owners. They are economically and politically conservative, but because of their

entrepreneurial spirit, would enthusiastically support this new venture. Self-reliance is a core value for this public but they are also aware of an obligation for community service and caring for the less fortunate, although many do not currently act on that awareness. They are tuned into local media and follow the news both print and broadcast. Combined memberships of the local Bar Association, the Dental Association, the Medical Association, Chamber of Commerce, and other such professional and business organizations is approximately 30,000, although there are closer to 40,000 area professionals because not all the associations are required memberships. Many community leaders and social service board members are included in this group of professionals. Because of the nature of United Way donation through the workplace and the nature of their employment in private practice rather than large companies, the members of this public who donate to local social service causes do not do so through traditional channels. In other words, most cannot say "I gave at the office."

Current relationship: A number of the members of this public are already giving and serving in the community, although many are not involved because the isolated nature of their small practices allows them to escape the traditional workplace giving involvement of larger companies. They are aware of pressing community issues, the agencies involved in the partnership, and will likely support our effort philosophically. We just need to change that support into a financial contribution.

Influentials: Peers, fellow professionals, business and civic leaders, spouses.

Self-interests: Professional reputation and success, clients, ability to support family, lifestyle, fitness, and appearance.

Health Care Workers: About 15,000 people are employed in health care in the Navajo Flats community, from doctors, nurses, and specialists to physical therapists and nursing assistants. They are at the hospitals, clinics, in doctor's offices, and working with home health care agencies. Many are in positions to recognize the critical need and the importance of this initiative in the community. Many work long hours in short-staffed situations.

Chapter 4 Teaching Case Continued...

Incomes of nurses, assistants, and therapists range from $35,000 a year to $85,000, with doctors and specialists typically earning in excess of $200,000 annually. The supporting staff is typically younger, with an average age of 29, while the average age of doctors is 46. Nearly 60% are married with families. They are strong participants in giving campaigns for local agencies, and will also volunteer time to support local health initiatives. They could be opinion leaders on this issue because they understand it well and are in what would be considered compassionate professions.

Current relationship: Strong. They understand the need and are typically giving and supportive of community health care efforts for the underprivileged.

Influentials: Peers, leaders of the social service agencies.

Self-interests: Strong altruistic motivation on this issue, patients, family.

College Students: The educational institutions in the valley enroll approximately 50,000 full- and part-time students with an average age of 22. About 50% are from Navajo Flats and the surrounding communities (within 100 miles). Another 40% come from elsewhere in Arizona, and 10% are from outside the state, most from the Southwestern states. Nearly 90% of students work at least part time. Schedules range from 10 to 40 hours per week at hourly jobs with an average wage of $8.50 an hour. Between school and work, students have very busy schedules, but they also tend to be activists, particularly on social issues. They are a tremendous source of volunteers in the community, but they have limited resources for giving. They have great energy and would stage fundraising events, but such events targeted at students typically yield more raised awareness and passion than money.

Current relationship: Students aren't particularly aware of the partnership or of the issue, but would be passionate supporters if informed.

Influentials: Peers, professors, parents.

Self-interests: Strong altruism and compassion, social good, education, social life, friends.

Hispanic Community: The Hispanic community in Navajo Flats is 60,000 strong, with 30,000 of those people in the workforce. Most are unskilled, hourly workers and some are illegal immigrants with phony social security numbers or who work for cash only. Most work either for the food packing plants or the golf cart manufacturer, or as manual laborers for landscapers, builders, or other such employers. Many of the women work in the fast food industry. Upwards of 70% are in a family unit of some kind, but others have left their families in their home countries. Most are religious, but few attend church because of cultural differences. The community is close knit and isolated from the mainstream in Navajo Flats. This public tends to be one that is served by the free clinic rather than one capable of contributing financially to it. Leaders within the Hispanic community include successful businessmen in Navajo Flats, primarily professionals in sole practice or entrepreneurs with small companies and few employees. These are few in number, but are opinion leaders for this public.

Current relationship: This public is aware of CAS because many have accessed its services in the past. They understand the problem, because they live it, but they are unaware of any planning for the free clinic.

Influentials: Hispanic community leaders, peers, family.

Self-interests: Survival, welfare of their families.

Community Leadership Givers: We can count on this public to support this project. They already give heavily to causes in the community and are typically in financial positions to be generous. They might be willing to make a commitment for a one-time gift of $1,000 (or perhaps more) to support this clinic. They are typically members of boards of directors for local nonprofits and formal opinion leaders in visible positions of authority in government or as leaders of community organizations. The United Way has directories of most of the nonprofit social service agencies' boards and a fairly complete list of other opinion leaders in the community. The integrated list contains about 2,500 names of these potential leadership givers. About half of these leaders are typical upper- middle-class or upper-class members of the Navajo Flats community working as professionals in private practice or in management positions in local corporations. (Most of these would be included in the membership of local professional associations.) The other half represents the wealthier segment of the Navajo Flats community, with assets well in excess of a million dollars. They are local philanthropists and benefactors, all with favorite causes. They are both male and female, almost all are married, but with grown children. They are heavily involved in the local social, political, and cultural scene. They are also well informed, both from mass media and from personal contacts who keep them abreast of important news and events. This group of philanthropists is well connected with one another. They all know each other well as they have together served the Navajo Flats community and each other for decades. It might be relatively easy to tap one or two of these benefactors to fully fund the free clinic, but the free clinic partnership would prefer that the financial support for the effort be a bit more broad-based so that the free clinic will be seen as a cooperative community venture, and not the pet project of one of the philanthropists alone. Nevertheless, support from among this group will be key to motivating the support of the rest of our community leaders and community members.

Current relationship: The members of this public are already giving and serving in the community. They are aware of pressing community issues, the agencies involved in the partnership and will likely support our effort. Whether they allow us to publicize their contributions will depend upon the effect on their other philanthropic activities.

Influentials: Peers, other community leaders, employees.

Self-interests: These individuals do have an altruistic attitude toward the community. While they are motivated by personal and business success and the ability to support their families, they are also compassionate towards the needs of the community and feel a responsibility to use their positions for the benefit of the members of the community. They like their status and enjoy the appreciation and honors others give them for their service, but they also recognize needs and use their position to help fill those needs. Finally, they are generous with their money, but their time is high-

ly valued. We need to make it easy for them to help us.

Current Donors: Because of the very active non-profit community and the giving and volunteer nature of the Navajo Flats community, a large number of community members currently give to one cause or another. Many companies feature annual United Way campaigns and their employees are generous supporters. The local United Way raises in excess of $8 million annually which is distributed among the local social service agencies that qualify. Many who already give will likely give another one-time donation to support the free clinic, but we need to make sure that we ask in such a way that they will give in addition to what they already give rather than diverting their current donations.

The United Way has a reliable profile of their current donors. They are employees of local corporations. Most are between 35 and 65 years of age. The older they are, the more they donate annually. Most are members of families with at least two children. About 25% of those families are in single-parent homes. The typical income of the majority of donors is between $32,000 and $60,000 annually. A lower percentage of members of other income groups are annual donors to their companies' United Way campaigns but probably give independently and more privately.

Current relationship: Very positive relationship with these individuals. They tend to appreciate the efforts of the nonprofits. But many feel they already do their part.

Influentials: Peers, family, community leaders, employers.

Self-interests: Some altruism here, they want to live in a healthy community and care for their neighbors. They are concerned about the welfare of their families. They like being among those who give.

Members of Local Churches: Approximately 75% of the adults in Navajo Flats consider themselves religious, but only 50% attend a church service at least once a year and 35% say they attend services regularly. Nevertheless, 60% identify themselves with a particular church and know

Chapter 4 Teaching Case Continued...

their spiritual leader by name. Nearly 85% of those who attend services do so as a family unit. Even among those who attend infrequently, most have children who are involved to some degree in youth groups affiliated with their church. There is a high correlation between regular church attendance and giving to and volunteering with community nonprofit organizations. This is one of the publics that the partnership will rely upon for volunteers to staff the free clinic. Most are in the lower- to upper-middle class income range.

Current relationship: Most of the churches are members of the Interfaith Council, but most of the members don't know that. The lay members are somewhat aware of the issue, but unaware of the effort to establish the free clinic.

Influentials: Church leaders, fellow members, spouses.

Self-interests: Some altruism, social good, status in their social circles, family.

Matrix: Research
Step Two—Situation Analysis

The community of Navajo Flats has a rare opportunity to fill a critical need for the less fortunate among them. Providing health care for this underserved population will eliminate other costly problems that stem from lack of access to medical treatment. Statistics show that lack of adequate health care is directly related to the demand for other social services such as welfare and aid to dependent children. Further, it contributes to

stress in families that can lead to domestic violence and even to rising crime rates. Community members in Navajo Flats are already very generous with money and time in support of local social service agencies and retired doctors, nurses, and technicians have volunteered their time and expertise to staff the clinic. CAS will be an ideal landlord for the clinic, but must fill the space and begin collecting on the lease relatively quickly in order to afford the building. We have a six-month window of opportunity to raise the $500,000 necessary to open the free clinic. The money must come from donations over and above what the community is already giving to support social services. If we are unable to raise the money and open the clinic, the need for health care among the migrant population, blue-collar families, and students will become more acute, exacerbating other social problems. Rallying community support to raise money for the clinic will also help people feel some ownership in helping to provide for their less fortunate neighbors.

Matrix: Research
Step Three—Core Problem/ Opportunity

Through the United Way partnership, establish the free medical clinic serving those members of the Navajo Flats community who would otherwise have no access to health care, by raising the $500,000 needed to build out the facility within six months.

Summary

Organizing background research according to the research checklist helps lay the foundation for decision making. The background, SWOT analysis, and public profiles help to focus everything we know into a solution or plan. It funnels research into the problem-solving and planning process because it has driven us to think analytically, to evaluate what is known, and identify how that will assist in the selection of publics and resources to solve the problem.

The situation analysis likely identifies some key factors not known when the challenge or opportunity was first discovered. Assessing the real situation after we have completed our background analysis helps us focus more clearly on the core challenge or opportunity and to marshal all knowledge, information, skills, and resources to succeed.

Exercises

1. Identify an organization with a communications and/or marketing problem. List everything you know about the organization, its environment, the problem, and the market. Then list everything you need to know to define the real problem and devise a solution. What research tools and information sources would you use to get that information?

2. Choose a public you are familiar with like university students. Create a profile with all the information you know about that public's values, attitudes, opinions, lifestyles, and media use. Identify their self-interests and influentials. Then identify what information you would need to complete the profile and how you would get it.

3. Find a nonprofit organization with a communications challenge that you can help solve. Using the research checklist, gather all the information you need to develop a solution to its problem. Using the strategic planning matrix, synthesize the information into the research section of a campaign proposal.

References and Additional Readings

Bruning, S., & Ledingham, J. (1999). Relationships between organizations and publics: Development of a multi-dimensional organization-public relationship scale. *Public Relations Review, 25(2):*157–170.

Bruning, S., & Ledingham, J. (2000). Organization and key public relationships: Testing the influence of the relationship dimensions in a business-to-business context. In J. Ledingham and S. Bruning (eds.) *Public relations as relationship management: A relational approach to the study and practice of public relations.* Mahwah, NJ: Lawrence Erlbaum Associates, Publishers.

Collett, S. (1999). SWOT analysis: quickstudy. *Computerworld,* July 19.

Klapper, J. T. (1960). *The effects of mass communication.* New York: Free Press.

Ledingham, J., & Bruning, S. (1998). Relationship management and public relations: Dimensions of an organization-public relationship. *Public Relations Review, 24,* 55–65.

McCombs, M. E., & Shaw, D. L. (1972). The agenda-setting function of mass media. *Public Opinion Quarterly, 36,*176–187.

McQuail, D. (1987). *Mass communication theory: An introduction.* Beverly Hills, CA: Sage Publications.

Stacks, D. W. (2002). *Primer of public relations research.* New York: Guilford Publications, Inc.

Setting Goals and Objectives

"If you fail to plan, you plan to fail."

—Unknown

LEARNING IMPERATIVES

- **To be able to turn problem statements into appropriate goals**

- **To understand the characteristics of good objectives**

- **To learn how to write specific objectives to support the accomplishment of a goal**

Planning

The process of using research to chart the step-by-step course to solve a problem, take advantage of an opportunity, or meet a challenge.

The second step of the RACE model—research, action planning, communications, evaluation—is action planning. Planning and the programming it generates is how we get from here to there. *Here* is where we are now. It is our current situation as we have described it after synthesizing our research and redefining the challenge or opportunity we face. *There* is where we need to be, having overcome the challenges and taken advantage of the opportunities. Planning helps us look ahead, to chart our course to ensure we get there. Like sailing a boat, planning must be flexible and open to alteration and correction as we receive feedback or obtain new information. Nevertheless, unless we know where we are going and have some idea of an appropriate course to get there, our arrival at the destination will be left to chance. The more complete our planning of the best course (based on good research), the better our chances of arriving at success.

THE MATRIX APPROACH TO PLANNING

The heart of the Strategic Communications Planning Matrix is the action planning section (Figure 5.1). The research process, the subsequent organization and analysis of data and the redefinition of the situation and the core challenge, all lay the foundation for the action planning process. Cutlip, Center, and Broom (2000) call this a "searching look backward," a "wide look around," a "deep look inside," and a "long look ahead."

The Strategic Communications Planning Matrix addresses each of the remaining three sections—action planning, communication, and evaluation—as discrete functions. Nevertheless, this is a planning matrix; the emphasis is on planning each step in the process before implementing. Thus, the resulting plan, although dynamic, becomes a document to drive both the communication and evaluation steps in the process.

Goal

The result or desired outcome that solves a problem, takes advantage of an opportunity, or meets a challenge.

Objective

Specific, measurable statements of what needs to be accomplished to reach the goal.

Planning occurs at two distinct levels within any organization. Long-term planning looks at the entirety of the organization and its mission. It identifies goals and objectives and publics and messages that address the long-term accomplishment of that mission. Planning at this level becomes a guide for planning more specific short-term campaigns or communication efforts. They are the second level of planning. Managing a crisis, launching a new product line, and repairing a damaged reputation are all more specific efforts within the overall long-term plan. Although they are focused on a more specific challenge, they always reinforce key messages to organizational publics and support the goals and objectives of the long-term plan. Nevertheless, by their nature, they may also address publics that may not be long-term key publics of the organization but that are crucial to the accomplishment of the short-term effort.

Research helps us define the challenge and the current environment within which the opportunity has occurred or will occur. Matrix planning identifies:

- What specifically needs to be accomplished (goal and objectives) to overcome the challenge,
- Who (key publics) we need to reach and/or motivate to accomplish the goals and objectives,

Figure 5.1

10-Step Strategic Communications Planning Matrix

Matrix: Action Planning

Step Four—Goal and Objectives

Goal

The goal is a one-sentence statement of the end to be achieved to resolve the core problem or seize a significant opportunity. The goal does not have to be stated in quantifiable terms.

Objectives

Objectives are numbered or bulleted statements of specific results that will lead to the achievement of the goal. Objectives must be: specific, measurable, attainable, time-bound, and mission-driven.

- What we need to convey (messages) to those publics to stimulate action and help us achieve our objectives, and
- How (strategies and tactics) to get those messages to those publics so they both receive and act upon them.

These are the four key decisions at the heart of matrix planning. The process is analytical, with the decisions made and actions planned in each step driving the decisions made and actions planned in each subsequent step. Further, the steps must be taken each in turn. For example, the key publics for a particular problem-solving effort cannot be selected until we have determined the goal and the objectives necessary to achieve that goal. Only then can we select the publics that are key to accomplishing those objectives. Similarly, we can only design effective messages after we have selected key publics and determined their self-interests. The decisions we make about the information a public needs, what will motivate it to act, and what opinion leaders can influence it are prerequisite to designing that public's message.

Effective informational and motivational messages cannot be designed for a given public without a thorough analysis of its research profile, examination of the status of the current relationship with that public, and knowledge of its self-interests as they pertain to the problem at hand and related issues. Strategies and tactics appropriate to send the designed messages to the selected publics cannot be determined until we know what those messages are. Quite simply, the matrix approach requires us to decide what we want to do, who we need to reach to do it, what messages we need to send to obtain cooperation, and how we can most effectively send those messages. The steps must be taken in order or our planning is left to chance and will most likely be flawed and off-track.

We have all seen campaigns that had good research but somehow misconnected in planning and implementation. One poignant example is Salt Lake City's campaign to win the bid for the 1998 (and subsequently the 2002) Olympic Winter Games. The Denver organizing committee had to withdraw its candidacy as the United States' representative in a previous Olympic games bid because of opposing public opinion in the Denver area. Consequently, the Salt Lake City organizers decided it was important to have a public referendum on the issue to demonstrate to the United States Olympic Committee (USOC) and to the International Olympic Committee (IOC) that the Utah public was fully supportive of Salt Lake's candidacy. With support running high in the state (upwards of 80%), the organizing committee expected the referendum would send a strong message from the Utah public in support of the effort. Nevertheless, their own polling showed they had weak support and even opposition among senior citizens, environmentalists, and ultra-conservative segments of the population. While these groups actually comprised only a small percentage of the Utah population, the organizing committee worried that, in an off-year election, those three segments of the population were the most likely to vote. Given that information, their goal and objectives were to get out the supportive vote.

The strategy was to air clever, creative, and visually appealing television spots (tactics) that gave people a good feeling about Utah hosting the Olympic games. At the end of the spots they showed a box with a check mark in it to indicate a vote supportive of the Olympic bid. But the ads were essentially still seeking intrinsic public support of the games. The ads didn't ask people to get out of their chairs and go vote. The bid already had a high public approval rating. What the committee really needed was to motivate those who approved to get to the polls and cast their supportive vote. But the committee (through

© Aron Hsiao, 2008.

its ads) never asked the approving public to actually go vote. So they didn't. The referendum ultimately passed by a very slim majority, and the organizing committee was plagued with explaining the low margin of public support to the IOC in almost every subsequent interaction.

Once the city won the opportunity to host the 2002 Olympic Winter Games, the organizing committee no longer had to address the issue of citizen support to the IOC. Nevertheless, the low voter support of the referendum was continual fodder for the active (albeit minority) opposition to the games in Utah. No public opinion poll could ever entirely dispel the results of the actual vote.

The Salt Lake City Olympic Organizing Committee had good research data and analysis. They knew what they had to do (get out the supportive publics who don't typically vote in an off-year election). They knew specifically the profiles of the publics they had to reach. Yet they designed a message that did not ask those publics to do what the committee needed done, and they sent it in a broadly targeted tactic through a mass medium ill-suited to the purpose at hand (reaching and motivating highly segmented publics). Each step of the matrix planning process must build on the previous step. The logic must flow consistently and coherently. Disregarding the information accumulated, the decisions made and actions planned in one step will almost always ensure that the decisions made and actions planned in the next step are off-target and headed for failure.

With this important lesson in mind, the next few chapters address the action planning steps of the Strategic Communications Planning Matrix. This chapter begins that discussion by identifying what needs to be done to meet the challenge or seize the opportunity at hand.

ESTABLISHING THE GOAL

Once the core problem or opportunity is accurately established, setting the goal is a simple task with the planning matrix. The goal is actually a positive restatement of the core problem. If your challenge is declining confidence among investors leading to a decline in stock price, your goal is to reestablish confidence so stock price will increase. If your problem is a lack of accurate information regarding the process of organ donation causing a shortage of available organs for transplant, your goal is to convey appropriate information in such a way as to increase the number of organs donated. The goal should be broader and more general than the objectives that follow. A goal also does not have to be specifically measurable. The measured achievement of strategic objectives should ensure that the overall goal is obtained.

Nevertheless, setting the goal may not be as simple as it appears. Too often, organizational communications and marketing personnel act unilaterally to set goals to solve problems. But those functions are not isolated within an organization; they should all be integral parts of the management function and team. Setting campaign goals in isolation, or without consideration of the organization's overall goals, is dangerous and can lead to a lack of support at critical junctures.

Tips from the Pros

What's a Goal and What's an Objective?

J. Michael Neumeier, APR, Principal and co-founder of Arketi Group, an integrated public relations and marketing consultancy, tips you off on how to tell a goal from an objective.

All too often, the terms goal and objective are used as interchangeable ways of saying the same thing. Plainly put, they are not—and the resulting lack of precision can be problematic. This lack of understanding can cripple a PR or marketing plan leaving it void of value.

Goals

A goal is a *statement of being* for the plan. Often, one goal is enough. PR and marketing goals should always be consistent with management goals and they should be carefully crafted with the end result in mind.

A marketing plan goal might be "to increase the level of government funding," or "to expand our industry leadership."

While the completion of the goal signifies the end of your plan, the objectives, strategies, and tactics are the means to that end.

Objectives

Compared to the goal, objectives are more focused and specific, and the best-formulated objectives express results as measurable outcomes. Think in terms of the awareness, attitude, or action that you hope to invoke. Often there are multiple objectives in support of a single goal. Meaningful objectives start with action verbs and have four parts; they:

- Identify a specific audience being addressed
- State a measurable outcome
- Set an attainment level
- Set a time frame

Examples of objectives are "to secure 20% more media coverage in trade publications in fiscal year 2007" or "to increase news flow from the company by 25% during 2007."

When writing objectives, keep these tips in mind:

Seek input from management. Output measurements, like distributing an average of two news releases a month, are sometimes very important to executives. And objectives that are easy to measure are as important as objectives that require complex and expensive metrics.

Don't force yourself into long time frames like a year. If you can tightly define a time frame to even a month or two, that will help you craft a stronger objective.

Get a second opinion. The best second opinions come from other PR professionals you know that are not working directly on the plan.

Audiences do not have to be limited to external targets. Many times getting internal stakeholders to understand and embrace a campaign can be a very worthy objective.

If you know you cannot measure it, don't build it into an objective.

Precautions

Two precautions can aid the practitioner in avoiding this problem.

1. If the daily communication function has been approached strategically, or planned in accordance with the organization's mission and goals (including the goals of various other departments such as public relations, advertising, and marketing), then communication is guided by the organization's mission. In other words, communications and marketing practitioners should always set and follow goals and objectives that support the overall organizational mission.

2. The practitioner should always verify the campaign goal's compliance with organizational goals and objectives. After setting the goal, take a moment to ask yourself if it supports the overall organizational mission. Does it mesh with marketing and communication goals and objectives? Does it cooperate to create an environment in which the organization progresses toward achievement of its goals? It is typically not enough to "not conflict" with the organization's communication and marketing missions and goals. Truly sound and defensible goals and objectives will enhance and support the overall organizational mission and goals.

Figure 5.2 identifies some examples of possible organizational goals. Remember that effective communication with key publics is necessary to create the environment in which the organization can reach its goals. Any single campaign, whether designed to solve a problem or to proactively position the organization, must be planned within the framework of the organization's goals.

Figure 5.2—Examples of Typical Organizational Goals

Business Sector
- Maintain profitability
- Maintain and gradually improve stock rating
- Achieve a positive trust ranking
- Maintain an operating environment with minimal government regulation

Public Sector
- Increase use of funded social programs
- Cut overhead and increase flow of funds to programs
- Decrease fraudulent use of social programs
- Improve citizen access to and use of information
- Increase government funding

Nonprofit Sector
- Expand research efforts
- Expand program reach
- Secure private financial support of programs

IDENTIFYING OBJECTIVES TO ACCOMPLISH THE GOAL

Once the goal is set, the challenge is to break down what you want to accomplish into smaller, more specific tasks. If your company's goal is to expand a research program, your communications campaign may need to set objectives that involve securing public approval, generating funding, attracting personnel, and building community support for the renovation of facilities. Objectives are specific, measurable statements of what needs to be accomplished for the goal to be reached. Whereas a goal may be somewhat ambiguous (i.e., not defining how much is enough funding or profit), objectives must be absolutely free from ambiguity.

Characteristics of Good Objectives

In the communications and business literature, the following eight characteristics emerge to guide the formulation of good objectives.

1. **Written.** This characteristic may appear to be obvious, but too often we begin planning by assuming everyone understands our purpose and objectives. Unless they are written, they have probably not been well considered, and there may be differing perceptions of what the objectives really are. One member of the team may be working toward something entirely different than the other members because his/her perception of the task is different than the rest of the team's. Putting the objectives in writing helps to avoid differing perceptions of what needs to be accomplished.

   Further, when objectives are written, they serve as reference points throughout the planning process. When you come to a point of disagreement on any element of the planning process or when you run out of ideas somewhere in the process, it often helps to go back and review exactly what it is you are trying to accomplish. Finally, written objectives serve as tangible guides for evaluation and evidence of success, not only for the program or project but also for you as a professional.

2. **Specific and clearly defined.** To be free from ambiguity, the task must be specific and clear. It helps to quantify the objective, and each objective should address only one task. You shouldn't write a single objective to increase awareness of both an issue and an organization. Moreover, sometimes simple name recognition is enough, but the majority of the time you need to be specific about what kind of awareness you are seeking. Do you want to increase awareness of an organization's existence or a specific product line? Are you specifically targeting HIV awareness, or the effect of its transmission to newborns? And what levels of awareness are you seeking based on current levels of public knowledge? Having task-specific objectives helps you more clearly understand what publics you need to reach and what you need each public to do. Those tasks actually become part of the strategies for key publics later in the planning process.

3. **Measurable and improvement-oriented.** It is a given that an objective should be improvement oriented. It must specify a task that works with other tasks to achieve the goal or meet the challenge. In order for an

objective to truly guide the program and demonstrate its ultimate success, it must also be measurable. Measurement can be in percentages or in actual figures (a dollar amount of funds needed, sales targets, total number of volunteer hours sought, number of votes necessary). Often times, it is helpful to indicate the measurable target in terms of improvement (sales increased 20% from $5 million to $6 million or inoculations increased 10% annually from 500,000 to 550,000).

When you work with percentages, remember to carefully state the percentage increase or decrease and use clarifying phrases. Otherwise, you might set yourself up to disappoint management's expectations created by your own objectives. If you want to decrease the percentage of high school students who have experimented with drugs by 50 percentage points, you should follow up that number by specifically stating the decrease (from 75% to 25%). If you really had in mind a 50% decrease (rather than a 50 percentage point decrease), you would have reduced the percentage from 75% to 37.5% (or 50% of 75). Similarly, a 20% increase in participation among a total population of 100 is not 20 people. The percent increase depends on the current level of participation, not the total population. If 50 of 100 people are currently participating, a 20% increase would be 10 people (20% of 50), from 50 to 60 participants, or a 10 percentage point improvement. Be very precise when you state your measurement.

Statistics on opinion or action may not always be readily available. If you are certain the level of knowledge or participation is minimal, just state the level it needs to be to accomplish the goal. If you don't have statistical measures for something, find another way to count the improvement.

4. **Credible.** Being credible simply means that the accomplishment can be directly attributed to your efforts. For example, if the advertising or public relations team members set an objective to obtain a 5% increase in product sales and then attempts to claim sole credit for that accomplishment, they will not only incur the disapproval of their marketing counterparts but also of top executives who recognize they are claiming credit for improvement for which they are not alone responsible. Set objectives and then design programs which can be directly credited with the success you claim. If your task is public relations, focus on creating the environment within which other organizational entities can succeed.

5. **Acceptable.** This characteristic refers to the acceptability of the objective to the organization and its management. To be acceptable, an objective must be in line with and support the organizational mission, goals, and objectives. It must address issues, problems, and improvements that management perceives as valuable.

6. **Realistic and attainable.** Can you really achieve what your objective specifies you will achieve? Keeping objectives specific and clear will also help to keep them realistic. But you still need to set your sights on significant improvement. Top management will scorn objectives that are too easily attainable. Executives have little respect for employees and managers who are unwilling to reach a bit, to take some risks, and to

© Frank Herzog, 2008.

challenge themselves. Nevertheless, if you shoot for the moon and just hit the stars, you may be branded as having fallen short, even if the stars were all you really needed to reach.

7. **Time-bound.** The duration of a communications or marketing campaign is determined by the problem or opportunity being addressed. Some may require short, quick efforts (a few weeks or months) while others may necessitate longer-range efforts. Some campaigns have built-in deadlines (i.e., special event for a product launch). Others seek to change perceptions and attitudes, which change very slowly. Good objectives must identify the time frame within which the program must be completed and include benchmarks for the measurement of long-range campaigns.

8. **Budget-bound.** Although you don't always know the budget available for a specific program when you are at this preliminary stage of planning, good objectives take into consideration the probable budgetary range. While you must set objectives to solve the problem and reach the goal, the objectives you set also shape the organization's expectations of you and your communications and marketing team. Budgetary limitations may necessitate objectives that create more modest expectations. They may also force greater creativity in your planning. Although larger budgets will lay the groundwork for a more ambitious program, the reality of today's business environment is that there is limited funding for communication.

In addition to the characteristics of good objectives, it is important to recognize the two basic kinds of objectives, each serving a different purpose but both integral to the overall accomplishment of any campaign. The first kind of objective lays a foundation of information and awareness necessary for any kind of persuasive effort. It addresses the dissemination of information and the increase in awareness necessary among publics before they can develop attitudes to drive the behavior you are seeking. Informational objectives are usually easy to accomplish because you are just spreading information, not attempting to change anything. In fact, much of today's corporate communications practice is heavily engaged in information dissemination and awareness- or consciousness-raising. Nevertheless, Wilcox, Ault, and Agee (2002) contend that it is difficult to measure the accomplishment of such an objective because you are trying to measure a cognitive function (increase in information or understanding) on a sliding scale (how much information or understanding).

Motivational objectives, on the other hand, are more easily measured and harder to achieve according to Wilcox et al (2002). It is a relatively simple matter to measure a desired behavior. People voted for your candidate or they did not; consumers bought the product or they didn't; children were inoculated or they weren't. Nevertheless, changing attitudes and opinions and creating the triggering event to move the public from attitude to behavior is much more difficult than just disseminating information and raising awareness of an issue or problem.

Use awareness objectives to lay the foundation for persuasive efforts or motivational objectives. People can't vote the way you want them to on an issue if they are not aware of the issue and its effect on their lives. Consumers cannot buy a new product that will make life easier or more pleasant if they are not aware of its existence. Set awareness and information objectives (with

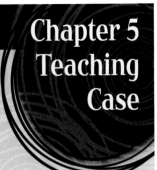

The Case of the Warehouse Welfare Health Care

Sample Campaign

Matrix: Action Planning
Step Four—Goal and Objectives

Goal

The United Way partnership's goal is to raise $500,000 from the community by the end of August to build out the space offered by CAS, without affecting the current level of support to other social service agencies.

Objectives

1. Raise awareness of the opportunity to 80% among key publics: to 20% within two months (by April 30th), to 60% within three months (by May 31st) and to 80% within five months (by July 31st).

2. Obtain $150,000 in new leadership gifts ($1,000 or more) within two months (April 30th).

3. Obtain $250,000 in new corporate sponsorships within four months (June 30th).

4. Obtain the remaining $100,000 within six months (August 31st).

all the characteristics of good objectives) that will lay the foundation to accomplish your motivational objectives. Keep in mind that disseminating information is easy but motivating behavior is more difficult. You will typically be able to reach a far higher level of awareness than you will behavior. You may be able to inform upwards of 90% of your target population on a particular issue. Nevertheless, 90% awareness does not translate to 90% motivated to act. The achievable percentage of behavior will always lag behind the level of awareness. On some issues it may be only slightly lower; on other issues there may be a dramatic difference.

Summary

The Strategic Communications Planning Matrix guides the planning process in communication and problem solving. It is the analytical tool that ensures research data and information are applied to solving the problem at hand. This matrix requires that good information, sound reasoning, and clear logic drive decisions regarding what objectives you need to accomplish to solve the problem, what publics you need to reach, what messages you need to send to motivate those publics to act, and what communication channels and tools (tactics) will ensure key publics select and act on your messages.

The matrix transforms each step of the RACE model into strategic functions. It ensures that the communication process is not just a succession of steps to be completed, but that it is an interactive, integrated methodology for finding the best and most timely solution for the most appropriate cost. The process must be guided by mission-oriented goals and clear, measurable objectives. Remember that a campaign goal is a positive restatement of the core problem identified in the research section of the matrix.

Objectives lay the foundation for the successful selection of key publics, their messages, and the strategies and tactics that will deliver the messages and motivate action. Well crafted objectives are written, specific and clearly defined, measurable and improvement-oriented, credible, acceptable, realistic and attainable, time-bound, and budget-bound.

Exercises

1. Based on your research, create goals and objectives for the nonprofit organization you identified in the previous chapter's exercises. Make sure you set a goal that overcomes the problem you identified, and set objectives to attain the goal that follow the eight characteristics of good objectives.

2. Select a local company and request a copy of its mission statement and goals. Then brainstorm the objectives necessary to reach the goals. Make sure your objectives meet all the criteria of good objectives.

References and Additional Readings

Cutlip, S., Center, A., & Broom, G. (2000). *Effective public relations* (8th ed.). Englewood Cliffs, NJ: Prentice-Hall, Inc.

Drucker, P. (1974). *Management tasks, responsibilities, practices.* New York: Harper and Row.

Hainsworth, B. E., & Wilson, L. J. (1992). Strategic program planning. *Public Relations Review, 18:1,* 9–15.

Koestler, F. A. (1977). *Planning and setting objectives.* New York: Foundation for Public Relations Research and Education.

Newsom, D., Turk J. V., & Kruckeberg D. (2004). *This is PR: The realities of public relations* (8th ed.). Belmont, CA: Wadsworth Publishing Company.

Norris, J. S. (1984). *Public relations.* Englewood Cliffs, NJ: Prentice-Hall, Inc.

Wilcox, D. L., Ault, P. H., & Agee, W. K. (2002). *Public relations: Strategies and tactics* (7th ed.). New York: Harper and Row.

Key Publics and Message Design

"An audience is not a demographic. Demographics are the boundaries, psychographics fill in the boundaries."

—Linda Hadley
Director of Research, Porter Novelli, 2002 PRSA International Conference

LEARNING IMPERATIVES

- To learn how to effectively select key publics
- To learn how to design effective messages for each key public that incorporate relevant self-interests

KEY PUBLICS

In Chapter 5 we discussed setting the objectives to be accomplished to meet the challenge of the core problem. Having done so, we can identify the key publics or audiences whose cooperation will be essential to achieving those objectives and design the messages that will motivate those publics to act, or to allow the organization to act (Figure 6.1).

We use the term public to describe a multidimensional active and interactive group of individuals with a few common characteristics that allow us to group them for the purpose of building relationships through communication and cooperation.

For some communicators, it has become habit to select key publics before setting objectives. As a result, objectives are determined by who you want to reach rather than what you need to accomplish. Every organization should have identified publics who are key to its long-term success, and it should systematically work to build relationships with those publics. But when a problem or challenge emerges, assuming the publics necessary to solve it will always be that same set of organizational publics is a prescription for failure. You may be successful at reaching the organization's existing key publics, but you risk missing other publics who are key to seizing the opportunity at hand.

A good example is an opportunity to expand the reach of your organization's influence. Such an effort will almost always require not only expanded reach to current publics, but also addressing publics the organization has not targeted before. You need to determine what it is you are trying to accomplish in expanding the influence, and then decide what publics are key to accomplishing that. While you may be able to rely somewhat on existing relationships, you will certainly need to cultivate relationships with new and different publics as well.

If you select publics and set objectives for those publics, you are also likely failing to identify some tasks that will be necessary to accomplish the goal. You may reach your designated target publics, but there is a real chance those publics will not be key publics, or the ones you needed to reach to complete the tasks that would accomplish your purpose.

Don't waste time and money informing and motivating publics that don't need informing or motivating. Success among them will not significantly contribute to accomplishing your goal. First identify the tasks (objectives) you need to accomplish and then select those publics that you need to reach and motivate to complete those tasks. Your strategies for a public then become the specific tasks you must accomplish with that public to achieve your objectives.

Key Publics

Segmented groups of people whose support and cooperation are essential to the long-term survival of an organization or the short-term accomplishment of its objectives.

Determining Key Publics

By this time in your study and practice of marketing communications and public relations, you should be well aware that there is no general public. Targeting a general public is useless because people won't pay attention to a message that isn't specifically targeted to their self-interests in a channel they use. Yet as communicators, our use of so-called mass media seems to perpetuate our tendency to generalize publics. In fact, communicators will often segment

Figure 6.1

10-Step Strategic Communications Planning Matrix   Matrix

Matrix: Action Planning

Step Five—Key Publics and Messages

Key Publics

Key publics include a description of each audience that must be reached to achieve the goal and objectives. Five elements should be identified for each public or audience:

1. Demographic and psychographic profile
2. Motivating self-interests
3. Status of current relationship with the organization and issue
4. Third party influentials and other opinion leaders
5. What objectives each public will help you accomplish

Messages

Messages are public-specific and appeal to the public's self-interests. They are designed as primary and secondary. Primary messages are one- or two-sentence summary statements similar to sound bites. Secondary messages are bulleted details that add credibility to and support the primary messages with facts, testimonials, examples, and other information and persuasive arguments.

---

publics and then devise a single message to reach all of their segmented publics through one of the mass media. The segmentation was a waste of time and resources, and the message sent even more so a waste. Remember that just because a medium is designated mass does not mean that the publics consuming the information provided therein are mass.

Think again of the example in Chapter 2 about how you read a newspaper. Do you read every word on every page? Probably not. When you read a newspaper you choose what you read based on headlines. Then you continue to read a story only as long as it is of personal interest. The same perceptual behavior applies to Internet tactics like Web sites and e-mail. You read a headline or subject line. If that draws you in by appealing to your self-interest, you continue to read. But the minute it loses its appeal to you personally, you hit the delete key. No matter the channel or tactic, people choose to perceive our message only when we design it specifically to appeal to them. It is clear that for a message to be selected, perceived, and retained by our publics from any kind of medium, it must be carefully and specifically targeted to a segmented public included within the viewership, readership, or listenership of that medium. If its appeal is general, no public will consider it for perception and retention. It may get sent, but if it doesn't obviously and openly address the self-interests of specific target publics, it will be ignored.

Segmenting Publics

There are lots of ways to segment publics. The way you choose to segment publics for a particular campaign depends upon the issue and your purpose. If you are addressing the quality of education in the community, public segmentation would include parents, teachers, administrators, and future employers. If the issue is zoning regulations within that very same community, your segmentation would recategorize the community members as nonproperty owners, residential property owners, commercial property owners or business people, and civic and government leaders. They are the same people, but how you segment or group and describe them for the purpose of reaching and motivating is based upon the issue at hand and their particular self-interest in that issue.

In the background step of the research section, you brainstormed a list of publics or audiences that might be involved in the solution to the problem or issue facing the organization. Then you used the primary and secondary data gathered to profile those publics—their demographics as well as their opinions, attitudes, values, beliefs, and lifestyles. You discovered their media habits and the best channels to use in communicating with them. You analyzed the potential publics' current relationships with the issue and organization, and you identified their self-interests and influentials. Because you have completed that analysis, you have a deeper understanding of each of those potential publics regarding your current challenge. Now, review your objectives and determine which objectives each potential public might help you accomplish. Remember that more than one public may need to be reached to accomplish each objective or task, and also that a key public may help you achieve more than one objective.

Key Public Combinations

Bear in mind that there may be several different combinations of key publics that can help you accomplish the goal. As described in Figure 6.2, your task is to discover the combination that solves the problem, builds long-term relationships, and is most cost-effective.

Consider, for example, a presidential election campaign. Political campaigns are probably one of the best examples of using thorough research to guide decision making. The research consultant to a presidential candidate has access to thousands of pieces of information from a variety of research techniques that include, at a minimum, focus groups, panel studies, and opinion polls. The consultant has divided the voting population into dozens of different segments and has an in-depth, research-based profile of each. The research profiles the attitudes, behaviors, and voting preferences of every demographically segmented public by age, income, education, gender, religion, geography, job, and any other descriptor you can imagine. Further, the consultant has included in the profiles their lifestyles, consumer preferences, habits, and other psychographic and value-based characteristics.

Figure 6.2—Priorities in Selecting the Best Combination of Key Publics

1. Which publics working together will produce the best overall solution?
2. Which publics make the most sense for long-term organizational relationships?
3. Which combination of publics will get the desired result for the least amount of additional time, money, and other resources?

With all those segments, there are literally hundreds of combinations of publics that could accomplish the task—election of the candidate for president. A strategist might, for example, choose a combination that includes, among others, 24- to 32-year-olds, Catholics, blue-collar workers, and Northeastern voters. The job of the strategist in a political campaign is to select, from the dozens of profiled segments, the combination of voter publics that will best assure victory in the election (priority one in Figure 6.2). In selecting publics to bring victory, the strategist should also consider those publics whose cooperation will be most crucial to the long-term success of the newly elected president (priority two). Finally, the strategist should consider the combination of publics that will bring the most benefit for the least cost (priority three).

Too often in the past, business has operated with that third priority as the first consideration. Leading our decisions with only cost considerations has landed us in the current crisis of trust among those publics most essential to survival of organizations in our society. The key publics selected to meet any challenge we face should be those best combined to facilitate proper resolution and long-term success. If cost considerations become a concern, they should be addressed in more creative use of resources rather than jeopardizing the long-term health of the organization.

Intervening Publics

An intervening public is one that carries our message to the publics we ultimately need to reach and influence. Media and opinion leaders or influentials are intervening publics that are often used in communications and persuasion. Teachers or PTA volunteers in school are sometimes good channels to get a message to a parental public. Health care workers are good intervening publics on health issues. Intervening publics are not typically designated as key publics unless you need to persuade them to help you. If you need to develop or strengthen a relationship with an intervening public to ensure its cooperation, then you might designate it as key. For example, if you've had a problem with media being hostile, unresponsive, or inaccurate, you may need to identify them as a key public and develop strategies and tactics that will improve your relationship with them. Otherwise, media are typically an intervening public or channel we often use to reach our key publics.

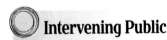 **Intervening Public**

An individual or public used as a message channel to reach and influence a key public.

Creating Synergy

A key public will often be helpful in accomplishing more than one of your objectives. Strategies for those publics should be planned with a complete view of all you need to accomplish with them. Otherwise strategies for separate objectives will be isolated from each other and may result in tactics that don't integrate well into the overall campaign plan and, in some cases, even conflict with each other. Separating publics and strategies by specific tasks or objectives tends to fragment your efforts and lose the advantage of overlap and reinforcement. Focus on each public and the whole of their contribution to create synergy among your strategies and tactics. Use the profiles you created for your publics in the research section. They will help you make decisions about messages, strategies and tactics that will bring results.

Remember that those profiles assessed your organization's current relationship with each public which gives you a baseline to know what you need to do and how to design your messages and strategies. The profiles also identified self-interests which are crucial in designing messages that publics will pay attention to and act on. Further, the profiles identified the influentials that may act as intervening publics or as opinion leaders to provide a personal appeal or challenge to action.

DESIGNING MESSAGE STRATEGIES

Now that you know what you need to do to resolve your problem and whom you need to reach to accomplish that, you are ready to design the messages to be sent to motivate your key publics to do what you want them to do. Remember that messages are public-specific. You cannot successfully incorporate a public's self-interest into a message generalized to all publics. Each public will need a different appeal based on its particular overriding self-interest.

Primary Messages

The message strategy is in two parts. The first is primary messages that resemble sound bites. The primary messages encompass what you are trying to motivate the public to do and include a short self-interest appeal. (See the teaching case at the end of the chapter.) For example, in a campaign regarding children's nutrition, one primary message might be: "Healthy adults come from healthy children. Ensure your child's future with a healthy diet today."

The number of primary messages for a key public will depend upon the number of tasks (objectives) you have set for that particular public. If you need this public's help and support in only one task, you may have only one primary message. Several tasks or desired actions will require more primary messages. Typically, a key public will have two to four primary messages.

Secondary Messages

The second part of message strategy is secondary messages. These messages contain all the facts, statistics, case studies, examples, and other information to support the primary messages. The secondary messages to support the primary message example above may include studies on childhood obesity and other statistics, and the components of a healthy diet recommended by the Food and Drug Administration (FDA). It may also include case studies or examples with emotional appeal and use the credibility of statements by opinion leaders or celebrities.

Remember that good motivational messages always tap into a public's self-interests. Never forget that people don't do what you want them to do just because you want them to do it. Individuals act in what they perceive to be their self-interests. You must determine and appeal to the shared and relevant self-interests of the public you are trying to motivate.

Slogans, Themes, and Tag Lines

We mentioned above that message strategies are typically public-specific. The exception to this rule is campaign themes or slogans, or advertising tag lines. A theme or slogan is a short, compelling, attention-getting phrase that reminds a public of the specific messages you have sent them in other channels. You are already aware of some of the pervasive slogans that have high retention value. The "Just Say No" anti-drug slogan or Nike's "Just Do It" are both good examples.

Advertising tag lines are similar to slogans. They summarize and add emphasis to the advertising message and almost always come at the end of a television or radio ad or appear at the bottom of a print ad. Developed in 1992 by the market research firm Wirthlin Worldwide, the tag line "Plastics Make it Possible," and the campaign built around this theme redefined the debate

Primary Messages

Sound bite statements that encompass what you need the public to do and an appeal to the public's self-interest.

Secondary Messages

Bulleted details that include facts, testimonials, examples, and all other information or persuasive arguments that support a primary message.

Slogan or Theme

Short, catchy phrase that brings to mind the public-specific messages sent in other channels.

Tag Line

A short summarizing theme that appears at the end of an advertisement.

Tips from the Pros

Massaging Your Message

Trevor C. Hale, Head of Communications for Daimler Northeast Asia, tips you off on how to craft a message that's crisp, cool, clean, and contains no trans fat.

Joseph Pulitzer gave some famous advice about writing, "Put it before them briefly so they will read it, clearly so they will appreciate it, picturesquely so they will remember it, and, above all, accurately so they will be guided by its light."

One of my mentors, University of Alabama at Birmingham's John W. Wittig, said, "A good speech should be like a skirt or a kilt: long enough to cover the subject, but short enough to be interesting." Whether drafting a press release, "dropping by to send love" on a MySpace page, trying to make your boss seem funny in his dinner speech, or sending an LOL text message re a gr8 d8, your message should be crisp, customized, memorable, and have purpose.

Where's the Beef? Garnish is nice, but messages need meat to be newsworthy. Don't make a journalist on deadline wade through filler to find something digestible. Yuck!

Tough crowd! Know thy audience. Using ancient words like "cool" or "hip" with teenagers in order to appear cool and hip will most assuredly be seen as neither cool nor hip. Can you D-I-G I-T? And if you ever find yourself addressing the communist leadership of the People's Republic of China at an important state luncheon, don't welcome them as the Republic of China (also known as Taiwan, China's "renegade" province).

There is no B-3 bomber. While not to be used lightly or frequently, according to the famous Chinese military strategist Sun Tsu, misdirection and ambiguity can be very useful in warfare.

It's cliché to avoid clichés. But avoid them like the plague or you'll sound like a broken record. Listen to your heart. Follow your instinct. Stick a fork in me—I'm done.

about plastics. The message of the campaign, summarized in the tag line, focuses key publics on the positive associations they have with plastic such as keeping food fresh, keeping people safe, and making possible many of today's lifesaving medical technologies. Instead of directly taking on the environmental concerns people have about plastic, the campaign works to generate appreciation for the material's unique properties. "Plastics Make it Possible" has been so successful the American Plastics Council continues to use the tag line and theme to drive its advertising—more than 10 years after its conception.

Notwithstanding their utility in summarizing key messages, slogans and advertising tag lines cannot stand alone as messages to your publics. They are useful in creating synergy among publics in a campaign and can dramatically affect recall of public-specific messages sent in other channels. A slogan like "Working Toward a More Healthy Community" will bring to mind public-specific messages regarding economic well-being to a business public, messages of physical and mental health to the health care public, and messages of combating drug and alcohol abuse to a parental public. The slogan in and of itself is not an effective message. It is only as good as the public-specific messages it supports.

Staged Events

Staged events often—but not always—use the same kind of appeal to several key publics as do slogans or themes. For example, a campaign to increase awareness of cancer prevention techniques and raise money for cancer research may target all of its publics with a staged event at a local hospital or cancer treatment center that includes blood screening, free mammograms for women, nutritional workshops, informational booths, family activities, food, children's games, a fundraising home crafts bazaar, and a five-kilometer fundraising run. Its slogan may be something like "Cancer Prevention in Cleveland: A Community Affair."

© 2008 JupiterImages Corporation.

Nevertheless, promotion of the event would still be reliant on public-specific messages, strategies, and tactics, because every public will have a slightly different motivation for attending the event. And the slogan, delivered to all publics through the event strategy, becomes a "big idea," but is only one of the messages (and one of the strategies) for reaching your key publics and accomplishing your objectives. You will need to separately and sufficiently plan other informational and motivational strategies for each public to fully accomplish your objectives and goal.

Using Research in Designing Message Strategies

At the heart of the planning process are the decisions we make about key publics, messages, and the best way to get those messages to those publics. It is in this central part of the process that we need most to be guided by our research and information. Yet, we are most tempted to rely on instinct alone. Not that instinct is necessarily bad. It is often a subconscious process of integrating bits and pieces of knowledge and information, and charting an appropriate course given the data. But, it can also be an unwillingness to believe information and data because it conflicts with limited personal observation. In the latter case, instinct usually leads us to follow courses that fail to solve, and often exacerbate, the problem. To avoid that error, we would be wise to always test our instinct against the information and data gathered through research.

If you identify that a public is motivated on a particular issue by its self-interest in quality of life for their children, your message must convey the importance of that result. Parents concerned about their children's safety from gang violence are motivated by messages and arguments that promise or affect preservation of safety, not by arguments of taxpayer cost. ("Can we place a monetary value on a child's life?") On the other hand, taxpayers concerned about growing demands on their income to solve social problems are motivated by messages that seek to moderate the cost as they propose solutions. ("Lock them up; we can't keep spending money on expensive programs for the socially deviant!")

How you segment publics to achieve your objectives and the self-interests you identify dictate the messages to be sent. The message strategy then contains two essential factors:

1. your purpose or what you need to accomplish
2. your appeal to the self-interest of those you need to motivate to accomplish your purpose

Messages will essentially be both informational and motivational. Designing primary and secondary messages in this way provides you an in-depth treatment of messages for those communication tactics that allow for length (like newspapers and brochures) while also creating short, memorable messages for time- and space-limited media.

The Case of the Warehouse Welfare Health Care

Chapter 6 Teaching Case

Sample Campaign

Matrix: Action Planning
Step Five—Key Publics and Messages

Four publics have been chosen for this campaign. Because of the limited time to raise $500,000, we have selected those with the greatest inclination and capacity to give. *Members of the boards of directors of the free clinic partnership* will be crucial not only in leadership giving, but in opinion leadership to persuade other community leaders to give. *Community leadership givers*, those who routinely support community efforts, will be fairly easily persuaded for a one-time donation and will set an example for their peers who are local area professionals. Many of the *local area professionals* are in independent practice and typically are not targeted for regular giving and could be persuaded for a one-time gift. Finally, *corporate executives* will be important for the corporate sponsorships which will not only provide a needed service for many of their blue-collar employees, but will spotlight their companies as community citizens fulfilling their corporate social responsibility.

Partnership Boards

The cooperation and visible involvement of these community leaders will be key to the success of our campaign. These leaders not only have the capacity to give a leadership gift ($1,000 or more), but more importantly, they are known and respected in the Navajo Flats community and will be highly influential in securing the support and contributions of other members of the community. They are truly committed to the community, and they value their status as community leaders. In most cases, we can count on their support both as leadership givers and as an intervening public, but we will need to make it easy and non-time-intensive for them to be involved. They already know about the free clinic, they have been involved in the negotiations to bring it about. But we must now convince them to become personally involved in the fundraising and to use their influence one-on-one and through mass media to raise the $500,000. The United Way board has 20 members, the CAS board has 15, the SWHC board has 24 members, and the Interfaith Council has 31 members for a total of 90 of these respected community leaders to personally ask other community leaders for their support.

Primary and Secondary Messages

Primary message: Because you are personally recognized and your name is known for good within this community, your visible support of this effort will be key to its success.

Secondary messages:

- To raise $500,000 in the next six months will require larger than average donations. In typical fundraising campaigns, we receive small donations ($25 to $200) from many generous citizens in Navajo Flats. But we will not be able to raise half a million dollars in six months from $25 donations. We will need to enlist the support of those able to give larger one-time donations in the range of $500 to $2,500.
- To accomplish this task, we will need to receive leadership donations ($1,000 or more). The publics in this community who are able to give that kind of donation are the business and civic leaders (many of whom are your friends and colleagues) and the members of the professional community (such as doctors, dentists, attorneys, and accountants). These individuals are in

Chapter 6 Teaching Case Continued...

an income range that would make it possible to give this kind of a one-time donation without difficulty.

- These potential donors will respond best to a personal approach for a one-time gift from someone they know and respect. You are more likely to get a positive response because they know you.
- A final public we will need to target to raise this much money quickly is corporate executives. Corporate donations will need to be a part of the effort if we are to succeed. You also know these individuals and have some influence on them. These executives will support the clinic because you support it and they trust your judgment.

Primary message: Commit to make the phone calls and personal visits/presentations. Our staff will work with you to identify five of your colleagues to contact and two corporate executives to visit with us.

Secondary messages:

- These professionals and executives are most likely to respond favorably to an appeal from a friend and colleague. They know you. They know you know this community. They respect your judgment and advice. They are likely to support causes in which you are involved.
- We know you are extremely busy so our staff will do all the legwork. We will do all we can to make this easy and painless for you. We will provide all the information you need to make the calls and will organize the visits and design and create the presentations and collateral material. All you have to do is show up and pitch the project to your professional and corporate executive colleagues.

Primary message: Commit to your own leadership donation of $1,000 or more.

Secondary messages:

- Your own donation will give you leverage when you ask your business and professional col-

leagues in this community to join you in supporting the free clinic.
- This one-time donation is a relatively small commitment that will pay big dividends for the community. There will never be a follow-up request because of your efforts and the efforts of everyone else on the partnership boards to create a self-sustaining entity that fills a critical community need.
- You demonstrate your personal integrity in monetarily supporting a project you have worked to launch for the good of this community.
- You reinforce your position as a respected and esteemed leader in this community with the ability to find real solutions to the most troublesome problems.
- Unless you direct otherwise, your support will be recognized as part of the Circle of Caring display in the free clinic and in associated publicity and media coverage.

Community Leadership Givers

We can count on this public to support this project. They already give generously to causes in the community, but are typically in financial positions to be generous and would likely accept a commitment for a one-time gift of $1,000 or more to support this clinic, particularly if asked personally by a partnership board member. They are aware of pressing issues in the community and trust the agencies involved in the partnership. They are committed to the community and value their status and recognition as generous supporters of community causes. They may allow us to publicize their contributions to encourage their peers and others to give as well. They are very busy, so we need to make it easy for them to support this cause. The United Way has a list of about 2,500 people in this category.

Primary and Secondary Messages

Primary message: The United Way, Southwest Health Care, Community Action Services, and the Interfaith Council have joined in a partnership to take advantage of an opportunity to establish a free health clinic to serve our area's low-income and uninsured citizens. We need your help as a leader in this community in a one-time effort to raise $500,000 within six months to open the clinic.

Secondary messages:

- One of the critical social issues in our community is affordable health care. While many have access and insurance, we have an underserved population (including 15,000 children) that has no access and a need too large to be met by the generous charity care provided by local health care facilities.

- Community Action Services (CAS), the local nonprofit that operates the food bank and housing and employment services for those in need, has an opportunity to purchase the vacated Wal-Mart building at a concessionary rate. CAS will use 70% of the facility as a warehouse and processing center for the food bank and related services, but it will need to lease the remaining 30% of the space to service the loans and maintain the facility. Working with CAS, the local United Way has leveraged partnerships in the community—health care providers and churches—to operate and maintain a free medical clinic in the remaining 30% of the warehouse facility, including the lease, a full-time administrator and assistant, and the necessary insurance coverage on volunteer medical personnel. Some of the equipment and furnishings will be donated by local health care providers as they upgrade and replace equipment, and an annual contribution from the United Way will provide renewable medical supplies. Local builders have volunteered their construction crews.

- The partnership lacks the estimated $500,000 that is required for materials to build out the space and initially equip it as a free clinic. It has been determined that, for the goal of a free medical clinic to be realized, the clinic partnership will need to raise $500,000 from the community.

- The partnership is comprised of entities you already support and trust: the United Way,

SWHC, CAS, and local churches. The leaders and members of their boards of directors are your friends and colleagues. You, like they, are a leader in this community involved in ensuring the quality of life for all our residents and businesses.

- Local retired health care workers and your friends Dr. Bill Tucker and nurse Eleanor Tucker, are leading the team of retired health care professionals who will volunteer their time to staff the clinic.

- The need for health care among the migrant community, blue-collar families and students is acute. The lack of affordable health care means many simply go without treatment and medication. Potentially 15,000 children in our community currently have no access to health care. When people do not receive necessary medical care, other social problems are compounded.

- For example, Estancia is the seven-year-old daughter of Guillermo and Maria Fuentes. Guillermo originally came to our community to work in the produce fields and sent his earnings home to his wife and family in Mexico. Through diligence and hard work, Guillermo eventually brought his wife and children to Navajo Flats. Now Guillermo and Maria work in one of the packaging plants for minimum wage. Their children attend public school and are good students, because Guillermo and Maria know the importance of education. But Estancia recently developed respiratory problems that affect her ability to do as well in school as her siblings have. She is often ill, as the lack of treatment of her asthma makes her susceptible to constant colds and infections. Doctors say her health problems are manageable, with proper treatment and medication. But Guillermo and Maria have no insurance, and while their frugality enables them to adequately support their family, they simply cannot afford the cost of asthma treatments and medication. Every time Estancia is too sick to go to school, one of her parents has to stay home from work and doesn't get paid. That's a burden we all end up bearing. Estancia continues to suffer with her condition, which affects her not

Chapter 6 Teaching Case Continued...

only physically, but threatens her future success. Your support of this partnership will secure Estancia's future, and help many more of our community's children grow up healthy and be successful.

- Because of your stature within our community, your visible support of this partnership is crucial to our success.

Primary message: In order to take advantage of this phenomenal opportunity to provide care, we need your leadership gift of $1,000 or more.

Secondary messages:

- Your gift will earn you a place in the clinic's Circle of Caring, a visible display in the lobby of the clinic highlighting those corporations and individuals whose leadership contributions made the clinic possible.
- Your gift will be an example to others in the community who will follow your lead in giving to support the free clinic. Knowing of your gift, they too will give.
- Your participation in this effort reinforces your civic leadership in Navajo Flats in addressing the needs of community members.
- Receiving your leadership gift by April 30th will allow us to leverage your support with other community members.

Local Area Professionals

These members of the business and professional associations in Navajo Flats are those we need to convert to leadership givers. They are prosperous, but many are not engaged in community service or giving because they are independent and somewhat isolated from charitable organizations that target larger companies and their employees. Through the local Bar Association, the Dental Association, the Medical Association, Chamber of Commerce, and other such professional and business organizations, we can potentially reach 30,000 professionals and persuade them to become involved in their community by supporting the free health clinic as a leadership giver and/or as a participant in the 5K run/bike/walk. They will be influenced to give by community

leaders and by their fellow professionals. Their motivations for giving will be less altruistic. We need to help them see the benefit of community involvement to their professional stature and success, and that their one-time gift is a fairly effortless way to be involved. The appeal of the 5K run/bike/walk will be both the visibility of their support to their peers and their employees, as well as an appeal to their fitness, a concern for many of those in this public.

Primary and Secondary Messages

Primary message: Many of your fellow citizens in Navajo Flats are in critical need of health care and are without insurance and without financial means to access it. Join us in helping them.

Secondary messages:

- Join your friends and colleagues who are leading professionals in Navajo Flats who are uniting to support this free clinic as a solution to needs in the community. Your one-time leadership gift will identify you to colleagues and clients as a caring member of the Navajo Flats community.
- As many as 15,000 children in our community are without the health care they need to succeed in school and become contributing members of our community.
- Community Action Services (CAS), the local nonprofit that operates the food bank and housing and employment services for those in need, has an opportunity to purchase the vacated Wal-Mart building at a concessionary rate. CAS will use 70% of the facility as a warehouse and processing center for the food bank and related services, but it will need to lease the remaining 30% of the space to service the loans and maintain the facility. Working with CAS, the local United Way has leveraged partnerships in the community—healthcare providers and churches—to operate and maintain a free medical clinic in the remaining 30% of the warehouse facility, including the lease, a full-time administrator and assistant, and the necessary insurance coverage on volunteer medical per-

sonnel. Some of the equipment and furnishings will be donated by local health care providers as they upgrade and replace equipment, and an annual contribution from the United Way will provide renewable medical supplies. Local builders have volunteered their construction crews.

- The partnership lacks the estimated $500,000 that is required for materials to build out the space and initially equip it as a free clinic. It has been determined that, for the goal of a free medical clinic to be realized, the clinic partnership will need to raise $500,000 from the community.

- The partnership is comprised of trusted local entities strongly supported by the community: the United Way, SWHC, CAS, and local churches. The leaders and members of their boards of directors are your friends and colleagues, leaders in this community involved in ensuring the quality of life for all our residents and businesses. They welcome you to join their circle of influence in the community.

- Local retired health care workers and your friends Dr. Bill Tucker and nurse Eleanor Tucker are leading the team of retired health care professionals who will volunteer their time to staff the clinic.

- The need for health care among the migrant community, blue-collar families and students is acute. The lack of affordable health care means many simply go without treatment and medication. Potentially 15,000 children in our community currently have no access to health care. When people do not receive necessary medical care, other social problems are compounded.

- For example, Estancia is the seven-year-old daughter of Guillermo and Maria Fuentes. Guillermo originally came to our community to work in the produce fields and sent his earnings home to his wife and family in Mexico. Through diligence and hard work, Guillermo eventually brought his wife and children to Navajo Flats. Now Guillermo and Maria work in one of the packaging plants for minimum wage. Their children attend public school and are good students, because Guillermo and Maria know the importance of education. But Estancia recently developed respiratory problems that affect her ability to do as well in school as her siblings have. She is often ill, as the lack of treatment of her asthma makes her susceptible to constant colds and infections. Doctors say her health problems are manageable, with proper treatment and medication. But Guillermo and Maria have no insurance, and while their frugality enables them to adequately support their family, they simply cannot afford the cost of asthma treatments and medication. Every time Estancia is too sick to go to school, one of her parents has to stay home from work and doesn't get paid. That's a burden we all end up bearing. Estancia continues to suffer with her condition, which affects her not only physically, but threatens her future success. Your support of this partnership will secure Estancia's future, and help many more of our community's children grow up healthy and be successful.

Primary message: As a leader in this community we are looking to you for a one-time leadership gift to help your less fortunate friends and neighbors.

Secondary messages:

- Your one-time leadership gift of $1,000 or more will earn you a place in the clinic's Circle of Caring, a visible display in the lobby of the clinic highlighting those corporations and individuals whose leadership contributions made the clinic possible. With your permission, your support will also be acknowledged in associated publicity and media coverage.

- Your gift will be an example to your fellow professionals who will follow your lead in giving to support the free clinic. Through planned recognition, your clients and peers will know of your generosity. Knowing of your gift, they too will give.

- Your participation in this effort reinforces your civic leadership in Navajo Flats in addressing the needs of community members.

- Receiving your leadership gift by April 30th will allow us to leverage your support with other community members.

Primary message: Participate in the 5K run/bike/walk to further reinforce your commitment to the welfare of your fellow citizens in Navajo Flats.

Secondary messages:

- To raise awareness of the clinic and the community support of this effort, a 5K run/bike/walk will be held on Saturday, May 20th, beginning at Liberty Park.
- We encourage you to participate, and to bring your colleagues and coworkers. We will provide a packet of information on organizing an office team to participate. The involvement of your office staff is good visibility for your professional practice.
- Office teams involved in this community benefit will increase camaraderie and unity among your coworkers. They will view you as a caring community leader.
- Leadership givers will be recognized at the event in collateral material and signage.

Corporate Executives

The CEOs (or local executives) of major corporations with operations in Navajo Flats and the CEOs of the mid-size companies (1,000 or more employees) are typically supportive of community initiatives, particularly those supported by the United Way of Navajo Flats. They know and have done business with many of the partnership board members. Most are in a position to recognize the health care issues because some of their own employees or the families of their employees are affected. These executives see their community involvement as playing a significant role in maintaining corporate reputation and employee morale. Some have even been involved in the planning as members of the partnership boards. We need to make sure they see a tangible reward for their corporate support of this initiative which will undoubtedly be popular among their employees. They may also give a personal leadership gift, but our primary focus with this public is a larger corporate gift.

Primary and Secondary Messages

Primary message: We appreciate your continual community support and need your help on a one-time opportunity to provide health care to underserved people in Navajo Flats.

Secondary messages:

- Your one-time corporate gift and personal leadership gift will give members of the community, some of whom may be your own employees, access to health care they otherwise could not afford. Your company will be recognized as part of an exclusive group of corporate contributors.
- Your corporate gift will earn you a place in the clinic's Circle of Caring, a visible display in the lobby of the clinic highlighting those corporations and individuals whose leadership contributions made the clinic possible. With your permission, your support will also be acknowledged in associated publicity and media coverage.
- One of the critical social issues in our community is affordable health care. We have an underserved population, including as many as 15,000 children, in our community who are without the healthcare they need to succeed in school and work and to become contributing members of our community.
- Community Action Services (CAS), the local nonprofit that operates the food bank and housing and employment services for those in need, has an opportunity to purchase the vacated Wal-Mart building at a concessionary rate. CAS will use 70% of the facility as a warehouse and processing center for the food bank and related services, but it will need to lease the remaining 30% of the space to service the loans and maintain the facility. Working with CAS, the local United Way has leveraged partnerships in the community—health care providers and churches—to operate and maintain a free medical clinic in the remaining 30% of the warehouse facility, including the lease, a full-time

administrator and assistant, and the necessary insurance coverage on volunteer medical personnel. Some of the equipment and furnishings will be donated by local health care providers as they upgrade and replace equipment, and an annual contribution from the United Way will provide renewable medical supplies. Local builders have volunteered their construction crews.

- The partnership lacks the estimated $500,000 that is required for materials to build out the space and initially equip it as a free clinic. It has been determined that, for the goal of a free medical clinic to be realized, the clinic partnership will need to raise $500,000 from the community.
- The partnership is comprised of trusted local entities strongly supported by the community: the United Way, SWHC, CAS, and local churches. The leaders and members of their boards of directors are your friends and colleagues, leaders in this community involved in ensuring the quality of life for all our residents and businesses. They appreciate all you have done in the past and welcome your involvement and support of this crucial initiative.
- Local retired health care workers Dr. Bill Tucker and nurse Eleanor Tucker, are leading the team of retired health care professionals who will volunteer their time to staff the clinic.
- The need for health care among the migrant community, blue-collar families and students is acute. The lack of affordable health care means many simply go without treatment and medication. Potentially 15,000 children in our community currently have no access to health care. When people do not receive necessary medical care, other social problems are compounded.
- Your gift will be an example to your fellow professionals who will follow your lead in giving to support the free clinic. Through planned recognition, your peers and your employees will know of your generosity and respect your support of the Navajo Flats community.
- Your participation in this effort reinforces your civic leadership in Navajo Flats in addressing the needs of community members.
- Receiving your leadership gift by June 30th will allow us to leverage your support with other corporate leaders.

Primary message: Involve your employees in your corporate support through corporate teams in the 5K run/bike/walk.

Secondary messages:
- To raise awareness of the clinic and the community support of this effort, a 5K run/bike/walk will be held on Saturday, May 20th, beginning at Liberty Park.
- We encourage you to participate and to host a corporate team. If you designate a corporate point of contact, we will provide a packet of information on organizing a corporate team to participate. Your employees will appreciate being involved in your corporate support of this effort and their involvement will bring visibility to your corporation as socially responsible and a good citizen in this community.
- Involving your employees as a team in this community cause will increase camaraderie and unity among your employees, and reinforce their pride in their employer. They will view you and your company as a caring community leader.
- Leadership and corporate givers will be recognized at the event in collateral material and signage.

Summary

Once objectives are set, we can select the most effective combination of publics to accomplish them. To be holistic in accomplishing the goal, we need to remember that more than one key public may be needed to reach an objective and that a key public may help satisfy multiple objectives. At this point, we may also select intervening publics to help us get our messages to the key publics.

To develop effective messages for each of our key publics, we rely upon the public profiles assimilated in the research. Using each public's overriding self-interest regarding the issue or effort at hand, those opinion leaders who influence them on the issue, and our assessment of the current relationship with each public, we will design primary and secondary messages to provide information and motivate our publics to action. Effective messages depend upon solid analysis of the publics selected to accomplish the objectives.

Exercises

1. Review matrix step five in the teaching case. Based on the analysis of publics and the profiles created in step one of the teaching case in Appendix A, suggest at least two different combinations of publics that could alternatively be used to accomplish the goal and objectives.

2. Select a local small business and do a brief analysis of its function and the issues routinely faced. Then identify the organization's key publics, the key publics' self-interests, the key publics' influentials, and the organization's current relationship with each key public.

3. Conduct some focus groups to discover the formal and informal opinion leaders and influentials of a couple of segmented publics on an issue of your choosing.

4. Identify a nonprofit organization and analyze the messages it sends to different publics. Identify primary messages and their supporting secondary messages and make recommendations for alterations or additions that would make the messages more effective.

References and Additional Readings

Cutlip, S., Center, A., & Broom, G. (2006). *Effective public relations* (9th ed.). Englewood Cliffs, NJ: Prentice-Hall, Inc.

Newsom, D., Turk, J.V., & Kruckeberg, D. (2007). *This is PR: The realities of public relations* (9th ed.). Belmont, CA: Wadsworth Publishing Company.

Wirthlin Worldwide (1997). The American Plastics Council Campaign. A Case Study of Award Winning Advertising Research and Strategy.

Designing Strategies and Tactics to Send Messages

> *"The roots of successful decisions often lie in obscure places. . . . The truly great decisions happen. They arise from spur-of-the-moment phone calls and from crazy ideas you try when you're desperate."*
>
> —Stuart Crainer
> Author of *The 75 Greatest Management Decisions Ever Made*

LEARNING IMPERATIVES

- **To design strategies that reach a public with a message to motivate a desired action or behavior**

- **To creatively select the best channels to deliver the tactics that support strategies**

- **To design creative and effective tactics delivered through specific channels**

- **To brainstorm creative strategies and tactics**

- **To use copy outlines to channel creative ideas into strategic communication tools**

Strategies

Public-specific plan specifying the channel to send messages to achieve an objective.

Tactics

Strategy-specific communication tools that carry the message to key publics.

Now that we have established what needs to be accomplished, who we need to reach to accomplish it, and what messages will motivate action, we can design our strategies and tactics to send those messages. Strategies and tactics are public-specific—they are designed with one public in mind. They are the best way to give a key public its own message to motivate desired behavior.

We again draw a simple analogy to military strategy. In an overall challenge to win a battle one objective might be to secure a certain piece of ground or a particular town. The strategy would then be devised to coordinate the effort to achieve that objective. The strategy may be to weaken the town's defenses and attack through a particularly vulnerable spot in the wall. The tactics supporting the strategy may be an artillery barrage, aerial bombing, a Special Forces patrol to plant explosives to create a breech, and a ground assault through the wall into the town. The strategy provides the overall approach to a particular objective answering what and, very generally, how. Tactics are the specific plans to achieve the strategy step-by-step.

In communicating with an organization's publics, the strategies are the approaches to reaching a designated public for a particular purpose with the message that will inform or motivate that public. Almost like mini-objectives for that public, strategies determine what purpose you are trying to accomplish in reaching the public with the message (i.e., to inform, to increase awareness, to persuade or to motivate to do something) and what channel you are going to use to send that message (i.e., influentials, mass media, social media, workplace communication). Because strategies are designed to reach a specific public with a specific message you created to appeal to that public's self-interests, strategies must be public-specific.

The tactics that support the strategies identify in more detail how you will send the message within the strategy (i.e., employee meetings, newsletter articles, bulletin boards, payroll envelope stuffers, and letters from the company president in a workplace channel). Tactics are strategy-specific because they support a single strategy targeted at a particular public.

Figure 7.1

10-Step Strategic Communications Planning Matrix   **Matrix** ◯

Matrix: Action Planning

Step Six—Strategies and Tactics

Strategies	Strategies identify approaches to send messages to each public through specific channels in order to motivate action. Multiple strategies may be required for each public.
Tactics	Tactics are communications tools and tasks required to support each strategy. Each strategy is supported by a number of tactics designed to convey key messages to a specific public through the communications channel outlined in the strategy.

CREATIVITY

Because of the importance of creativity, we'll take a short detour here to help you enhance your creative efforts. Step six in the matrix (Figure 7.1) requires high levels of creativity to devise strategies and tactics that break through all the other information and persuasion clutter with which your publics are bombarded. You must design creative strategies and tactics that will cause the target public to choose to perceive your messages, choose to retain them, and choose to act upon them. The matrix process provides the framework or strategic structure to focus your creativity, ensuring it is on target in terms of meeting your challenge. Once you have focused efforts on a particular public and you know what messages you need to send to motivate the desired action within that public you must draw on creativity to deliver those messages. Focus your creativity to determine the best strategy and channel for getting your message to your public. Then, let your creativity loose again on detailing the tactics to accomplish the strategy.

Creativity

The process of looking outside ourselves and our routine to discover new ideas and innovative solutions.

Avoiding a Common Mistake

Only by channeling your creativity within the analytical process will you avoid a common mistake: allowing a creative tactic to drive your campaign. Just because you have a great opportunity to use a celebrity in a campaign doesn't mean that approach will serve your public, purpose, and message. Great creative ideas not founded in logical reasoning and analysis of public, purpose, and message result in lots of money wasted on campaigns that accomplish nothing. Remember the lesson of the Salt Lake City Olympic bid committee. Its television spots were extremely creative and visually appealing. But the issue passed by only two or three percentage points, denying them the public referendum of overwhelming support they sought. If you get a creative idea that doesn't work for a specific purpose, public, and message, put it on the shelf to be adapted and used in a later communication effort. The idea isn't wasted if you can use it appropriately at a later time. It will be wasted, and perhaps even harmful, if used inappropriately now.

Looking Outside the Familiar

French naturalist Jean-Henri Fabre writes of the processionary caterpillar. Processionary caterpillars feed on pine needles as they move through the forest in a long procession, with one head fitted snugly against the behind of the caterpillar before. In his experiments, Fabre enticed a group of these caterpillars onto the rim of a flower pot where he got the first one connected with the last so they were moving in unending procession around the top of the pot.

Fabre expected the caterpillars would catch on to their useless march and move off in a new direction, especially since he had placed food nearby. Not so. The force of habit caused them to continue moving in their unending circle, round and round the rim of the flower pot. Even though food was visible nearby, the caterpillars continued their march for seven days and nights, and probably would have continued longer had they not collapsed from sheer

Tips from the Pros

Stoking Creativity for Award-Winning Ideas

Grace Leong, APR, Fellow PRSA, Managing Partner of Hunter Public Relations, who leads a team that services the nation's top consumer products companies, tips you off on coming up with "big ideas."

Be an everyday student of creativity. Build a database of great ideas. The best brainstormers are those who read, see, and retain good ideas daily. Keep a file of "great ideas" that catch your eye: a new product launch that used an innovative strategy or a clever idea for a press kit or Web site. Your own library of ideas will serve you well when you are asked to be creative "on the spot."

Never respond to the question: "What's the Big Idea?" To get to the big idea in a brainstorm you need to put people's minds at ease: play creative games, ask seemingly unrelated questions, make the environment fun. When minds are stimulated in a creative atmosphere, ideas flow and the big idea will emerge naturally.

Strive for singles and doubles and you will hit more home runs. Hank Aaron was the home run king of baseball, but he also ranks high on the all-time strike-out list. Allow yourself hundreds of strikes, singles, and doubles for every home run. People who are not afraid of striking out are more likely to hit the ball out of the park.

Create an environment that inspires your creativity. At Hunter PR, we build a staff of people with diverse backgrounds and outlooks on life and we inspire each other to look at opportunities from multiple perspectives. We are a culture that regularly permits people to slay the sacred cow. No idea is a bad idea even if it goes against convention. If you do not live in a culture like this, fix that first, and then watch the creativity flow.

---

exhaustion and ultimate starvation. The food was outside the range of the circle, off the beaten path. They followed instinct, habit, custom, tradition, precedent, and past experience. They confused activity with accomplishment. They were in constant motion, but they made no progress.

Creativity is the process of looking outside ourselves, our habit, our custom, and tradition to find new solutions and innovative ideas. The strategic communications planning process is designed to analytically drive our planning and decisions. But it should not limit our creativity in searching for new ideas, channels, and tactics to get our messages to key publics. In fact, unless we develop creative strategies and tactics, our publics are not likely to perceive the messages we have designed to motivate them.

Most of us think that creativity is inborn, you either have it or you don't. But the greatest scientific discoveries and inventions came out of years of experimentation, trial and error. The Royal Bank of Canada tells its employees that innovation is like playing hockey: the best players miss more shots than they make. But they also try more often. The more you shoot, the more you score. That's why one of the rules of brainstorming (Figure 7.2) is not to evaluate or criticize while in the brainstorming process. The object is to get as many ideas on the table as possible, no matter how ridiculous they might initially appear. Those ridiculous ideas, reevaluated, rearranged, and combined, frequently become the innovative solutions that are praised, awarded, and used as examples of phenomenal creativity.

In 2006, a newly hired marketing and communications director at Blendtec, a manufacturer of commercial blenders for the food service industry, walked by the Research and Development (R&D) suite and noticed wood shavings on the floor. Inquiries led to the discovery that one of the R&D guys liked to play around blending odd things to test the sturdiness of their heavy duty blender. The marketing director got a video camera and began shooting as they blended rakes, IPods, golf balls, and everything else imaginable. He posted the videos on YouTube to launch their new line of home blenders. Less than a year later, the "Will It Blend?" series is Internet history. More than 30 million people to date have viewed the videos. Sales of their blenders doubled in a month. They now sell a DVD of the first 50 "Will It Blend?" videos and have responded to thousands of e-mailed suggestions on what they should blend next. And now their experiments are being duplicated. Abazias Diamonds copycatted and blended a diamond ring and posted the video on YouTube. The Blendtec viral campaign cost less than $100 to initiate. A savvy marketing and communications director saw an opportunity and took a chance. With a supportive CEO, it paid off big time.

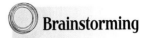

Brainstorming

A structured group creative exercise to generate as many ideas as possible in a specified amount of time.

Figure 7.2—Rules for Brainstorming

© Marcin Balcerzak, 2008.

1. Assemble a diverse group of people (at least three).
2. Set a time limit for the brainstorming session. Plan no less than five minutes but no more than 20 minutes to ensure urgency and, hence, a rapid flow of ideas.
3. Record the session for later transcription.
4. Do not evaluate ideas while in the session. Even laughter can be an act of evaluation that may stifle the flow of ideas (although in a truly free flowing session, it is difficult not to laugh).
5. Engage in freewheeling. Verbalize any idea that comes into your mind. Otherwise you are silently evaluating your own ideas and perhaps censuring those that are most creative.
6. Reserve the details for the post-session evaluation. Use your time to generate as many ideas as possible, not to explain your ideas in any detail.
7. Piggyback on ideas. For example, if someone mentions a tactic like bumper stickers, try to spiral off with similar transportation-related ideas like bus boards or sun visor wraparounds.
8. Take some time as a group after the session to evaluate each idea for its merits. Try to find ways that each might work. Try modifying, combining, and rearranging before discarding an idea.

Thomas Edison said that creativity is "10 percent inspiration and 90 percent perspiration." It may well begin when you realize that there is no particular benefit in doing things as they have always been done. It also does not require complete originality. Creativity often means borrowing and adapting ideas. Modify and rearrange, make them bigger or smaller. Brainstorm ways to change and adapt an idea. In fact, practice brainstorming on a topic just to see how many different ideas you can generate. Try free-association. Piggyback on ideas. Practice saying whatever idea comes into your head.

These are all good exercises, but to be creative, you must first believe that you can be. Break the barriers to creative thinking identified in Figure 7.3. Explore your imagination. Think. Create fantasies and play with ideas. And then cultivate the habit. The more you challenge yourself to think creatively, the better you will become.

Figure 7.3—Roger von Oech's Mental Locks to Creativity

Mental Locks to Creativity

Be Practical
Don't disregard impossible suggestions, rather use them as stepping stones to workable solutions.

That's Not My Area
Specializing causes us to miss out on a lot. Interdisciplinary answers are better solutions.

Don't Be Foolish
Poking fun at proposals provides feedback that prevents group think.

I'm Not Creative
Self-fulfilling prophecy. Allow yourself to be creative.

To Err Is Wrong
Get over the stigma that being wrong is all bad. Use mistakes to learn.

The Right Answer
Looking for the one right answer keeps us from realizing that there may be many possibilities.

Follow the Rules
Creativity is often enhanced by breaking the rules, going outside the normal parameters.

That's Not Logical
Don't disregard thinking outside the boundaries because it doesn't fit the analytical approach.

Play Is Frivolous
Fun environments are productive, creative environments.

Avoid Ambiguity
Introducing ambiguity into a creative session can help generate answers. Also use humor and paradoxes.

Challenging the Parameters of Your Thinking

In her book, *Teaching Creative Behavior*, Doris Shallcross (1981) provides a number of exercises that require you to challenge the parameters of your thinking. For example, how many squares do you see in the figure below? The expected answer would be 16, but count all the squares.

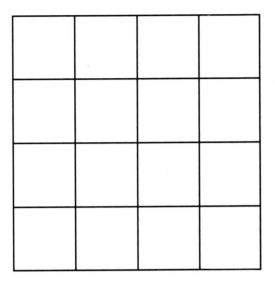

Assuming this figure is on a flat plane, there are 30 of them, all different sizes. One is the outside square. You will also see squares formed by two smaller squares across combined with two squares down, and three squares across combined with three squares down. A door is opened to our creative brain when we obtain permission, indeed are given direction, to look outside the traditional boundaries and expected perception!

The next test from Shallcross is one you may have seen before, but that powerfully illustrates the need to go outside the boundaries we set for ourselves. Connect all nine dots with four straight lines. Go through each dot only once and do not lift your pencil from the paper. Take a few minutes to take this test before reading on. (The solution is located at the end of the chapter.)

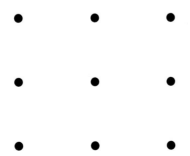

This test is specifically designed to show us that we set our own artificial boundaries. There was no instruction indicating the connecting lines had to be kept within the invisible boundary set by the dots in the diagram. Yet we are accustomed to setting those boundaries ourselves. One of the greatest marketing ploys of all time was to print a margin line an inch in from the edge of notebook paper. Most of us automatically observe that margin and leave the space on the left side of the line blank. Most notebook paper is used for taking notes no one else will ever see. What does it matter if we observe the margin? But much more notebook paper is sold to students in any given year because the artificial boundary limits what fits on the page.

Where did we learn to set these kinds of invisible boundaries? Remember when you began coloring? What are some of the first lessons—or rules—you were taught? One was to always color inside the lines. That rule was so ingrained that some of us even traced the lines with the crayon before coloring to make sure we didn't accidentally breach the boundary. We were also taught to choose the appropriate colors. Frogs are green, not purple or blue. So we always had to choose the right color for the item pictured, so much so that fights erupted in grade school over color crayons. Now grade school kids buy their own set of crayons so they don't have to fight with anyone to get the green crayon for their frog. But in a graphic design, wouldn't a purple frog get more second glances than a green one?

Creative ideas and solutions are, by nature, out of our typical range of experience. Problems with obvious, traditional solutions seldom require much time. To find truly innovative solutions to challenges we face, we must reach outside our comfort zone, those boundaries we have created for ourselves.

Fear is probably the single greatest barrier to creative behavior. Author John Holt has said that the real test of intelligence is "not how much we know how to do, but how we behave when we don't know what to do." What do we fear? We fear failure and rejection. No one likes their ideas to be rejected, laughed at, or ridiculed. We often fail to contribute our ideas for fear we will look silly or stupid. We think that people who fail do not get promoted. They do not get raises. But if we never take a risk we will also never succeed.

Remember the hockey player and work to create an environment friendly to creativity. Accept that mistakes will be made, but praise the effort to find new ideas and solutions, even if you frequently miss the mark. Companies that foster this kind of environment are typically known for their creative products and solutions. Some even give annual awards for the most spectacular failure because management recognizes that if employees are afraid to be creative, the company will lose its competitive edge in the marketplace.

While you may not be working for an organization with such policies, you can still create that kind of environment within your work area. Make your workplace safe for creativity. Praise creative efforts even if the ideas don't or won't work. Celebrate new ideas and ways of doing things. Color a few frogs purple.

DESIGNING STRATEGIES AND CHOOSING APPROPRIATE CHANNELS

As we said earlier, your strategy for message delivery is public-specific. In other words, you don't determine how you are going to send a message until you know who you are trying to reach and what you are trying to tell them. The strategy inherently identifies the public, and then addresses what you are try-ing to do in support of your objectives and the channel you propose to use to send the appeal.

As has been mentioned, strategies are like mini-objectives for each public. They identify what action or behavior is desired. Just like objectives, the action part of a strategy may be informational or motivational. Informational strate-gies (also known as awareness or educational strategies) lay a significant foun-dation of information for the motivational strategies that ask the key public to act in some way.

As with objectives, it may not be necessary to have a separate information-al strategy. If a public is already sufficiently educated and is ready to act, neces-sary information can be carried by the motivational strategy to avoid fragment-ing your strategies and messages. All motivational strategies will contain some information messages either in separate tactics or within each tactic. A tactic that appeals for a citizen's vote will almost always include some information to justify the action. Your job is to determine whether a separate informational strategy is necessary for that public. If there is a significant lack of knowledge and understanding, you probably need an informational strategy to lay a foun-dation before you can implement strategies to motivate behavior. If the infor-mation is already pervasive and people just need to be reminded, the informa-tional tactics within a motivational strategy will be sufficient.

For example, many people still do not understand that mental illness—like depression—has a physiological cause that must be addressed by medica-tion. Any effort to motivate people with mental illness to see a doctor would require creating a better informed public environment. But to motivate people to give blood, just tell them where and when to show up. Virtually everyone understands the need and the process.

As you know, objectives always require a metric of some kind. Each objec-tive must specify improvement that can be measured. The action identified in a public-specific strategy may also be stated in measurable terms. While not all strategies will detail the action this specifically, it may be necessary for some to do so. If a campaign supporting a local municipal bond requires 55% of the vote to pass, public-specific strategies may break that overall percentage down into manageable pieces for each public. A 55% overall vote may translate to 85% of business leaders, 65% of white-collar workers, 45% of blue-collar workers and 58% of stay-at-home parents. The strategies for each public may include the measurements to support the overall objective.

Determining the right channel to send the message in a strategy is depend-ent upon both the message itself and the public being targeted. Take a look around. Some marketing and communications strategies have become so per-vasive in our society that we don't give them a second thought. What has become the almost exclusive strategy to market beer to the age-segmented male audience? The primary strategy is to use sporting events as the channel to deliver beer-drinking messages to that target public. And that channel has literally hundreds of potential tactics, many of which employ humor, to carry the message within the channel. What is the predominant fundraising strate-gy of your local United Way? It is the workplace campaign. The strategy pro-vides the channel within which messages are focused at a specific public with the ability to give using tactics that overlap and reinforce one another to accomplish the purpose.

Channel

The conduit or medium through which tactics carry messages to a specific public to accomplish a specific purpose.

A more specific example is an objective to raise participation in educational programs for handicapped children. Parents of handicapped children would be a key public (the who) needing an informational message regarding the resources available and a motivational appeal to use them. One strategy for that public would be to raise participation in available programs (the purpose or objective) using the Parent-Teacher Association (PTA) network in schools (the channel). Tactics would necessarily include printed collateral materials explaining the programs available. Other tactics may involve using the personal influence of PTA leaders in a meeting, presentation, or home visit to introduce parents to the literature and encourage them to take advantage of the resources available. As is clear from the last chapter, opinion leader influence is best exerted by people the parents perceive to be operating credibly in a relevant issue environment. The PTA would have credibility in the area of educational programs for children. The individuals functioning in those leadership roles will probably also be known to the parents, perhaps as friends and neighbors, perhaps as community leaders. Study the strategies and tactics for the key publics in the teaching case at the end of this chapter and in Appendix A for examples of public-specific strategies and tactics.

The channel stipulated in the strategy should be the best way to get the message to the public for the outlined purpose (i.e., staged events, workplace communication, or opinion leaders). In order to be sufficiently planned, each strategy requires the development of specific tactics within the channel (communication tools like signage and t-shirts at staged events, newsletters and e-mail in the workplace, and meetings or personal visits with collateral material for opinion leaders). In the previous example, we decided it was necessary to use opinion leaders or personal influence and printed collaterals to reach the key public with the message. The tactics specify the communication tools within the channel more clearly, perhaps a brochure on available programs and an application to participate. Other possible tactics might be a booklet explaining the learning techniques most successful with handicapped children, a fact sheet on local programs and funding, a listing of support groups, and a contact sheet for more information. The written tactics would be introduced and/or distributed through personal contact with PTA leaders, like a phone call or a personal visit. Perhaps a follow-up tactic or some other kind of supportive tactic will also be necessary. By focusing tactics within a specific channel, you ensure the members of the key public will receive the message at least once, but likely more than once. Such focused overlap makes it more certain the message will be selected to be perceived, retained, and acted upon.

The point is that you must carefully consider your public in determining the best ways to reach them. How this particular public best receives this message for this purpose is the relevant question. You must also carefully consider the message being sent to ensure the channels and media selected are appropriate for the message.

Alternative Channels and Related Tactics

It is critically important here to recognize that our effective and extensive use of the mass media to communicate with target audiences may belong to past decades. While mass media are highly effective in generating name recognition, even their information-disseminating utility is not as great as before because of declining trust. In the Golin/Harris 2002 Trust Index, the communications business sectors all had negative trust scores (Golin, p. 240). Of them all, public relations had the least negative score (–31), followed by journalism (–38), and then advertising/marketing (–41). In the 2007 Edelman Trust Barometer, media ranked 14th of 14 industries on trust. As sources of information, business magazines are the most credible source, but only 37% rank newspapers as credible sources, 39% rank radio, and 35% rank television news as credible. While mass media channels have their place, in an environment where media are not trusted, it is unwise to rely on them too heavily. In fact, with peers or "someone like me" being the most credible source of information today, social media is quickly overtaking traditional media as the best channel for messages.

We are accustomed to segmenting publics for the purpose of persuasion. We have long recognized that identifying a group of people who share common interests and lifestyles (and who may interact with one another) is the best way to devise an appeal that will motivate them. Now, segmentation is required not just to persuade, but to reach our desired publics. Readership of that traditionally broad print communication medium, the newspaper, is declining. Among those who still read a newspaper, their selectivity in what they read has increased. Broad audience magazines are also disappearing, replaced by highly segmented special-interest and professional or trade publications. The explosion in cable and satellite television technology is already creating highly segmented viewership, which will continue to increase. And radio has long been segmented by the preferences of listeners for differing formats and music.

Segmentation

Defining and separating publics by demographics and psychographics to ensure more effective communication.

The lesson to be learned is that the mass media (which arguably never did reach a mass public) are declining in their ability to reach our publics with the messages we need sent. The good news is that as a medium becomes more specific and segmented, it becomes a better buy in terms of reaching the public segments we need to target. So while our jobs may be a bit more difficult in that we need to exercise a greater range of creativity and expertise in using differentiated communication tools, we are promised higher rates of success because of the narrowing of mass and multimedia audiences.

Similarly, with the widespread use of technologies that make production and distribution of communication materials easy and inexpensive (like desktop publishing and Web publishing), the range of diversified and alternative media has burgeoned. The Internet has nearly eliminated the use of stand alone fax machines. Telephone technology has become so innovative that we hardly personally speak at all through our ubiquitous cell phones. Our print runs of hard copy tactics are significantly reduced by the growing number of people who access information electronically. The range of Internet capabilities helps us creatively reach a highly segmented public at an incredibly low cost.

Print Media

As readership of newspapers declined—some newspapers have been driven out of business—the readership and number of newsletters has exploded, and the percentage of newsletters delivered electronically is steadily increasing.

Hardly an industry or organization can be found that doesn't produce at least one newsletter and many produce a separate newsletter for a number of their publics. Local United Way organizations have separate newsletters for their volunteers, corporate contributors, organizations wanting to participate in volunteer opportunities, and for their funded agencies. Corporations have newsletters for employees, for shareholders and investors, for stakeholders, and for customers. Professional societies and trade associations also publish newsletters. Special interest groups produce newsletters. Sports fans have hundreds of newsletters and magazines to which they can subscribe, some of which address only the performance of their favorite college or professional teams. The opportunities provided by specific channels of communication for segmented publics are endless. And all of those publications to very specifically segmented publics are constantly looking for copy that is relevant to their readership.

Internet

The opportunities now provided by the Internet include a growing range of options to creatively communicate a message. As in the early days of radio, advertisers now create online programming, similar to soaps and sitcoms, to secure vehicles for product promotion. Audio, video, and online conferencing has been made relatively inexpensive through the Internet. Affinity portals, Web sites visited often by a particular group of especially interested individuals, are an excellent way to reach some targeted publics. A 2006 TEKgroup, International, survey of journalists found that 99% believe a company should have an online newsroom. Chat rooms, listserves, online forums, and many other Internet features are effective tactics to be considered. Smart use of search engines and Web site links can also provide opportunities to communicate a message to publics already predisposed to be receptive.

The astronomical growth of social media has changed the face of communication in our society. Recently, an executive of a major global public relations firm boarded a plane with a stack of resumes to review for an entry-level position. As he reviewed resumes, he searched the names on Facebook. One applicant's site caught his eye. Rather than the typical frivolous college student banter, he found her plans, passion, and preparation for a career in public relations. She got the job. Online media have changed the communications and marketing industries forever.

According to a Vocus, Inc., white paper, "in 2006, the blogosphere had grown 100 times in three years. . .[with] 50 million blogs." In February of 2006, "YouTube attracted nine million visitors who viewed 176 million pages" in one month. In April of that year, 35,000 videos were posted daily to their site. In September of 2006, the majority of traffic to a British online music retailer was referred to them from MySpace rather than from search engines. Vocus concludes that "the Internet has blurred the lines between production, distribution, and consumption of media content."

Figure 7.4 identifies and describes some of the newest kinds of social media pervasive in today's communications environment. Vocus asserts that they share some characteristics.

- **User-driven.** Content is generated and controlled by users themselves.

- **Organic content.** Content is constantly changing as users edit, mix, and repurpose it.
- **Community-oriented.** Social media is collaborative with participation based on shared interests creating a community of users.
- **Easy to use.** The sites are simplified so anyone can use them and post to them, regardless of technical skill level.

As trust in traditional media declines, social media have the power to attract publics that have tuned out traditional advertising and marketing message channels. The viral nature of social media—or word-of-mouse campaigns—means peer opinion leader endorsement of key messages that spreads faster and farther than traditional efforts could hope. Social media have become highly visible on the Internet. And the interactivity—the dialogue between user and source—allows for continual update and improvement.

Nevertheless, the Internet brings both possibilities and problems. While making it easier, faster, and less expensive to send messages to certain publics, the Internet also makes it easier for opposing publics, or just someone with a grudge, to attack your organization or products online. Especially with social

Figure 7.4—New Social Media

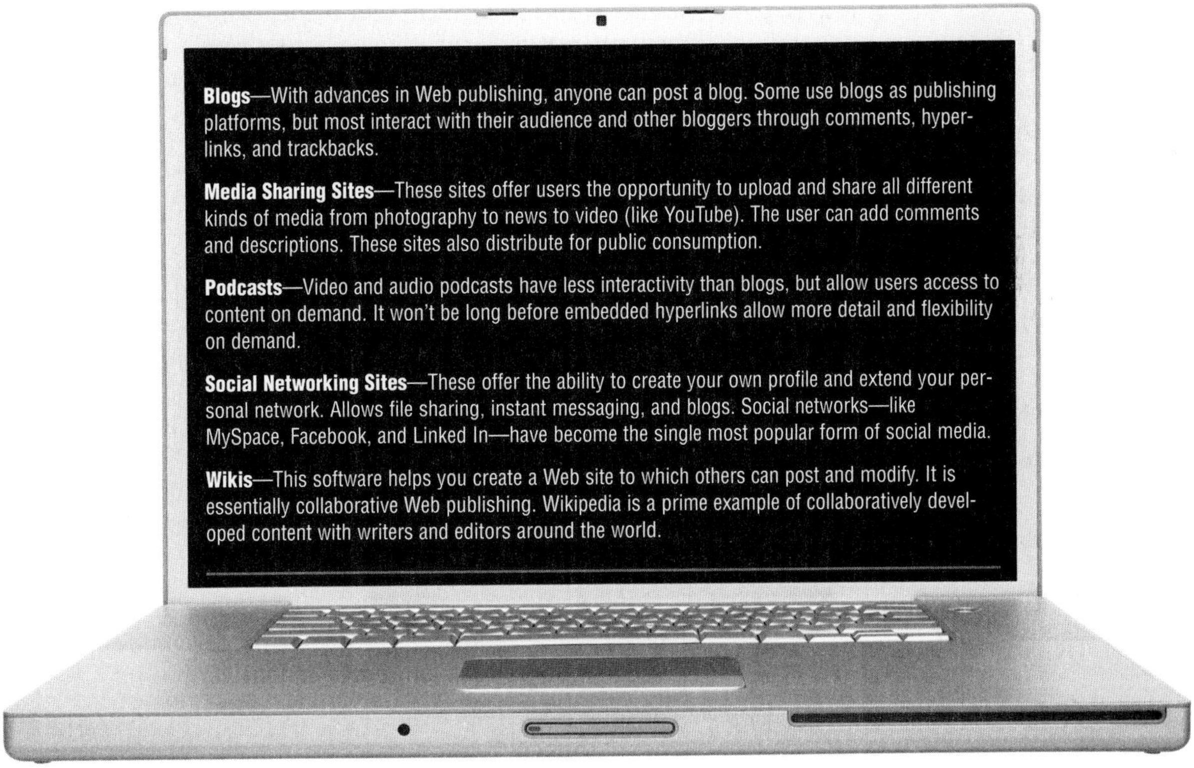

Blogs—With advances in Web publishing, anyone can post a blog. Some use blogs as publishing platforms, but most interact with their audience and other bloggers through comments, hyperlinks, and trackbacks.

Media Sharing Sites—These sites offer users the opportunity to upload and share all different kinds of media from photography to news to video (like YouTube). The user can add comments and descriptions. These sites also distribute for public consumption.

Podcasts—Video and audio podcasts have less interactivity than blogs, but allow users access to content on demand. It won't be long before embedded hyperlinks allow more detail and flexibility on demand.

Social Networking Sites—These offer the ability to create your own profile and extend your personal network. Allows file sharing, instant messaging, and blogs. Social networks—like MySpace, Facebook, and Linked In—have become the single most popular form of social media.

Wikis—This software helps you create a Web site to which others can post and modify. It is essentially collaborative Web publishing. Wikipedia is a prime example of collaboratively developed content with writers and editors around the world.

Image © ifong, 2008.

media, the backlash can be brutal. It is virtually impossible to block or even monitor everything anyone wants to post regarding your organization. And there is no filter or screen for lies and misrepresentations. No one asks whether or not the attack is credible—sometimes not even the media whose responsibility it is to ask. It is tremendously difficult to deal with false information that can be published so broadly, freely, and anonymously. This dilemma underscores the importance of continual trust building efforts among all key publics.

Communication Channels that Reach Segmented Publics

Even with all the drawbacks, new technology has indeed provided us myriad channels to reach our publics. The key in writing creative strategies is to break out of our traditional mode of using broadly based mass media and find communication channels and tools that reach segmented publics. Our publics are far more likely to read a newsletter to which they subscribe than a direct mail piece that goes to every postal customer. They are far more likely to respond to advice given through a segmented channel from an organization to which they choose to belong than to counsel given broadly in the mass media. They will be even more responsive to messages delivered by a special interest cable channel than through the major television networks. Break the barriers that cause you to choose the traditional media channels for all your communication. Take off the blinders and use some creativity in devising strategies and tactics to reach your publics with messages to which they will pay attention and respond. Try something different, something never before done.

There are literally dozens of channels we might use to reach a key public. Put yourself in the place of one of your publics and see through your mind's eye how they receive information throughout the day. What communication channels do they encounter and pay attention to as part of their daily routine? Figure 7.5 may help you begin to see how numerous and differentiated those channels can be.

Choose channels that will cause a key public to perceive a specific message about a particular issue. Remember that communication in most channels can be supplemented with printed collateral materials (as in the previous example regarding parents of handicapped children and the PTA). And viral communication or social media should be used to support your messages in more formal channels. Focus several tactics in the chosen channel to reinforce the message. This way, the message is delivered in several rifle shots, rather than scattered by multiple shotgun blasts. The next section should help you get started on designing channel-specific tactics to deliver the message.

DESIGNING COMMUNICATION TACTICS

Designing communication tactics is perhaps what most communicators do best . . . and worst. Most of us seem to be fairly adept at inventing catchy slogans and creative visual events and displays. The problem is not typically too little creativity in tactics, it is rather too little channeling of that creativity to

Figure 7.5—Examples of Possible Channels for Some Potential Key Publics

Possible Key Publics

Business Executives

© Wolfgang Amri, 2008.

Teachers

© PhotoCreate, 2008.

Mothers of Elementary School Children

© Jason Stitt, 2008.

College Students

© digitalskillet, 2008.

Possible Channels*

Political and Community Opinion Leaders
Community Business and Service Clubs
Professional Associations
Professional/Trade Media
Commuter/Transportation Media
Long Distance Travel Media
Country Clubs and Golf Courses
Online Media

Parents
School Districts/Government
Professional Associations/Unions
School Supply/Services Retailers
Textbook/Classroom Resource Wholesalers
Educational Travel Providers
Alma Mater Colleges

Medical Professionals and Facilities
Children's Retail Stores
Schools and Teachers
Parent-Teacher Associations
Religious Organizations
Food and Household Retailers
Homemaking/Women's Media

Campus Media and Collaterals
Alumni
College Sporting/Entertainment Events
National Preprofessional Associations
Fitness and Recreation Facilities/Retailers
Financial Institutions
On- and Off-campus Housing Units
Social Media

* These represent only a very few of the possible channels for these publics. Literally dozens of channels exist for those creative enough to discover them.

ensure that our tactics are those best suited to deliver predetermined messages to specific publics. It is not usually our creativity that fails; it is our ability to strategically use that creativity that has been problematic.

Another problem has been the tendency to rely on the same tactics or communication tools over and over. Although there is nothing wrong with reusing tactics that work well with particular publics, communicators should be careful not to fall into the routine of the processionary caterpillars described earlier. Using a tactic repeatedly sometimes causes us to select that tactic without thinking about its appropriateness to get a particular message to a particular public for a particular purpose. We fall into a pattern of selecting tactics because we've always used them, or because the tactic has always worked before.

Remember to review the analytical process to select communication tools each time you design messages and strategies for publics. Change is one of the only constants in business and marketing. Publics change, circumstances change, purposes change, messages change, and communication channels change. If communicators stay with the same plan for the same publics without recognizing the constantly changing environment, communication efforts will miss their targets. A practitioner will be left (possibly without a job) wondering why it didn't work this time since it had always worked before.

The other inherent danger in using the same tools continually is stifling creativity. Communicators may ignore new creative and innovative ways to get messages to publics. But in a society flooded with messages in the typical media channels, creative and innovative delivery of messages is necessary to cut through the message clutter to reach our targets. Remember your challenge is two-fold: You must motivate the members of your key public to choose to perceive the message (and retain it), and to choose to act upon it. Both require an appeal to the public's self-interests, but self-interest appeals alone will not get you over the perception hurdle. We may not find a solution to our specific need in the textbooks that teach us how to design communication tactics. We must be able to create innovative delivery systems and then follow the principles of good communication to send our messages in creative ways that command attention.

How to Select Tactics

The diversity of tactics available is limited only by the imagination. Nevertheless, there are abundant numbers of books, articles, and other references that identify a variety of some of the standard communication tools and their appropriate uses. We refer you to a broad range of easily available literature (some of which is identified in this chapter's references) that suggests dozens of tactics and instructions on their preparation and use. Because of the vast resources which give specific direction on preparing and using communication tools, it is not our purpose here to review specific tactics. Rather, it is more important to provide a process to assist communication professionals in determining how to select the tactics most appropriate for a specific public, purpose, and message.

Most popular introductory textbooks in communication segment tools and tactics into written, spoken, and visual categories. But today's communication professionals focused on key publics and messages recognize that, in the radically changed communication environment, such divisions are artificial, especially considering that the most effective tactics combine at least two, and often all three, of those senses. Further, that type of categorization puts undue emphasis on the medium or channel, with less thought of the purpose, the target audience, and the message itself. Such categorization may be partially responsible for communications practice that is excessively tactic-driven rather than strategic. It perhaps encourages creativity focusing on media, developing award-winning pieces for print, broadcast, and now the Internet, rather than on using media as tools to get messages to the publics you need to reach for your campaign.

Figure 7.6—The Interactivity Grid of Communication Tactics

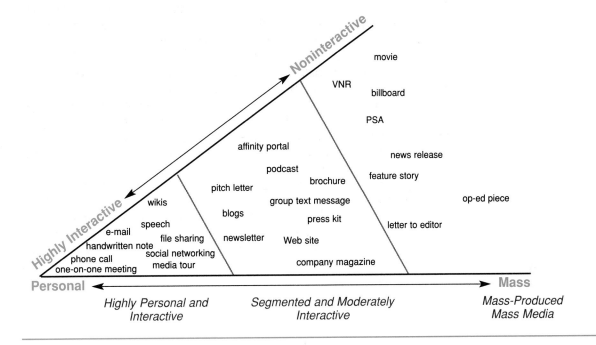

It might be more reasonable to address tactics in a grid (see Figure 7.6) with one axis ranging from personal communication to mass-produced messages, and the other measuring the level of interaction (two-way communication) from highly interactive to noninteractive. The grid visually depicts how we design tactics for a specific public. When we need a highly interactive approach, we also make the tactic highly personal—increasing the likelihood of selection and retention. The other end of the grid forms a megaphone which depicts a wide distribution of a message with little or no interactivity. For example, if the public and the specific message to be delivered requires a personal or peer influence, the tactics will be designed to invoke personal interaction and may include phone calls or handwritten notes or invitations. If, however, a breadth of coverage rather than personal influence is needed, a medium with a broader reach to publics may be more appropriate, including tactics such as public service announcements, radio actualities, or Internet broadcasts. In the middle of the grid would be highly segmented media like newsletters or special interest magazines, annual reports, and speeches with moderate opportunity for interaction.

Identifying communication tactics in this fashion helps us select the best communication tools for the public, purpose, and message. Otherwise, the medium (print/broadcast/Internet) and budget tend to determine what tactics we use rather than which tool would best accomplish our purpose. Using the grid, tactics fall into three categories:

1. highly personal and interactive
2. segmented and moderately interactive
3. mass-produced mass media

Highly Personal and Interactive Tactics

The basis of the relational or cooperative community approach to public relations is the overwhelming power of personal and interactive communication. The personal influence of opinion leaders and peers is particularly important in a persuasion campaign. It is in this area of tactics that creativity and innovation are most needed. This type of tactic is very specifically tailored to the public (usually made up of identifiable individuals) and personalized in its delivery. It is typically direct human-to-human communication, often handwritten, spoken one-on-one, and/or delivered in person by an influential.

A personal delivery system engenders interactivity. Interactivity is important in several ways.

Interactivity

The degree to which the tactic provides interaction between the sender of the message and the receiver.

- Interaction is a basis of strong relationships and cooperation
- It is a key to the crystallization of opinion
- It provides a personal commitment and stimulus for action

For these reasons, this kind of tactic is highly effective. Nevertheless, it is also time consuming and often expensive. The advantages must be weighed carefully against the costs (time and money) to determine the best circumstances in which to use personal communication channels and tools.

In some situations, it's possible to create the one-on-one communication hierarchically. A good example is the United Way's workplace giving campaign. Companies that support the United Way in their community by running workplace campaigns identify a company representative who is trained by local volunteers to hold an employee information meeting and to subsequently personally ask each person in the company to support local community social service efforts through monthly payroll deductions. In larger organizations, the company representative trains a representative in each department to make the personal ask. This hierarchical system uses opinion leadership, personal influentials, and one-on-one communication supported by collateral materials to reach hundreds of thousands of people within a community. Nevertheless, it is highly labor intensive, even though the laborers are volunteers.

More recently, a lot of social media has emerged as highly personal and interactive. The viral nature of many of these tactics makes them less labor-intensive and less expensive. The tradeoff for those benefits is that we largely relinquish control of the message and its distribution.

Segmented and Moderately Interactive Tactics

This kind of tactic combines the best of both worlds. Although not nearly as personal, it still provides a highly targeted message to a larger target audience than personal communication typically can. This category of tactic uses, or sometimes establishes, a channel that is specifically designed for an already segmented public. Good examples include newsletters and special interest magazines that have analyzed and been designed to meet the needs of a very specific group. Another example might be a stockholder meeting for all stockholders which, in some companies, can be thousands of people. The segmentation of cable channels also allows for the effective use of this kind of tactic.

These types of tactics are also typically more interactive than the mass media. Because the target audience is an interest group, it tends to be more responsive in publication surveys, and more active in initiating feedback letters, phone calls, and faxes. This environment is perfect for communicators to build in response mechanisms that provide the interactivity necessary for symmetry in communication with the organization's key publics.

Further, because the segmented channel has already identified the needs of its audience, it is a fairly simple matter for the public relations practitioner to tap into and help satisfy those needs. Such channels are often shorter on funding than traditional media channels and are therefore hungry for material that honestly meets the needs of their audiences. It is to the practitioner's advantage to identify such channels that target the organization's typical key publics, and to include them within the plan to build strong, mutually beneficial relationships.

Internet tactics will often fall into the segmented and moderately interactive category. Tactics using the Internet have proliferated such that the primary question is not whether we can use one to reach our publics but how and when it is appropriate to do so. Penetrating ethical questions surround the use of blogs and other Internet tactics. Some just irritate, but others tend toward the unethical. We must always remember that the fundamental basis of a relationship with a key public is trust. In our zeal to communicate and motivate, anything we do that erodes trust comes at too high a price.

In 1997, a Middleberg/Ross Media in Cyberspace Study reported that 91% of surveyed journalists were online to some degree. Now, almost all journalists prefer this method of communication. In fact, the most common method of pitching a story to a journalist now is by e-mail. The credibility of online communication has risen as well. Journalists search the Web for verifiable facts and for the opportunity to interact with a source. The Media in Cyberspace Study also reported that journalists were more interested in the interactivity of a company Web site than with the audiovisual bells and whistles we spend so much money to create.

More recently, Web sites have become the first organizational point of contact for all key publics. Web sites must be carefully planned to communicate the organization's messages to its key publics. The elements of the Web site should be mapped out like separate tactics with particular publics, purposes, and messages in mind. From Frequently Asked Questions (FAQs) to corporate histories and product information pages, the needs and self-interests of various key publics should drive the messages and their delivery. It is important for communicators to include Internet habits in the profiles of their key publics to know what online tactics will be effective.

Mass-Produced Mass Media Tactics

This type of tactic is perhaps the most familiar to communicators. The use of electronic media (which with today's technology includes print as well as broadcast media) to broadly disseminate messages will undoubtedly characterize communication for years to come. The technology facilitates broad coverage of certain publics that probably would not be reached any other way. Nevertheless, it is important to remember the advantages and disadvantages of specific mass media channels and to use them appropriately (see Figure 7.7). Further, just because we use mass media does not mean we are targeting a mass audience. It is just as important to segment publics and design public-specific messages for mass media as it is for segmented media.

Mass media provide immediacy, credibility, and a strong impact. Nevertheless, practitioners often take a passive approach to mass media placement. While we don't directly control news placements, there are communication

Figure 7.7—Advantages and Disadvantages of Primary Mass Media Channels

	Advantages	Disadvantages
Television	High impact because it combines sight, sound, and motion. Immediacy and credibility of message. Popular medium with large audiences. Worldwide coverage. Access to segmented special interest channels.	Time limits message content. High production costs. Expensive for advertising. Sometimes difficult to access and provides little feedback. TV news declining in credibility.
Radio	Good saturation of local markets and geographical selectivity. Relatively low cost and easy to change copy. Well targeted by listener profiles. Daily use by large numbers of people. Local endorsement. Fast and flexible placement.	Short time segments place limitations on message. Limited opportunity for feedback restricted primarily to talk format. No visual appeal. Radio news declining in credibility.
Newspapers	Geographical targeting. Broad reach of income groups at low cost. Immediacy if newsworthy and timely features. Highly accessible and credible.	High cost for national advertising. Short message life. Primarily black/white, but with some color opportunity especially with photos. Newsprint is a low quality, dirty medium. Declining readership but still high among older public.
Magazines	Highly segmented audience, typically more affluent. High quality, visual with color and credibility. Lengthy messages. Pass-along readership. Issues often retained.	Usually not dominant in a local market. No immediacy, early deadlines. Duplicate circulation. High production costs.
Internet	Expanding use and savvy users increase credibility of legitimate messages. Broad usage and easy to use. Comparatively inexpensive as a channel. Fast and flexible. Visual medium with high interactivity. Social media explosion with peers as message sources enhances credibility.	Some public segments still not online. Potentially high technology and start up costs. Can also be expensive to establish and maintain a prominent Internet presence, and to monitor it. Little control of the message in social media.

tools available that will help us be more active in building relationships with media. Satellite media tours, syndicated columns or programs, radio actualities as part of news releases, B-roll accompanying video news releases, and other techniques can help get a message used more readily than it might otherwise have been. We have the ability now to send photos over the Internet and even to stream video. Such tactics can be quite effective if we will remember a few important guidelines.

National Archives and Records Administration.

- Become acquainted with your media contacts (including Internet contacts) and work to meet their needs as they meet the needs of their audiences. Be familiar with their past work and what kind of material they prefer. You should make their jobs easier.

- Know the media market or audiences and adapt your material to meet their needs. Don't expect media to accept copy or programming that is blatantly self-serving. You must provide solid news.

- Localize your material. Whether it is a video news release, a feature story, or a public service announcement, unless it specifically targets the local community it will not be used. For special interest media—print, broadcast, and online—the community is not geographical, but it is still a community.

- Provide quality media products. Use their writing style and make sure to provide error-free copy well in advance of deadline. Provide a consistent point of contact and train people for interviews. Select interviewees who are knowledgeable and personable.

- Don't call a news conference unless you have a story that legitimately requires one. If it can be handled in a news release, use a news release.

Communicators will continue using mass media extensively for message dissemination. Make sure to establish strong media relationships based on honesty, trust, and ethical practice to enhance your ability to use mass media to target key organizational publics.

Other Considerations in Selecting Communication Tools and Devising Tactics

Although tactic selection should depend primarily on the public and the best way to reach them to accomplish your purpose, the content of the message will also be a determinant. For example, detailed messages with lots of information usually require a printed or online medium that allows a receiver the luxury of rereading or studying. Similarly, broadcast messages must typically be simple and highly memorable because they cannot be reviewed at will unless they are posted on the Internet. In both of these cases, the content and length or difficulty of the message are factors in media selection.

Tips from the Pros

Working with a TV News Service

George Tamerlani, Reuters Senior Producer and Washington, D.C. Bureau Chief, tips you off on working with a television news service and placing your story.

Do your research. I get a lot of calls from people who clearly don't know who we are or what we do. Look at media placement from a freelance perspective. If you were doing a magazine article about gardening, you wouldn't send it to *Soldiers of Fortune* magazine. You can make 50 calls and get three hits or make seven calls and get five hits.

Remember TV is an audio as well as visual medium. Sound is everything. There's nothing worse than a mute VNR or mute b-roll. We want natural sound only, without commentary. We also prefer blandly edited stories where each shot is 15- to 30-seconds long. We won't use your wipes, your quick cuts, or your music. We want to cut it and put it back together ourselves.

Include logistics and other key facts. Press releases tend to have a mark against them. But I welcome a release that gives me logistics information—where something will be and when it will happen. Tell me who's speaking—the heaviest hitter you have. What does your b-roll show and why is the story important?

Timing matters. I get calls from people who have never worked in journalism and they don't know my mindset. My responsiveness has a lot to do with the time of day you call. We have deadlines—crunch periods—and at a certain point in the day the agenda is set.

Drop the PR voice. Your success can sometimes just be in your delivery. Some people call and act like we're old mates, like we've spent two years in some foxhole together under artillery fire. Journalists joke and laugh about the tone of the PR pitch. "Hi, it's Jack calling." "Oh, hello Jack. Who are you Jack?"

Learn from those that do it well. The American Petroleum Institute has one of the best PR shops around. What they do is dull as dishwater but they deal in numbers. When the oil companies posted huge profits, the largest in history, they responded forthrightly with two messages: "We made a lot of money, but we earned it" and "We're not manipulating the market." The API is great because I can always reach someone in minutes and their numbers and statistics are verifiable facts.

Become a general expert. Read. Be current experts in two dozen or more subjects. PR professionals should broaden their scope on what's happening in the world. Read newspapers, both domestic and foreign. Read books and magazines. You build your gravitas by being well-read and articulate enough to handle my follow-up questions, which may not be on your bullet points. You cannot pitch me some new pharmaceutical drug without being conversant on the practices of pharmaceutical distribution in Africa. I may ask you about that and you have to have an answer. You have to be able to keep up.

Further, the practitioner should consider the degree to which they control the medium selected. Heitpas discusses two types of media channels: controlled and uncontrolled. Controlled channels allow the practitioner to dictate the content, timing, and placement or distribution. Examples are paid advertising, trade shows, and brochures. Such tactics are entirely designed and written by the communicator. No intervening gatekeepers affect the final product and its placement. Nevertheless, that advantage is tempered by a typically higher cost and lower credibility. Publics are well aware that controlled tactics convey exactly what the organization paying for the space wants said. There is no doubt in the consumer's mind that when they are reading paid advertising that the advertiser is telling only one side of the story to motivate consumer purchase.

On the other hand, uncontrolled channels are typically more credible because of the intervention of a third party, most often a reporter or blogger. They are usually less costly because much of the work is done by the "objective" third party. But the practitioner is unable to dictate the exact copy or message, placement, or timing. The risk that the message may be buried or distorted is the price paid for credibility gained through perceived third party objectivity.

Finally, you should remember that combinations of tactics are often preferable to tactics used individually or in isolation. If you determine that a critical company policy statement included in a press kit may not be fully appreciated by key opinion leaders unless you use a more personally interactive tactic, mail it to them separately with a handwritten note from an organizational executive or some other influential indicating key points that may specifically interest them. If you think your key investors need more personal attention regarding the latest stock jump, send them a copy of the news clipping with an FYI (for your information) corner notation from the president of the company. There are a number of ways to personalize a mass media (or even a segmented media) message.

On the other hand, some personal and interactive messages may be made mass through media coverage, editorial comments, or online posting. However, use care when deciding whether or not to turn a personal message into a mass message. It may not only dilute the appeal, it may alienate those originally touched by the personal message.

Some communication tools lend themselves to all three categories of tactics. A special event, for example, may be designed to be personal and interactive (like a private dinner for a major donor), segmented and moderately interactive (like a media tour of facilities or an award ceremony), or mass-produced mass media (like the Democratic or Republican national conventions). Turning a special event into a media event requires that care be taken to stage the event with messaging for the immediate attendees, but package it in such a way that the messages will appeal over the airwaves to listeners and viewers. Just remember that even though a special event is organized as a celebration or some other routine commemoration, you've wasted the organization's opportunities and resources if you don't also use it to convey primary messages to key organizational publics.

Further, combining tactics stimulates greater care in assuring our full array of tactics are integrated to support and enhance each other. Even using name tags at a staged event can be planned to strategically support other tactics. You might color code the tags to identify separate key publics and prepare separate packets of supporting materials to be distributed based on name tag color. All tactics should be developed to magnify the effect of other tactics. They should be timed to support and enhance each other. The whole of the tactics supporting any strategy should be greater than the sum of the parts. They are like pieces to a puzzle that must interlock and intertwine for the complete picture to appear.

For example, at a United Way campaign kickoff luncheon for the company representatives described earlier, the new theme was "Helping the Dream Come True." Literature at the place settings provided a written explanation of the theme selection and its focus on people and agencies working together to realize the dreams of the community to eliminate illiteracy, domestic violence, and other social problems. The table centerpieces reinforced the theme which was printed on a ribbon woven through the piece. Sparkling confetti around the centerpiece provided twinkling stars associated with dreaming. The entertainment was a group of handicapped children singing a song about dreams. And the dessert was served with fortune cookies whose fortunes had been replaced with the goals of the local United Way-supported social service agencies worded as community "dreams" for the coming year. The dream theme was carried throughout the year (and into the next year) in all communication efforts. Each member of the United Way team and the directors of supported agencies were trained to include the community's dreams in specific terms in every communication opportunity. The communication tools were all designed to reinforce each other and to send the message resonating throughout the key publics in the community.

DEVELOPING INDIVIDUAL TACTICS

As was mentioned at the beginning of the chapter, the process of developing communication strategies and tactics must employ creativity and innovation. The Strategic Communications Planning Matrix provides the analytical framework necessary to channel creativity in the planning process. But it is also necessary to channel creativity at the tactical level. Otherwise, the creator may lose the proper focus on public, purpose and message.

Copy Outlines

Copy Outline

An analytical tool that extends strategic planning to creation of effective tactics.

The secret to maintaining focus in the creative process at the tactical level is to employ an analytical tool to plan the necessary content of a tactic or communication tool before actually writing or designing it. Copy outlines have been devised for this purpose (see Figure 7.8) to supplement and extend the strategic planning matrix. The copy outline plans the specific details of the communication piece to make sure it is consistent with the overall plan, and to ensure that all important details are included in the copy. Similar to an outline used to organize and detail a paper or presentation, the copy outline is an analytical piece that joins the public, purpose, and message in logical persuasive fashion.

Figure 7.8—Sample Copy Outline: Brochure

Key public (audience):

    Secondary publics (audiences), if any:

Action desired from public(s):

    How that action ties to the primary public's self-interest:

Primary messages: (usually 2–3, short statements/selling points to be conveyed)
    Secondary messages: (bulleted supporting data, facts, cases, testimonials, etc.)

    1. Primary Message:

        Secondary: •
                 •
                 •

    2. Primary Message:

        Secondary: •
                 •
                 •

    3. Primary Message:

        Secondary: •
                 •
                 •

Third-party influentials and how they will be used (testimonials, quotes, etc.):

Proposed cover title and cover copy:

    Proposed cover photos/figures/art (if any):

Method and timing of distribution (self-mailer, point of purchase display, etc.):

Brochure size and paper (weight, finish, etc.):

Print quantity and number of colors:

Other graphics to be used (other than cover):

Timeline/deadline:

Identifying the Key Public and Action

The copy outline begins by identifying the key public, which must be one of the publics identified in the campaign plan and the public for which the strategy supported by the specific tactic was designed. It also states the desired action and identifies the public's self-interest as part of the appeal.

Messages

Then the copy outline gets specific in terms of details. Keeping in mind the public and purpose identified in the copy outline, what are the primary and secondary messages that public needs to receive to understand and perform the desired action? These become the copy for your tactic and, in effect, become the first draft of the communication tool. The messages are pulled from those you previously designed for this public in step five of the matrix and should be stated specifically enough that another member of your campaign team, your firm, or your department in an organization can edit and produce the communication tool without much other information. The messages contain each piece of information necessary to inform the public and motivate them to act. That means, for example, that you must be specific and accurate about dates and times of events you are publicizing, provide contact information for individuals to request more information, and include statistics when supporting logical arguments.

Make sure to include specific details in the copy outline. When the brain is in the analytical mode, you can determine exactly what information must be included to accomplish your purpose. But when the brain shifts to the creative mode, you may fail to include critical information in the process of creating great copy. You must channel your creativity by knowing the public, purpose, and message, and then you must check the resultant creation against the copy outline your analytical mind created for effectiveness. The most frequently omitted detail is the information that provides a way for the public to do what you have asked them to do. Be sure to include the specific action desired from a public and how that action relates to its self-interest. Nothing is more frustrating to people than to be persuaded to act but not be given the information necessary to do so. Provide a phone number to call, a Web site to get more information, or specific instructions on what to do.

Third-Party Influentials

After identifying the messages to be used in this product, the copy outline requires you to list third-party influentials and how they are used either as part of the messages or in distributing the tactic. For example, in a brochure on personal hygiene for low-income parents, you might use testimonials or information from a recognized health care provider. You may also use nurses at free clinics to distribute the brochure. Both methods use third-party influentials or opinion leaders to strengthen the appeal.

Distribution

Next, the copy outline details your planning for distribution. If it is a media product, designate each specific media channel (broadcasting station, newspaper, or other publication) that will receive the communication product. Indicate the delivery method and if any follow-up is required. If it is a brochure or flyer, indicate how it will be distributed. If it is a billboard, indicate size and location, as well as describing any visual appeal or art.

Appendix B contains copy outlines for a variety of communication products; each has been appropriately altered to request the specific information that must be determined in the analytical process to help drive the creative process and to check its accuracy and completeness. Although the copy outlines provided herein will help you when designing communication tools, you will use a vast array of tools for which copy outlines are not provided. Make sure you understand each communication tool or product well enough to custom design your own copy outlines for other communication tools. That shouldn't be a difficult task. For each tactic you use, you should plan the key public or target audience and secondary audiences, the action desired and the self-interest appeal to motivate that action, and then the primary and secondary messages that carry that appeal. Identify third-party influentials and how they will be used. Some tactics will include art or photos. Describe what they should be and how they support your messages. Some tactics require distribution. Indicate how that will be accomplished. For each communication tool identify specific production needs like print colors and quantity. Always include a deadline to keep you on task.

Remember that the copy outline is the analytical tool to make sure your creative products follow your strategic plan and stay on target with your public, purpose, and message. It contains the specific detail you determined was necessary to inform, persuade, and motivate the public to action. It is important to shift your thinking to an emphasis on the process of analytically creating the copy outline. The majority of your time spent on tactic creation should be in developing the copy outline. It is the most important task in the creation of tactics and should receive the bulk of the time expended. A good copy outline actually becomes the first draft of your product. You will find that, if you plan your copy outlines carefully and completely, your communication tools will always be on target and will take less time to create.

Once a communication product is completed, the copy outline becomes a cover sheet to explain your product's purpose and proposed use to your client or manager. It demonstrates the quality of your planning and the strategic thought behind the development of the piece, and it convinces your clients or managers that the product was the result of systematic planning and thought. They will be more assured of the wisdom of committing resources to production because the product has been designed to achieve the purpose identified in the planning to reach goals and objectives already established. Using copy outlines will ensure that your research-based planning carries into product development. This tool will help to keep your efforts strategic and on target.

The Case of the Warehouse Welfare Health Care

Sample Campaign

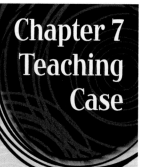

**Chapter 7
Teaching
Case**

Matrix: Action Planning
Step Six—Strategies and Tactics

Four publics have been chosen for this campaign. Because of the limited time to raise $500,000, we have selected those with the greatest inclination and capacity to give. *Members of the boards of directors of the free clinic partnership* will be crucial not only in leadership giving, but in opinion leadership to persuade other community leaders to give. *Community leadership givers*, those who routinely support community efforts, will be fairly easily persuaded for a one-time donation, and will set an example for their peers who are local area professionals. Many of the *local area professionals* are in independent practice and typically are not targeted for regular giving and could be persuaded for a one-time gift. Finally, *corporate executives* will be important for the corporate sponsorships which will not only provide a needed service for many of their blue-collar employees, but will spotlight their companies as community citizens fulfilling their corporate social responsibility.

Partnership Boards
Strategies and Tactics

Strategy one: Secure the participation of these board members in the presentations, personal visits and phone calls to colleagues through a presentation by the chair of each clinic partnership board to respective board members that also provides all necessary information, resources, and support to make their involvement easy without taking a lot of their time.

Tactics:

- Ten-minute presentation by the board chair at the March board meeting of each organization (United Way, CAS, SWHC, and ICNF).

- A written invitation for each of these board members to give at some level to make it easier for them to ask others to give.
- Information on the Circle of Caring recognition.
- Campaign event outline.
- Resource packet that includes: Half-page flyer listing in bold each task we are asking them to perform and the desired completion date, one-page instruction sheet for each task providing all necessary information and suggested approaches to accomplishing the task, proposal leaflet, fact sheet on the free clinic and on the partnership, 24/7 contact information for all individuals leading the partnership and the partnership staffers, and donation card.
- Print copy of Web portal for online information and giving.
- Information packet about the free clinic partnership's 5K race and how their organizations can get involved to support the event. The packet will contain information on how to organize a team and participate in the 5K run/bike/walk that includes a fact sheet on the event with all particulars including entrance fees and deadlines, a fact sheet on health care in the community and the proposed free clinic, templates for flyers and posters and other collateral to promote the run within their own companies, template of story for company newsletter, template of an e-mail to employees, templates for t-shirts or arm/wrist bands for the run, employee pass-along cards promoting the cause and the event with the Web address for online donation, team-building benefits, entrance applications and other necessary information, and a CD of all templates and collateral in electronic format.
- Follow-up e-mails reminding board members of the importance of the tasks and the deadlines.

Strategy two: Reinforce personal commitments to help raise the money through staff communications from the respective boards.

Tactics:

- Personally written thank you from each board's chair for the member's commitment and effort to support the free clinic.
- Circle of Caring paperweight delivered to the office with a note of appreciation and reminder of tasks to be completed.
- Personal thank you note from the director of one of the nonprofits involved in the partnership (United Way, CAS, SWHC, or ICNF).
- Report of campaign's progress and reminders at each monthly meeting of each board.
- Monthly e-mails reporting on campaign progress and highlighting what board members are doing.
- Phone calls from partnership directors to board members not making progress offering personal or staff assistance in helping them complete their tasks.
- Electronic packet of resources to encourage their organization's participation in the 5K run/bike/walk and a reminder to organize early.
- Advance invitation to the free clinic's grand opening Circle of Caring Celebration.

Community Leadership Givers

Strategies and Tactics

Strategy one: Solicit leadership contributions from local business and civic leaders, particularly those serving on boards of directors or as officers in the local social service agencies, through personal contact by partnership board members.

Tactics:

- Each partnership board member will call and ask five people whom he/she knows on the list of community leadership givers. (Coordinated by the United Way staff to assure no duplication.) The board member will tell them he/she is putting some information in the mail and ask them to consider supporting the free medical clinic as a leadership giver. Some partnership board members may prefer to host a lunch for their assigned asks so their appeal will be in person.

- Package mailed (or personally given) to each potential donor includes the leaflet proposal for the free clinic, the Circle of Caring brochure, and the donation card with return envelope. The package will also contain a pass-along card with statistical information on the health care need in the community, the free clinic, and a Web site address for more information or online giving.
- The board member will send a follow-up e-mail (template provided by the partnership staff) requesting support or thanking for support. E-mail will also contain hot link to the Web portal for online information or giving.

Strategy two: Express gratitude and give recognition to all who contribute through community opinion leaders.

Tactics:

- Thank you card written and signed by a well known United Way Board member or the Tuckers sent to all who contribute as soon as they contribute. Enclose an updated Circle of Caring brochure with their names included.
- Invitation to the grand opening of the free clinic.
- Circle of Caring display in clinic lobby with engraved nameplates of leadership givers, both companies and individuals.
- Final Circle of Caring brochures distributed to all at the grand opening.
- Recognition at the grand opening by those conducting the ceremony.
- Opportunities for media sound bites and interviews at the grand opening.
- A full-page ad in each community newspaper replicating the Circle of Caring display with thanks from the partnership to individually recognized contributors.
- Thank you flyer at 5K run/bike/walk listing all contributors.

Local Area Professionals

Strategies and Tactics

Strategy one: Seek support of the free clinic and leadership contributions among local area professionals through presentations to members of local

Chapter 7 Teaching Case Continued...

professional associations, business, and professional organizations like Chamber of Commerce and local service clubs and civic organizations like Lions and Rotary.

Tactics:

- PowerPoint presentation by partnership board members who are also members of the association to which they are presenting.
- Information packet for each professional at the presentation with proposal leaflet, Circle of Caring brochure describing the program, pass-along card with statistics on health care and the free clinic and information on how to give, and a donation card and return envelope with information on contributing by phone or online.
- Copy (for each professional) of an article in a related trade or professional journal about the business and reputation benefits of investing in your local community.
- Print copy of Web portal for online information and giving.

Strategy two: Reinforce the asks at the presentations and provide the information to professionals not in attendance at a presentation through the established communication channels of business, professional, service, and civic membership organizations.

Tactics:

- Story in the organization's newsletter on the opportunity to be involved.
- Letter from the president of the professional/civic organization enclosing the leaflet, Circle of Caring brochure, and donation card and envelope.
- E-mail copy of the trade or professional journal article on the benefits of investing in your local community.
- Video e-mails of partnership board members encouraging professionals to invest in the free clinic to support the community (TV PSAs sent electronically).
- E-mail reminder and health care statistics with facts on free clinic. Include a hotlink to the Web portal for online information or giving.
- Posting on organization's member Web site.

Strategy three: Enlist the support and contributions of local area professionals through targeted mass media.

Tactics:

- Pitch the story of the clinic and current professional community support to the TV/radio news with press kit.
- TV PSAs during news and prime time with recognizable partnership board members enlisting the support of the professional community and promoting the 5K run/bike/walk.
- Drive-time radio PSAs on the Circle of Caring using partnership board members as voiceovers and featuring local professionals who have contributed.
- Press release to the business section of the local newspapers.
- Facility tour (as build-out begins) featured on Sunday afternoon's local business and professional hour on television.
- Pitch to local financial columnist on local professionals investing in the community.

Strategy four: Engage professionals and motivate donation through a 5K run/bike/walk.

Tactics:

- Invitation from professional association to personally participate or to organize an office team to participate in the 5K run/bike/walk.
- Reinforce the invitations with TV announcements of the event and Web site for more information and registration.
- Pass-along cards in all local gyms, athletic clubs, bike shops, and similar locations promoting the cause and the event.
- Announcements of the event on the Web sites of the above shops.
- Event registration Web site with organizing information and collateral templates. Include access to an electronic information packet on organizing a team including a fact sheet on the event with all particulars including entrance fees and deadlines, a fact sheet on health care in the community and the proposed free clinic, templates for flyers and posters and other collateral to promote the run within their own

companies, template of story for company newsletter, template of an e-mail to employees, templates for t-shirts or arm/wrist bands for the run, employee pass-along cards promoting the cause and the event with the Web address for online donation, team-building benefits, entrance applications, and other necessary information.

Strategy five: Thank and recognize professionals who have contributed and encourage others to step up to contribute and be recognized through mass media.

Tactics:
- Media coverage of 5K run/bike/walk with opportunities for vignettes of local professionals supporting the cause.
- Race signage and collateral material for participants thanking and recognizing those community leaders and professionals who have contributed to the free clinic.
- Drive-time radio PSAs on the Circle of Caring using partnership board members as voiceovers and featuring local professionals who have contributed.
- Full-page in localized newspapers replicating the Circle of Caring display with thanks from the partnership to individually recognized contributors.
- Pitched series of feature stories (TV, radio, and newspaper) on local area professionals who are investing in the community by supporting the free clinic.

Corporate Executives
Strategies and Tactics
Strategy one: Motivate a corporate gift through a personal visit from a director of one of the partnership organizations and a couple of board members.

Tactics:
- Set appointments with CEOs and corporate executives to ask for a corporate gift. The visit should include a director from one of the partnership organizations and one or two board

members from partnership organizations who have an established relationship with the CEO or executive being visited.
- Provide a fact sheet detailing the local health care problem and the resulting social costs. Provide statistics specific to that company's workforce as appropriate.
- Provide the free clinic proposal leaflet at the meeting.
- Include a pass-along card with statistics on health care and the free clinic.
- Provide a Circle of Caring brochure and fact sheet detailing the public recognitions to be given donors through events (grand opening and the 5K run/bike/walk) and through mass media.
- One member of the visit team should follow up with a phone call to those not making an immediate commitment.

Strategy two: Motivate participation of corporate teams in the 5K run/bike/walk through personal contact and standardized collateral to make team organization easy.

Tactics:
- At the above corporate visits, provide a 5K run/bike/walk organizing packet as detailed in tactics above.
- Provide a fact sheet of benefits and publicity planned.
- Partnership organization's staff make phone calls to appropriate points of contacts within local corporations to request they host at least one team of employees in the event.
- Send electronic organizing packets to all interested corporations.
- Provide the organizing packet and template download from the event Web site.
- E-mail the television PSAs on the 5K run/bike/walk to corporate points of contact.

Strategy three: Reinforce the gift commitment through public recognition and thanks.

Tactics:
- Thank you card written and signed by a well known United Way Board member or the Tuck-

ers sent to all who contribute as soon as they contribute. Enclose an updated Circle of Caring brochure with their corporation recognized.

- Invitation for executives to the grand opening of the free clinic.
- Circle of Caring display in clinic lobby with engraved nameplates of leadership givers, both companies and individuals.
- Final Circle of Caring brochures distributed to all at the grand opening.
- Recognition at the grand opening by those conducting the ceremony.
- Media coverage of 5K run/bike/walk with opportunities for interviews and sound bites from corporate participants.
- Race signage and collateral material for participants thanking and recognizing those commu-

nity leaders, professionals, and corporations who have contributed to the free clinic.

- Drive-time radio PSAs on the Circle of Caring using partnership board members as voiceovers and featuring local corporations who have made donations.
- Full-page in localized newspapers replicating the Circle of Caring display with thanks from the partnership to individually recognized contributors.
- News releases to the business section of newspaper and to broadcast news directors on the corporate support of the free clinic.
- Video series following the renovation of the clinic and the start of operation, recognizing those corporations and philanthropists responsible for the negotiations to get it set up and the donations to fund the renovation.

Summary

Carefully planned strategies and tactics will ensure not only that your messages reach your target publics but also that they motivate a desired action or behavior. Strategies determine which channels are most appropriate to reach key publics. Tactics detail the creative tools designed to convey your messages and solicit action from your key publics. They are the tasks that must be done to implement the campaign or project. Copy outlines are used to create communications pieces that are consistent with our overall strategy and plans. They also make sure important details are included in the copy and the desired action from key publics is clearly stated.

Because many practitioners often find themselves choosing and implementing the same strategies and tactics over and over, it is important to remember the need for creativity. Use brainstorming and other techniques to look outside yourself, your habits, your customs, and your traditions to discover new solutions and innovative ideas. Experiment through trial and error. Creativity is often the result of borrowing ideas from others and reshaping them into your own new ideas. Strategic communication requires creative thinking and implementation particularly in the planning of strategies and tactics.

Exercises

1. Review step six of the teaching case. Based on the analysis of the publics and the profiles in step one of the teaching case in Appendix A, suggest alternative strategies and tactics for each public that would also accomplish the goal and objectives.

2. Watch local media to discover a local organization running a campaign to solve a problem or meet a challenge. Try to identify all the strategies and tactics being used to send messages to the publics. Evaluate the effectiveness of the strategies and tactics, and think about how you might have designed them differently or sent them through different channels to make them more effective.

3. Using the nonprofit organization you analyzed in the Chapter 6 exercises, design new strategies and tactics to send the messages of the organization.

4. Using a local or national organization with which you are familiar, identify two or three publics of that organization. Then brainstorm for each a list of six to eight unique channels within which to send messages. Then brainstorm a list of at least 10 different tactics for each channel.

Solution to Shallcross Test

How easy the answer appears when we give ourselves the permission to breach the perceived boundaries.

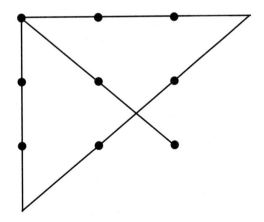

References and Additional Readings

Benn, A. (1982). *Twenty-three most common mistakes in public relations.* New York: AMACOM.

Blendtec. (2007). Will It Blend? Retrieved October 16, 2007 from http://www.willitblend.com.

Cutlip, S., Center, A., & Broom, G. (2006). *Effective public relations* (9th ed.). Englewood Cliffs, NJ: Prentice-Hall, Inc.

Edelman Worldwide. (2007). Edelman Trust Barometer. Retrieved October 16, 2007, from http://www.edelman.com/trust/2007.

Golin, A. (2004). *Trust or consequences: Build trust today or lose your market tomorrow.* New York: AMACOM.

Hainsworth, B. E., & Wilson, L. J. (1992). Strategic program planning. *Public Relations Review, 18:1*, 9–15.

Howard, C., & Mathews, W. (2000). *On deadline: Managing media relations* (3rd ed.) Prospect Heights, IL: Waveland Press.

Lenhart, A. et al. (2003). The evershifting Internet population: A new look at Internet access and the digital divide. Pew Internet and American Life Project. Retrieved October 16, 2007, from www.pewinternet.org.

Newsom, D., Turk J. V., & Kruckeberg, D. (2007). *This is PR: The realities of public relations* (9th ed.). Belmont, CA: Wadsworth Publishing Company.

Norris, J. S. (1984). *Public relations*. Englewood Cliffs, NJ: Prentice-Hall, Inc.

Shallcross, D. J. (1981). *Teaching creative behavior*. Englewood Cliffs, NJ:Prentice-Hall, Inc.

Tucker, K., Derelian, D., & Rouner, D. (1994). *Public relations writing: An issue-driven behavioral approach* (2nd ed.). Englewood Cliffs, NJ: Prentice-Hall, Inc.

Vocus, Inc. (2007). Optimizing your public relations with social media. Vocus White Paper.

von Oech, R. (1990). *A whack on the side of the head: How to be creative.* New York: Warner Books.

von Oech, R. (1983). *A whack on the side of the head: How to unlock your mind for innovation.* New York: Warner Books.

Wilcox, D. L., Ault, P. H., & Agee, W. K. (2006). *Public relations: Strategies and tactics (8th ed.).* New York: Harper and Row.

Calendaring and Budgeting

"Do not squander time, for that is the stuff that life is made of."

—Benjamin Franklin (1706–1790)
American Inventor, Journalist, and Statesman

LEARNING IMPERATIVES

- To learn a format for calendars and budgets that supports strategic planning
- To understand the importance of calendaring interactivity among tactics
- To learn the value of creativity in the calendaring and budgeting processes

In all relationships, timing is everything. Whether responding to a crisis or pursuing an opportunity, timing plays a crucial role in the strategic planning process.

The next two steps in the strategic planning matrix (Figure 8.1)—calendaring actions and budgeting for their cost—both require very specific detail. With so much information available in the communications and business literature about calendaring and budgeting, only a few important points need to be emphasized here.

Primarily, it is important to remember that a calendar and a budget are strategic planning tools. They must be considered carefully so that timing and cost are addressed within the overall framework of the organization's goals as well as the plan's objectives. Electronic tools for calendaring and budgeting abound. One of the best for a calendar is a Gantt chart (see Figure 8.2) that allows you to view the schedule for each public by day, week, or month.

Both the calendar and budget should detail tactics by public and strategy so your client or executive can quickly determine what tactics will target a specific public and how much each will cost. It also makes you much more aware of the cost of information and persuasion efforts among each of your key publics, and you are conversant in the interactive scheduling of the campaign by public. It provides an easy "line item veto" when your client or executive wants to eliminate a public or strategy for any reason. It is a simple matter to delete that section of your plan and subtract the cost from the total.

CALENDARING

Never forget that a calendar is strategic. When you calendar a plan, you are not just picking dates; you are finding the premier moment for an event to be held, a mailing to be sent, an ad campaign to launch. Timing is critical to success. To ensure effective calendaring, keep in mind interactivity, conflicts, tradition, lead time and planning.

Figure 8.1

10-Step Strategic Communications Planning Matrix   **Matrix**

Matrix: Action Planning

Steps Seven and Eight—Calendar and Budget

7. Calendar	Calendaring should be done with a time-task matrix (such as a Gantt chart) used to plan and strategically time implementation. The calendar should be organized by public and strategy with scheduling for each tactic.
8. Budget	Budgets should also be organized by public and strategy. The budget projects the specific cost of each tactic. It should also indicate where costs will be offset by donations or sponsorships. Subtotals should be provided for each strategy and public.

Figure 8.2—What Is a Gantt Chart?

A Gantt chart is a horizontal chart (usually a bar chart) developed as a production control tool in 1917 by Henry L. Gantt, an American engineer and social scientist. Frequently used in project management, a Gantt chart provides a graphical illustration of a schedule that helps to plan, coordinate, and track specific tasks in a project. Gantt charts may be simple versions created on graph paper or more complex automated versions created using project management applications such as Microsoft Project or Excel. Dozens of other software packages are also available to help build quick, effective Gantt charts.

Sample Gantt Chart

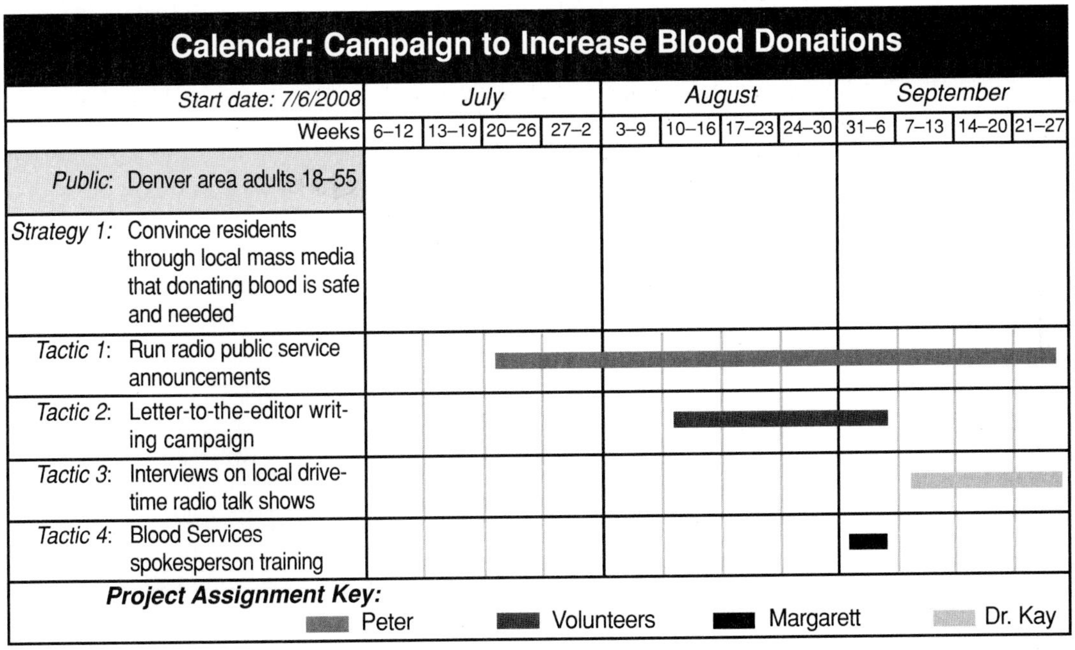

Calendar: Campaign to Increase Blood Donations												
Start date: 7/6/2008	July				August				September			
Weeks	6–12	13–19	20–26	27–2	3–9	10–16	17–23	24–30	31–6	7–13	14–20	21–27
Public: Denver area adults 18–55												
Strategy 1: Convince residents through local mass media that donating blood is safe and needed												
Tactic 1: Run radio public service announcements			▓	▓	▓	▓	▓	▓	▓	▓	▓	
Tactic 2: Letter-to-the-editor writing campaign						▓	▓	▓				
Tactic 3: Interviews on local drive-time radio talk shows										▒	▒	
Tactic 4: Blood Services spokesperson training									■			

Project Assignment Key: ▒ Peter   ▓ Volunteers   ■ Margarett   ▒ Dr. Kay

Interactivity Is Key

The timing of tactics should be such that you magnify, reinforce, and build on other tactics within publics and across publics. Schedule the grade school poster contest to conclude in time to use the winning posters in your efforts to solicit sponsorships from local businesses. Time your viral communication to peak when publics are getting messages in more formal channels.

Check for Conflicts

Check for conflicts seasonally and within communities. It is difficult to compete with traditional events and efforts. The annual Oktoberfest is probably not the time to schedule the launch of the hospital's new alcoholic rehabilitation program.

Build on Tradition

Build on tradition and other regularly scheduled events. While you need to avoid conflicting events, building upon related traditions can leverage awareness and motivation. The beginning of a new school year might be a great time to launch an effort to change a habit or routine. Perhaps when the kids go off to school is the best time for the local library to start a women's readers' circle.

Provide Lead Time

Always provide enough lead time for production and other arrangements. Plan for collateral material to be complete far in advance of the time it is needed. Make all reservations and invitations to key participants well in advance of the event. Doing so will leave time to reprint if needed or even to reschedule.

Plan Backward

Plan backward from the implementation date. If the launch is in July, when should the media pieces be prepared and placed? Is the media element a promotion or a follow-up? When should collateral material be completed? When should invitations be printed and mailed?

A calendar for implementation is obviously much more detailed than a calendar for a proposed plan. While the latter simply schedules the date each tactic will be used, the former requires scheduling of all efforts leading up to the date of implementation. For a brochure, for example, you would calendar deadlines for copy, art, design, approvals, and final printing.

BUDGETING

The budget should also be considered strategically. The issue should not only be total cost but also who should pay and how. Really creative plans find solutions to budgetary limitations that actually result in greater persuasive power. Recruiting volunteers to do work that would have been a budgetary item results not only in lower cost but also in greater support and advocacy from influentials in a community. Building partnerships between organizations—whether business to business or corporate to nonprofit—often strengthens the credibility of the appeal. Combining with other actors in a cooperative effort sharing costs provides a unity of action that is more persuasive and far reaching than acting unilaterally. Even requesting small contributions from target publics (like $1 admission to an event with the proceeds donated to a relevant local charity) can be effective. Making something free doesn't always make it appealing. In fact, many people consider that something free may not be worth their time. Among certain publics, you are more likely to get attention and participation if there is some monetary investment—no matter how small.

Partnership

A mutually beneficial short- or long-term cooperative relationship to reach common goals.

Strategic Budgeting

Judith T. Phair, APR, Fellow PRSA, Vice President of Communications for the Graduate Management Admission Council and former PRSA President, tips you off on budgeting so your first-rate public relations programs don't end up as exercises in "what might have been."

Effective budgeting is one of the most strategic things you can do to advance your department, your organization—and your career. To be valued as a trusted adviser and counselor, a public relations professional needs to know the business side of the client or organization. Carefully building, justifying, maintaining, and monitoring a budget is a critical part of strategic planning. A well-constructed budget provides a built-in method for setting expectations and evaluating results. Here are some things to keep in mind when crafting a financial scenario that will truly show return on investment and set the stage for gaining funding for future projects.

Know the organization's business plan and understand the relationship of your work to key elements. What are the top priorities, including financial priorities?

Budget strategically. Think about why dollars will be spent, as well as how. Justify each expenditure with measurable results.

Budget realistically. Match the budget to expectations. If the organization doesn't have the resources to meet its expectations, show what would be required as well as what can be done within existing boundaries. Offer alternative scenarios, along with a strategic analysis of what the return on investment would be with greater expenditures.

Consider both direct and indirect costs. Staff labor is not "free," nor is the use of equipment, office space, and the like.

Measure the return on investment. Remember also that the return does not need to be monetary to provide real value. Is your program creating the climate for an effective fundraising campaign or boosting public support for (or against) legislation that may affect your organization? That value can be calculated and ultimately contributes to the organization's bottom line.

Your budget should have six columns. The first is actually the public, strategy, and tactic under consideration and the second is the detail associated with that (i.e., how many brochures at how much each and any discount percentages or sponsors). The next column is the per item cost and the fourth is the total projected cost, the fair market price of this good or service. The fifth

The Case of the Warehouse Welfare Health Care

Sample Campaign
Matrix: Action Planning
Step Seven—Calendar

		March				April				May		
Key Public	**Community Leadership Givers**	Wk 1	Wk 2	Wk 3	Wk 4	Wk 1	Wk 2	Wk 3	Wk 4	Wk 1	Wk 2	Wk 3
Strategy	**Gratitude/recognition.**											
Tactics	Written thanks with C of C brochures				x——						—x	
	Invitation to C of C Celebration											
	C of C Celebration/clinic opening:											
	Final C of C brochures											
	Verbal recognition as sponsor											
	Engraved nameplate C of C											
	C of C paperweight											
	Media interviews of donors											
	C of C banners											
	Fresh flowers											
	Refreshments											
	Venue set-up											
	Full-page C of C thanks in papers											
	Thank you flyer with names at 5K										x	
Key Public	**Local Area Professionals**											
Strategy	**Get gifts through professional assoc/civic clubs.**											
Tactics	PowerPoint presentations								x——			
	Info packet:								x——			
	Leaflet proposal											
	C of C brochure											
	Donation card and envelope											
	Pass-along stats and clinic card											
	Copy of journal article								x——			
	Print copy of Web portal								x——			
Strategy	**Reinforce through mass media.**											
Tactics	Pitch stories to news directors											
	Press kit:											
	Release											
	Fact Sheet											
	Leaflet proposal											
	C of C brochure											
	Pass-along card											
	Campaign event outline											
	TV PSAs on 5K production								x			
	Placement								x——			—x
	Drive time radio C of C PSAs prod								x			
	Placement										x——	
	Release to business section											
	Facility tours for media											
	Pitch financial columnist											
Key Public	**Corporate Executives**											
Strategy	**Motivate corporate 5K team through personal contact.**											
Tactics	Packet to organize 5K team						x					
	Fact sheet on benefits and publicity						x					
	Phone calls offering help							x——		—x		
	Electronic 5K organizing packets						x					
	5K packet on Web site					x——				—x		
	E-mail TV PSAs on 5K						x					

Chapter 8 Teaching Case

Note: This calendar is abbreviated for space. It serves only as an illustration. Calendars must include all strategies and tactics for every public.

	Wk 4	June				July				August				September			
		Wk 1	Wk 2	Wk 3	Wk 4	Wk 1	Wk 2	Wk 3	Wk 4	Wk 1	Wk 2	Wk 3	Wk 4	Wk 1	Wk 2	Wk 3	Wk 4
														x			
														x			
																	x
																	x
																	x
																	x
																	x
																	x
																	x
																	x
														x			
								x									
								x									
								x									
								x									
	x				x				x								x
	x				x				x								x
									x								
				x								x					
						x								x	x		

The Case of the Warehouse Welfare Health Care

Sample Campaign

**Matrix: Action Planning
Step Eight—Budget**

Key Public	Members of Partnership Boards	Detail	Per Item Cost	Total Projected	Sponsored Credit	Actual Projected
Strategy	Secure participation through board presentation.					
Tactics	PowerPoint presentations	Prepared by UW staff	$0.00	$0.00	$0.00	$0.00
	Written invitation to give	90@.10/ea Each partner sponsors	$0.10	$9.00	$9.00	$0.00
	C of C recognition brochure	90 2-color @ .35/ea Printer @ 20% off	$0.35	$31.50	$6.30	$25.20
	Campaign event outline	90 @ .02/ea	$0.02	$1.80	$0.00	$1.80
	Resource packet:	90 covers @ .10/ea	$0.10	$9.00	$0.00	$9.00
	1/2 page flyer on tasks	90 @ .01/ea	$0.01	$0.90	$0.00	$0.90
	1-page instruction on each task	90 @ .02/ea	$0.02	$1.80	$0.00	$1.80
	Leaflet proposal for free clinic	No color/trifold 90 @ .25/ea	$0.25	$22.50	$0.00	$22.50
	Fact sheet on clinic/partnership	90 @ .02/ea	$0.02	$1.80	$0.00	$1.80
	Contact sheet on all staff/chairs	90 @ .02/ea	$0.02	$1.80	$0.00	$1.80
	Donation card/envelope	90 (3 per cardstock @ .10/ea) + env.	$0.08	$7.20	$0.00	$7.20
	Print copy of Web portal	90 @ .02/ea	$0.02	$1.80	$0.00	$1.80
	Resource packet to organize 5K:	90 covers @ .25/ea (5K fee covers)	$0.25	$22.50	$22.50	$0.00
	Fact sheet on event	90 @ .02/ea (5K fee covers)	$0.02	$1.80	$1.80	$0.00
	Fact sheet on clinic	90 @ .02/ea (5K fee covers)	$0.02	$1.80	$1.80	$0.00
	Templates for flyers	3 styles 270 @ .02/ea (5K fee covers)	$0.06	$5.40	$5.40	$0.00
	Templates for posters	3 styles 270 @ .25/ea (5K fee covers)	$0.75	$67.50	$67.50	$0.00
	Template for newsletter story	90 @ .02/ea (5K fee covers)	$0.02	$1.80	$1.80	$0.00
	Template of employee e-mail	90 @ .02/ea (5K fee covers)	$0.02	$1.80	$1.80	$0.00
	Logos for t-shirt, arm/wrist bands	90 @ .02/ea (5K fee covers)	$0.02	$1.80	$1.80	$0.00
	Pass-along cards on clinic and 5K	90 (10 per cardstock @ .10/ea) 5K fee	$0.01	$0.90	$0.90	$0.00
	Fact sheet/team building benefits	90 @ .02/ea (5K fee covers)	$0.02	$1.80	$1.80	$0.00
	Apps and new registration forms	90 @ .02/ea (5K fee covers)	$0.02	$1.80	$1.80	$0.00
	CD of all template materials	90 @ .25/ea (5K fee covers)	$0.25	$67.50	$67.50	$0.00
	E-mail reminders of tasks	90 @ .02/ea	$0.02	$1.80	$0.00	$1.80
		Strategy Subtotal	**$2.47**	**$267.30**	**$191.70**	**$75.60**
Strategy	Reinforce commitments through board comms channels.					
Tactics	Board thank you notes	90 @ .10/ea Each partner sponsors	$0.10	$9.00	$9.00	$0.00
	C of C paperweight with tasks:					
	Paperweight	90 @$15/ea (Local supplier 30%)	$15.00	$1,350.00	$405.00	$945.00
	1/4 sheet task list	90 (4 per slickstock @ .20/ea)	$0.05	$4.50	$0.00	$4.50
	Nonprofit director thank you note	90 @ .10/ea + .41 to mail (nonprofits)	$0.51	$45.90	$45.90	$0.00
	Progress report at board mtg	PowerPoint—no cost	$0.00	$0.00	$0.00	$0.00
	E-mailed progress reports	No cost	$0.00	$0.00	$0.00	$0.00
	Director phone calls	No cost	$0.00	$0.00	$0.00	$0.00
	Electronic resource packet on 5K	No cost	$0.00	$0.00	$0.00	$0.00
	Invitation to C of C and opening	90 @ .25/ea + .41 to mail	$0.66	$59.40	$0.00	$59.40
		Strategy Subtotal	**$16.32**	**$1,468.80**	**$459.00**	**$1,008.90**
		Public Subtotal	**$18.79**	**$1,736.10**	**$651.60**	**$1,084.50**
Key Public	Community Leadership Givers					
Strategy	Gratitude/recognition.					
Tactics	Written thanks with	250 @ .10/ea + .41 Asker mails	$0.51	$127.50	$127.50	$0.00
	C of C brochure	300 @ .35/ea Printer 20% off	$0.35	$105.00	$21.00	$84.00
	Invitation to C of C Celebration	600 @ .25/ea + .41 to mail	$0.66	$396.00	$0.00	$396.00
	C of C Celebration/clinic opening:					
	Final C of C brochures	750 @ .35/ea Printer 20% off	$0.35	$262.50	$52.50	$210.00
	Verbal recognition as sponsor	No cost	$0.00	$0.00	$0.00	$0.00
	Engraved nameplate C of C	250 @ $5/ea	$5.00	$1,250.00	$0.00	$1,250.00
	C of C paperweight	250 @ $15/ea Supplier 30% off	$15.00	$3,750.00	$1,125.00	$2,625.00

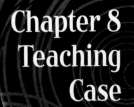

Chapter 8 Teaching Case

Note: This budget is abbreviated for space. It serves only as an illustration. Budgets must include all strategies and tactics for every public.

Key Public	Detail		Per Item Cost	Total Projected	Sponsored Credit	Actual Projected
Key Public	Community Leadership Givers					
	Media interviews of donors	No cost	$0.00	$0.00	$0.00	$0.00
	C of C banners	1 outdoor/1 indoor @ 150/4' x 6' ea	$150.00	$300.00	$0.00	$300.00
	Fresh flowers	3 sprays at $100/ea Florist comped	$100.00	$300.00	$300.00	$0.00
	Refreshments	400 @ $3/ea Local bakery comped	$3.00	$1,200.00	$1,200.00	$0.00
	Venue set-up	No cost/UW and CAS	$0.00	$0.00	$0.00	$0.00
	Full-page C of C thanks in papers	Daily @ $900/3 Weeklies @ $500/free	$900.00	$2,400.00	$1,500.00	$900.00
	Thank you flyer with names at 5K	500 @ .02/ea (5K fee covers)	$0.02	$10.00	$10.00	$0.00
		Strategy Subtotal	$1,174.89	$10,101.00	$4,336.00	$5,765.00
		Public Subtotal	$1,174.89	$10,101.00	$4,336.00	$5,765.00
Key Public	Local Area Professionals					
Strategy	Get gifts through professional assoc/civic clubs.					
Tactics	PowerPoint presentations	Prepared by UW staff	$0.00	$0.00	$0.00	$0.00
	Info packet:	500 @ .79 per packet (above)	$0.79	$395.00	$40.00	$355.00
	Leaflet proposal					
	C of C brochure	Printer 20% off (.07/ea)				
	Donation card and envelope					
	Pass-along stats and clinic card	5K fee covers (.01/ea)				
	Copy of journal article	500 @ .10/ea (club prints)	$0.10	$50.00	$50.00	$0.00
	Print copy of Web portal	500 @ .02/ea	$0.02	$10.00	$0.00	$10.00
		Strategy Subtotal	$0.91	$455.00	$90.00	$365.00
Strategy	Reinforce through mass media.					
Tactics	Pitch clinic story to news directors					
	Press kit:	5 covers @ .50/ea	$0.50	$2.50	$0.00	$2.50
	Release	5 @ .02/ea	$0.02	$0.10	$0.00	$0.10
	Fact Sheet	5 @ .02/ea	$0.02	$0.10	$0.00	$0.10
	Leaflet proposal	5 @ .25/ea	$0.25	$1.25	$0.00	$1.25
	C of C brochure	5 @ .35/ea Printer 20% off	$0.35	$1.75	$0.35	$1.40
	Pass-along card	5 @ .01/ea (5K fee covers)	$0.01	$0.05	$0.05	$0.00
	Campaign event outline	5 @ .02/ea	$0.02	$0.10	$0.00	$0.10
	TV PSAs production	1 30-sec @ $20K/comped prod.	$20,000.00	$20,000.00	$20,000.00	$0.00
	Placement	10/wk 4 wks $400/ea 2 sta/comped	$400.00	$16,000.00	$16,000.00	$0.00
	Drive time radio PSAs production	5 30-sec @$150/ea comped prod.	$150.00	$750.00	$750.00	$0.00
	Placement	10/wk 12 wks $100/av 2 sta/comped	$100.00	$24,000.00	$24,000.00	$0.00
	Release to business section	5 @ .02	$0.02	$0.10	$0.00	$0.10
	Facility tours for media	No cost	$0.00	$0.00	$0.00	$0.00
	Pitch financial columnist	No cost	$0.00	$0.00	$0.00	$0.00
		Strategy Subtotal	$20,651.19	$60,755.95	$60,750.40	$5.55
		Public Subtotal	$20,652.10	$61,210.95	$60,840.40	$370.55
Key Public	Corporate Executives					
Strategy	Motivate corporate 5K team through personal contact.					
Tactics	Packet to organize 5K team	40 visits @ $1.48/ea (5K fee covers)	$1.48	$59.20	$59.20	$0.00
	Fact sheet on benefits and publicity	40 @ .02	$0.02	$0.80	$0.00	$0.80
	Phone calls offering help	No cost	$0.00	$0.00	$0.00	$0.00
	Electronic 5K organizing packets	As many as needed—no cost	$0.00	$0.00	$0.00	$0.00
	5K packet on Web site	No cost	$0.00	$0.00	$0.00	$0.00
	E-mail TV PSAs on 5K	No cost (produced for area pros)	$0.00	$0.00	$0.00	$0.00
		Strategy Subtotal	$1.48	$59.20	$59.20	$0.00
		Public Subtotal	$1.48	$59.20	$59.20	$0.00
		CAMPAIGN TOTAL	$21,848.75	$73,694.25	$65,946.20	$7,748.05

column is the dollar amount of any discount, donation, or sponsorship and the final column is the actual projected cost to your client or organization (fair market price less the discount or sponsorship).

Budgeting by public, strategy, and tactic and subtotaling each public are particularly important. In your planning it is critical to assess the cost of reaching a particular public for a particular purpose and then to decide if the expenditure is worth the gain (cost-benefit analysis). If it isn't, then you will need to find a more cost-effective way to reach that public or find another solution that doesn't require its cooperation. Executives expect that kind of analysis.

Nevertheless, don't automatically reject a public because of cost. Be creative in finding ways to do what you have planned in more frugal ways, like using volunteers. Also, engage in partnerships. They are win-win relationships and in many ways even more important than cost savings.

Summary

Strategic planning does not end at tactics. Your approach to calendaring and budgeting must also be strategic. Tactics should be timed to gain maximum benefit from other tactics in the plan and from external events and annual community calendars. Strategic budgeting allows you to creatively manage cost while leveraging other relationships. The calendar and budget should be just as much a part of your strategic and creative planning as are the other elements of the plan.

Exercises

1. Examine a local annual event and identify what publics are being targeted. Sketch out the calendar for preparations and tactics. What are all the elements of the event including partnerships, media, and collateral materials? Design a calendar that incorporates the preparation and implementation of every element of the event by public and examine what the lead time would need to be for each tactic.

2. Make some phone calls to cost out the elements of the above event. Categorize the budgetary items by public to determine a cost per public. Identify where the organizers might have negotiated discounts or contributions and where partnerships have mitigated the cost.

References and Additional Readings

TechTarget, Inc. (2004). Gantt Chart. Retrieved October 17, 2007, from whatis.techtarget.com/definition/0,,sid9_gci331397,00.html.

Implementation and Communications Management

"There is a logic of language and a logic of mathematics. The former is supple and lifelike, it follows our experience."

—Thomas Merton (1915–1968)
American Monk, Writer, and Poet

LEARNING IMPERATIVES

- To understand the use of the strategic calendar in managing the tactics for each public and across all publics

- To learn to synthesize a plan into a table and check its logic

- To understand the importance of monitoring and flexibility in the process of implementation

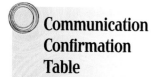

Communication Confirmation Table

A visual tool used to validate the logic of a communications plan.

Two of the most valuable tools for managing the implementation of a plan are the strategically planned calendar and the communication confirmation table. The calendar keeps all strategies and tactics for all publics coordinated and on schedule. The communication confirmation table helps you check to make sure you are accomplishing what your analysis and plan said you needed to accomplish with each public to reach the goal. Nevertheless, remember this is a planning matrix; you should complete every step of the planning—through evaluation criteria and tools—before you begin to implement the plan. Once you have done that, use the calendar and the communication confirmation table as your management maps.

MANAGING BY CALENDAR

To manage a project well, you must be able to visualize the outcome. You must be able to see how an effort comes together to communicate messages to an individual public and across publics. The Gantt chart format for a calendar helps you identify tasks and preparation by public throughout the entire time frame of the project or campaign. You can manage (or delegate management) by public if needed. The same format allows you to identify a selected time frame and consider every tactic being implemented among all publics within that time frame. It provides a holistic view of every tactic integrating across all publics; it displays the whole picture. As a management tool, it helps you keep all the balls in the air because you visualize the entirety of events, but still allows you to narrow your focus to one public as needed.

MANAGING BY COMMUNICATION CONFIRMATION TABLE

The steps in the planning section of the Strategic Communications Planning Matrix have required an analytical approach to answer these four questions:

1. What needs to be accomplished to achieve the goal?
2. Who needs to be reached and motivated in order to accomplish that?
3. What messages need to be sent to those publics to motivate them through self-interest appeal?
4. How can the messages be sent so our publics will receive them and act upon them?

The planning is analytical and is completed one public at a time using your research and knowledge about a particular public to formulate and deliver messages to that public. Because planning is naturally linear, it is helpful—particularly to students learning the strategic process—to create an abbreviated and more visual tool to validate the viability of the plan and to make sure it follows logically from the analysis of publics. That is the purpose of the communication confirmation table. It presents the logic across a single line of

Tips from the Pros

Managing Integrated Marketing Communications Campaigns

Andy Hopson, Managing Director of Ruder Finn's Chicago office and previously the President of Publicis Dialog, a "holistic" agency he helped launch in the U.S. in 1998, tips you off about how to integrate public relations, marketing, and advertising to create more successful campaigns.

Consumers are barraged with marketing messages from the time they get up in the morning until their heads hit their pillows at night. From television spots to billboards to the Internet, the onslaught of information is overwhelming. Consumers don't segregate where they get information; they take it in holistically to form opinions, brand preferences, and to make decisions. Brands are built through consistent messaging in every communications channel, and successful public relations practitioners understand the need to integrate all communications and marketing disciplines. While advertising builds brand equity, public relations establishes credibility and tells the brand story more completely. Database marketing touches consumers one-to-one and sales promotion motivates them to action. The most powerful campaigns are those that share a consistent message across all communication channels, touching consumers wherever they are in ways most meaningful to them individually. Following are components of successful integrated campaigns.

Holistic training. Marketers from all disciplines must be trained to think more broadly. They must possess an open mind to recognize the role each discipline can play in an integrated campaign.

Holistic planning. Successful integrated marketing communications campaigns start with planning, extending to the creative process and ultimately through execution. Advertising, marketing, and public relations must have equal status as each plays a role in creating equity and brand preference among consumers.

Multi-disciplinary creative development. A really big idea is one that can be effectively applied across many marketing disciplines and extended to all channels of communication. Ideas must be drawn from a broader range of perspectives, not devised by one discipline and later adapted to others.

Whole-picture measurement. An integrated campaign can be more readily held accountable for business performance. Holistic strategists must measure the effectiveness of each channel of communications so they can modulate the marketing mix for optimal return on investment.

vision to confirm that planning decisions employ good reasoning. By abbreviating your analysis in key words across the matrix categories, the communication confirmation table shows your logic as it answers the four questions above (Figure 9.1).

The communication confirmation table summarizes the self-interests of a public and shows in the next column how those self-interests are incorporated into the message appeal. It identifies from your overall objectives those that this particular public will help you satisfy and uses key words to highlight the strategies and supporting tactics necessary to achieve the objective. Viewing this short-hand version of your plan helps you confirm that the analysis has been applied, that the plan flows logically, that all elements of the matrix action planning process are aligned. It is not unusual for the confirmation table to reveal discrepancies in logic that were not apparent while the plan was being written. Have you selected mid-day television talk shows to reach high school students? Did you plan to run PSAs during drive time to reach housewives? Have you designed a message about money-saving features to target a public that is less concerned about money and more concerned about safety? Are you using video news releases to send a complicated message better conveyed in newspaper features or op-ed pieces? Check your logic, and then go back and make any appropriate changes before you begin your implementation. As intimated in the quotation at the beginning of the chapter, language is fluid and logical—especially words defining a strategic plan that effectively builds on itself.

Figure 9.1

10-Step Strategic Communications Planning Matrix   Matrix

Matrix: Action Planning

Step Nine—Communication Confirmation

9. Communication Confirmation   The communication confirmation table confirms the logic of the plan by converting it into short statements for each public in tabular form. This format (see below) aids in checking strategies and tactics to make sure they are appropriate to reach the public, that messages appeal to the public's self-interest, and that the planning for each public meets the objectives.

Key Public Self-Interests Primary Messages Influentials Objectives Strategies Tactics

Ongoing Monitoring and Feedback

These two management tools—the strategically planned calendar and the communication confirmation table—add the flexibility that is often missing from the planning process. When you plan the evaluation (the final step in the Strategic Communications Planning Matrix), you will plan for measurement throughout the implementation phase. These measurements provide checkpoints for your progress toward reaching the objectives and the goal. But what if your measurements reveal that you are not on track? Because you have strategically planned a calendar and thoughtfully prepared the communication confirmation table, you have the flexibility to go back to those two documents to rework and refine your plan to get back on track.

The necessary alteration may be as simple as adding or changing a single tactic or as grand as revamping an entire public. The confirmation table also provides the flexibility to quickly add or delete a public. You don't have to rewrite the whole plan. You have a summary of your plan by public, most particularly of the logic of the plan based on your analysis. Use it to determine what you need to change to reach your objectives on time and within budget.

The Case of the Warehouse Welfare Health Care

Sample Campaign

Matrix: Communication
Step Nine—Communication Confirmation

Key Public	Self-interests	Primary Messages	Influentials
Members of Partnership Boards	Opinion leadership/peer esteem, funding clinic for community, not spending a lot of time to do it.	1. Because of your community leadership, your visible support is key to our success. 2. Commit to make contacts. Staff will provide all materials and coordinate visits. 3. Commit to a leadership gift of $1,000 or more as an example and leverage.	Peers on boards, board chairs, professional colleagues.
Community Leadership Givers	Community status and respect, sincere care for community's welfare.	1. As community leader, you know the health care needs. Support the free clinic partnership. 2. We welcome your leadership gift of $1,000 or more.	Peers, other community leaders, employees, family members.
Local Area Professionals	Professional reputation, financial success.	1. Many Devon neighbors in need of health care. They need your help. 2. Show your leadership with a one-time gift. 3. Participate in 5K benefit to show your commitment to community.	Peers, business and civic leaders, fellow professionals.

Chapter 9 Teaching Case

Note: The Communication Confirmation Table (CCT) confirms the logic of the plan by converting it into short statements for each public in tabular form. This CCT is abbreviated for space. It serves only as an illustration. CCTs must include the complete planning for every public.

Objectives	Strategies	Tactics
1. Raise awareness to 80%. 2. Raise $150K in leadership gifts. 3. Raise $250K in corporate gifts. 4. Raise $100K in other gifts.	1. Secure participation through presentation by respective board chair and make involvement easy.	10-min. pres. at next board mtg. with collateral: written invitation for them to personally give, info on C of C recognition, campaign event outline, resource packet, flyer and instruction sheet on required tasks, proposal leaflet, info on clinic and staff contacts, print copy of Web portal. Resource packet to organize 5K team. Follow-up e-mails on tasks and deadlines.
	2. Reinforce commitments through their respective boards established communication channels.	Personal thank you from board chair. C of C paperweight with task reminders delivered to office. Personal thank you from director of one of the involved nonprofits. Campaign progress report at monthly board mtg. E-mailed progress reports. Phone calls from directors to those not making progress. Electronic resource packet on 5K team organization. Advance invitation to C of C celebration and clinic opening.
1. Raise awareness to 80%. 2. Raise $150K in leadership gifts.	1. Solicit leadership gifts through personal contact of partnership board members.	Each board member asks five leaders on leadership givers list. Info packet with leaflet proposal, C of C brochure, donation card and envelope, pass-along card with stats and case for clinic, and Web site address to give. Follow-up e-mail from board members thanking or reminding.
	3. Gratitude and recognition through community opin. ldrs.	Written thanks with updated C of C brochure. Invitation to C of C Celebration and clinic opening. Engraved C of C nameplates at opening. Final C of C brochures at opening. Recognition at opening by dignitary speaking. Media interviews at opening. Full-page C of C w/names in all local papers. Thank you flyer w/names at 5K.
1. Raise awareness to 80%. 2. Raise $150K in leadership gifts. 4. Raise $100K in other gifts.	1. Seek support and contributions through pres. to local professional associations and civic/service clubs.	Pres. at mtg. by partnership board member also a member of the association presenting to. Info packet w/proposal leaflet, C of C brochure, pass-along card with stats and info on free clinic and how to give, donation card/return envelope. Copy of article in professional journal about career benefits from investing in community. Print copy of Web portal.
	2. Reinforce mtg. asks and ask those not attending through established comms channels of each organization.	Story in organization's newsletter. Letter from pres. of the org. w/proposal leaflet, C of C brochure, and donation card/envelope. E-mail copy of professional journal article. Video e-mails of partnership board members encouraging gift. E-mail reminder and stats on clinic w/hotlink to Web portal for online giving. Post notice on organization's Web site.
	3. Enlist support through targeted mass media.	Pitch story of clinic and current professional community support to news directors w/press kit. TV PSAs during news and prime time featuring partnership board members encouraging local area professionals to give and do 5K. Drive time radio PSAs on C of C featuring professionals who give. Release to business section of all local weeklies and daily paper. Facility tour pitched to Sunday TV business program. Pitch local financial columnists on professionals investing in community.

Summary

The communication confirmation table is a planning tool that becomes a management tool once you have begun the actual implementation of your communications plan. As a planning tool, it confirms the logic of your plan for each public according to the analysis completed in your research. As a management tool, it provides the flexibility to change your plan quickly and effectively to make progress toward your objectives. The strategically planned calendar becomes the other key management tool in the implementation process. Use it to manage your plan for each public as well as to manage the whole effort from a macro perspective. In the implementation process, these two management tools provide the capability for measurement and feedback to adjust the plan and keep it on track.

Exercises

1. Use one of the partial plans or analyses completed in the exercises from prior chapters and create a communication confirmation table that will help you evaluate the logic of the plan. Make any appropriate corrections.

2. Now select a public that was not selected in the above plan and add them to the confirmation table as a viable part of the plan.

Effective Communications Measurement and Evaluation

"Unless evaluation becomes less of a mystery and a more accessible process, it would appear that a generation of better educated practitioners is needed to break the technician mold."

—Tom Watson
Author, *Integrating Planning and Evaluation*

LEARNING IMPERATIVES

- To understand the importance of evaluation in demonstrating results
- To understand how to plan evaluation that meets the standards set by an organization's management
- To understand how to determine evaluation criteria and the appropriate measurement tools

With the new vigor with which communications research is finally being pursued, another step in the RACE process moves in to take the "most neglected" title: evaluation. Evaluation has long been cast into the pot with research and, consequently, its specific nature and conduct ignored. In fact, surveys among public relations professionals found that they generally "lacked confidence to promote evaluation methods to employers and clients" (Watson, 2001). Lack of knowledge and understanding of evaluation models and techniques seemed to be the primary reason practitioners did not propose or conduct evaluation.

Nevertheless, how can the organization's communicators hope to be taken seriously if they shrink from measurements of their effectiveness? For too long, the communications function has been viewed as a kind of mystical intangible: intangible methods, intangible effects, and intangible results. But an organization focused on building strong relationships with key publics cannot afford to spend resources on intangibles. We have often claimed that our benefit to the organization was indirect, but that they would really miss us if we weren't there. It is a wonder more organizations haven't taken that challenge.

Organizations—commercial, governmental, and nonprofit—are managed to produce results, to accomplish missions. Each function of the organization must be able to demonstrate its contribution to the accomplishment of its mission. The ability to prove results is critical not only for the organization but also for the employees doing the work. It is little reward to work daily in efforts that you cannot be sure are making a difference.

EVALUATION MODELS

Standards of Success

The literature of communication contains several models of evaluation. They basically all evaluate success along three standards:

1. success that justifies the budget expenditure
2. effectiveness of the program itself
3. whether or not objectives were met

While these standards are all worthwhile, they may leave you and your organization wanting. Put yourself in the chair of the CEO. What are they looking for? In a word, results.

Results may mean meeting the objectives, they may mean success that justifies the budget expenditure or they may mean effectively carrying out a program. But what we should focus on as our organization's marketing, public relations, and advertising communication specialists is setting objectives that are measured in terms of results, justifying budget expenditures in terms of results, and determining program effectiveness in terms of results.

Tips from the Pros

Measuring Social Media

Katie Delahaye Paine, founder and former President of The Delahaye Group (sold to Medialink in 1999) and founder and CEO of KD Paine & Partners LLC, publisher of The Measurement Standard and The One-Minute Benchmarking Bulletin, tips you off on rethinking your approach to measurement.

The Internet revolution means consumers continue to seize power from the marketers. A new blog is created once every two seconds. Most journalists now check facts and look for story ideas and breaking news in blogs. People have access to so much information, the likelihood of your message penetrating the clutter is virtually nil. We used to say, "If you can't measure it, you can't manage it." But the nature of blogs renders management impossible. Here are some tips to guide your measurement in this new reality.

Tools and techniques for measuring your own blog are typically financial in nature. Basically you are assessing return on investment (ROI), impact on sales, or lead generation.

Think of the blogosphere as one enormous focus group. Customers, potential customers, employees, and potential employees use blogs to share their thoughts with the world. You can listen in on their conversations and gain a much better understanding of how your publics are responding to your initiatives.

Use content analysis of blogs to look for messages and themes. Determine how your constituencies perceive your organization or brand.

Measure links to rank the importance and credibility of various blogs. The generally accepted practice is to consider the number of links, track backs, and comments and roll them up to a ranking or authority index. Look up the URL of the blog on Technorati to see the ranking. Some firms are using panels to determine blog readership. However, this only reflects readership of major blogs. For the vast majority, there is no way to accurately count the number of eyeballs that view each blog. Statistics that show the number of visitors are usually hugely overstated. The owner of the blog itself and/or the blog host service has the data, but may not choose to share it.

Tease insight from the data and draw actionable conclusions. Look at trends over time. Are complaints going up or down; are relationships getting better or worse? Read the blogger's prior postings. If there are only one or two links, comments, or track backs, don't do anything but watch the numbers. If they start to grow quickly, you may have an emerging crisis. If it's already in the hundreds, and/or if this blog is on Feedster's top 500 list, then you need to respond. If someone is consistently writing about you, see what kinds of comments are made and how the blogger responds, then start a dialog. Offer information, a perspective, or insight on something the blogger will find relevant.

The Preparation, Implementation, and Impact (PII) Model

To simplify the process here, we refer the reader to a model of evaluation constructed by Cutlip, Center, & Broom (2000, pp. 436–454). The Preparation, Implementation, and Impact (PII) model is a straightforward approach to evaluating communication programs at all required levels. It provides guidelines to evaluate the preparation and planning process within the organization, the tactical implementation, and the impact or results of any given effort. In evaluating the planning process, it asks if the research collected was sufficient and complete, if it was organized and analyzed in a way that it could be used effectively, if the process was timely and inclusive, and other key questions that assess whether the process functioned to produce a workable plan to meet the challenge.

Evaluation of the implementation process tracks the success of tactics by counting media placement, event attendance, and other such measures of our tactical abilities. The final evaluation is the impact of the program. What were the results? Did the program meet the objectives? Were attitudes, opinions, or behaviors changed? And finally, did those changes produce the desired result and satisfy the goal (assuming the objectives were met) within the allocated budget? Evaluation that does not measure end results simply cannot stand the test of today's organizational managers. And communication professionals who cannot demonstrate that their efforts produce the desired results within acceptable expenditures are themselves expendable.

Evaluation is actually relatively easy if it is planned from the beginning of an effort using the Strategic Communications Planning Matrix (Figure 10.1). Good evaluation owes much to good objectives. If the objectives are written as outcomes to be accomplished in order to reach the goal, then the evaluation will be results-oriented and satisfy the organization's management. Two steps must be considered in evaluating any plan. First, by what criteria should we judge success; and second, how are those criteria best measured?

Figure 10.1

10-Step Strategic Communications Planning Matrix   Matrix ◯

Matrix: Evaluation

Step Ten—Evaluation Criteria and Tools

10. Evaluation Criteria and Tools   Evaluation criteria are the specific measures used to determine the success of each objective. Evaluation tools are the specific methods used to gather the data identified by each criterion. The evaluation tools should be included in the calendar and budget.

EVALUATION CRITERIA

Evaluation criteria are automatically set when objectives are set. Objectives are designed to provide direction to planning and to identify the results that determine success. Clients and managers will judge success by the criteria (objectives) you have set. In this step of your plan, you should restate your objectives in terms of success and designate an appropriate method for measuring each one including a date. For example, if one of your objectives is to increase name recognition of your client from 30% to 80%, the criterion for success would be written: "Achieve 80% name recognition of the client among key publics by June 30th."

The successful achievement of all campaign objectives should result in the accomplishment of the goal, which may or may not be directly measurable. If you have followed the strategic planning matrix, accomplishing the overall goal will signify to management that you have achieved success in all three standards identified above. You can justify the expenditure because you reached your goal within proposed budget. You demonstrate effectiveness because your strategies and tactics combined to accomplish the goal. And, you met the campaign objectives which resulted in the accomplishment of the goal.

Make sure to establish meaningful measures of success. Message exposure doesn't mean message receipt. Always keep in mind that behavior is the ultimate measure. Figure 10.2 provides some tips for measuring social media that can be translated to other channels as well.

Evaluation Criteria

Standards set to measure success.

Criteria for Evaluation of Plan Effectiveness

In addition to evaluating results by measuring performance on each objective, you should establish criteria for evaluation of the effectiveness of your plan and communication tactics. While the ultimate evaluation is results, you are also being personally evaluated by supervisors and clients on your professionalism,

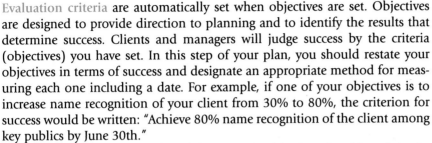

Figure 10.2—Katie Paine's Nine Immutable Laws for Measuring Social Media

1. Size doesn't matter.
2. ROI doesn't mean what you think it does.
3. HITS = How Idiots Track Success.
4. Stop screaming, start listening.
5. It's not how many eyeballs, it's the right eyeballs.
6. Be who you are and see who is pleased.
7. Be there when they need you.
8. Match the measurement tool to your objective.
9. It will all change tomorrow.

ROI = return on investment.
From Katie Delahaye Paine, founder, KD Paine & Partners LLC.

creativity, and ability to direct a communication effort. You should add evaluation factors that specifically address your success and effectiveness in community relations, media relations, or other skill areas. While media placement is
not a measure of whether a public received and acted upon a message, it is still
a factor to be evaluated within the context of effective strategies and tactics.

Although it is not recommended to set an objective for specific media
placements because it tends to force manipulative tendencies which are
expressly forbidden in some codes of ethics (PRSA's specifically), it is perfect-
ly acceptable to set an evaluation criterion that measures your success at placement couched in terms of media relations. While an objective for front-page
coverage in the *Wall Street Journal* may set a manipulative course that is fatal to
good relationships with media, evaluation criteria that measure such coverage
and placement as a whole across the campaign would examine the number of
front page placements in nationwide publications. The first course is manipulative; the second seeks to evaluate and improve media relationships across the
board.

Similarly, you may seek to evaluate your performance at staging and promoting events or any other accepted marketing or public relations communication tool. Although these evaluations are not specifically determining
whether or not you achieved your objectives, they are crucial to improvement
of your communication efforts and demonstrating your expertise, professionalism, and value to the client or organization.

Converting your objectives to evaluation criteria is your primary evaluation
of results. Additional criteria that address your team's specific capability and
expertise are highly useful secondary criteria to measure your effectiveness.

EVALUATION TOOLS

Each objective must be converted to an evaluation criterion and each criterion
must be measurable by an evaluation tool. Measurement tools are essentially
research tools. They are the same methodologies used in research but focus on
evaluation. They may include surveys or measure sales or count votes. But they
also tally results: dollars raised or saved, legislative bills passed or failed, and
other concrete outcomes. The rules of research apply in evaluation more particularly because the evaluation of your communication effort then becomes
part of the background for subsequent efforts.

Typically, evaluation measurements require a benchmark measurement
prior to the program, during the program, or both. Without adequate planning for the evaluation process, the benchmarks are often not taken in the
beginning, resulting in no data for comparison. Unless you know where you
started, you cannot determine how far you've come.

Although measurement tools are essentially the same as research methods, many research organizations have specialized in evaluative methods. It
would be wise to access the Web sites and newsletters on evaluation and
measurement produced by specialty firms like KD Paine & Partners or Cision.
While evaluation tools for some objectives may be obvious, others may

Evaluation Tools

Methods used to gather
data needed to assess
whether or not evaluation
criteria were met.

require complicated formulas that would, for example, combine measures of sales, media placements, and trade show referrals in some kind of sliding scale that measures the effect of marketing communications and media relations on product sales.

Clearly articulated evaluation tools must include the source of information and how it will be obtained. Include all necessary tasks when describing the evaluation tool for each criterion. If you are measuring the criterion mentioned above, your evaluation tool would read something like this: "Conduct a random, statistically viable, telephone survey of the key public population June 28–30, 2008, to determine what percentage recognize the client's name." This data could then be compared to the survey conducted at the beginning of the campaign, which indicated 30% name recognition for the client.

CALENDARING AND BUDGETING THE EVALUATION

The evaluation process points out the necessity of reviewing your calendar and budget to ensure that all evaluation tools are scheduled. You can designate a separate section of the calendar and budget to specifically address the planned evaluation. Another option might be to include evaluation as part of the planned strategies and tactics for each public. Only with this kind of planning can you ensure that appropriate benchmark research is done in the beginning and throughout the campaign to compare with evaluation research. It also enables you to incorporate appropriate evaluation in the detailed planning for tactics. For example, if you need to measure the number of attendees at events, or number of visitors to a trade show display, you will build into the tactic a method for tracking those numbers. Trying to guesstimate such figures later only causes your evaluation to be inadequate and your claim to success suspect. Finally, including the evaluation tools in the calendar and budget for each public ensures that the funding is available for this critical function.

The Case of the Warehouse Welfare Health Care

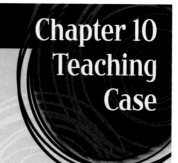

Chapter 10 Teaching Case

Sample Campaign

Matrix: Evaluation
Step Ten—Evaluation Criteria and Tools

Objective 1

Criteria

Awareness of the opportunity rose to 80% among key publics by March 31st.

Tools

Partnership board staff members will determine the total target public by combining the 2,500 community leaders from the United Way list and the number of professional and civic association members (approximately 30,000) to arrive at the total campaign target population. They will then keep track of presentations and mass media coverage to estimate whether 80% were exposed to the message (because of limited time and money, exposure is the only measure to be used although it doesn't measure message penetration).

Objective 2

Criteria

Collection of $150,000 in new leadership gifts by April 30th.

Tools

Records kept of donations from leadership appeals.

Objective 3

Criteria

Collection of $250,000 in new corporate sponsorships by June 30th.

Tools

Records kept of corporate donations.

Objective 4

Criteria

Collection of the remaining $100,000 by August 31st.

Tools

Records kept of revenue from 5K run/bike/walk and all other general donations.

Summary

Communication and marketing professionals cannot expect to be taken seriously unless they positively demonstrate the results of their efforts. Measuring the effectiveness of communication efforts can be a straightforward process if you use the Strategic Communications Planning Matrix. The matrix focuses your efforts to set objectives that are the outcomes which will combine to reach the end result desired. Evaluation of the objectives should be as strategic a function as any part of the process. Objectives become the evaluation criteria and must meet the highest standards of evaluation measurement. Your planning will also facilitate setting criteria to measure the effectiveness of the communications strategies and tactics.

Tools for measuring success are basically the same as the methodologies used in research. Nevertheless, many professional research firms now specialize in evaluative research and can design specific tools for your needs. Make sure to include the evaluation process in your tactics and in the calendar and budget for each public so this critical process is not overlooked.

Exercises

1. Ask a local nonprofit to share with you its objectives from an old strategic plan and check to see if evaluation measurement is included in the plan. Ask about the process for evaluating success and assess whether the tools used were appropriate to determine if the goal was truly achieved.

2. Examine several of the research methodologies identified in Chapter 3 and determine how each could be converted to an evaluation methodology.

3. Do a Web search for research companies and find those that advertise evaluation measurement. Try to find specific descriptions of those measurements on their sites. Also search for communications research and/or evaluation newsletters that are available on the Web.

References and Additional Readings

Cutlip, S. M., Center, A. H., & Broom, G. M. (2000). *Effective public relations* (8th ed.). Upper Saddle River, NJ: Prentice Hall.

KD Paine and Partners. The Measurement Standard. Retrieved October 17, 2007, from www.measuresofsuccess.com.

Newsom, D., Turk, J. V., & Kruckeberg, D. (2007). *This is PR: The realities of public relations* (9th ed.). Belmont, CA: Wadsworth Publishing Company.

Watson, T. (2001). Integrating planning and evaluation: Evaluating the public relations practice and public relations programs. In Heath, R. L. *Handbook of public relations* (pp. 259–268). Thousand Oaks, CA: Sage Publications, Inc.

Executive Summaries and Business Presentations

"The ability to present is probably the number one skill lacking today. If you can't present well, you're not going to move up in the company."

—Cindy Peterson

Founder of Presentations for Results, a coaching and consulting firm in Boise, Idaho

LEARNING IMPERATIVES

- **To understand the components and characteristics of effective executive summaries**

- **To understand how to create and give a business presentation that achieves positive results**

The reality of today's business environment is that few executives have the time or patience to read lengthy reports. In fact, nearly all written material targeted at executives contains a short executive summary. Hopefully someone on the project team will read the entire report or, in your case, the communications plan, but that cannot be guaranteed. The only two probable points of exposure to your plans, campaigns, or ideas are the executive summary and the business or client presentation. If these are engaging and to the point, an executive might take the time to look deeper into your plan. If not, you will lose his/her attention and support.

KEYS TO SUCCESS

The key to success for both executive summaries and business presentations is a strategic planning approach. Your goal is to grab their attention and convince them to adopt your proposal. With that goal in mind and specific objectives to support that, analyze the public(s) to be addressed, your relationship with them, and their motivating self-interests. Then design your summary or presentation to deliver the messages and lead your audience—perhaps only one key decision maker—to the conclusions you want it to reach. Remember, you must appeal directly to the audience's self-interests. Weaving in the influence of opinion leaders may also be useful.

Knowing your audience has little time, you must get to the key points and solutions quickly while capturing and retaining interest. You must show the logic and the creativity that make the proposal workable. Give just enough detail to sell the plan but not so much as to lose the interest of the target audience. Always include the cost in terms of time and resources (money). Remember that executive decision makers typically have only two questions that matter to them:

1. Is this the best solution or plan (i.e., is there really a need and will it work)?

2. How much will it cost?

To convince an executive to spend time and money on your plan, you must address the core of the challenge or opportunity and the macro-level logic, creativity, and appropriateness of the solution proposed. Your grand idea may be in the form of branding, identification with a key societal issue, a change in the logo or slogan, a new focus on community relations, or a number of other overarching ideas. Just remember that executives usually have a broader, more holistic view of problems, opportunities, and programs. Their vision encompasses the whole organization, not just your part of it. They want to see the grand solution and creative integration of that solution across organizational functions and publics. They also want to know if it is the most cost effective approach to the situation and why they should support the plan. Remember, in order for them to internalize your plan, you must first capture their attention.

EXECUTIVE SUMMARIES

A typical executive summary should be no more than four pages; two to three pages is best. It needs to be written directly to the target audience so it will be brief, comprised of short sentences and bullet points. It must be concise, focusing on solutions and referring to additional details in appropriate sections of the report or plan. It should also be written with words and phrases that invoke visual images of the proposed plan.

Characteristics

A good executive summary has five basic characteristics.

1. **It immediately engages the attention of the reader.** Either by an incisive restatement of the problem or challenge, a vision of what could be created, or some other attention-getting device, the executive summary must grab the reader and entice him/her to read on.

2. **It provides a broad solution to the problem** that integrates across the organization and its publics and/or creatively takes advantage of an opportunity. The executive summary must provide just enough creative detail to keep the reader engaged but not so much that he/she will lose interest.

3. **It contains visual words and phrases** that will enable the executive to actually visualize the plan including the creative work that will secure the attention of key publics.

4. **It provides concise rationale for acceptance of the solution.**

5. **It identifies the cost** of the plan and puts it in the context of the cost of not accepting the plan.

Executive Summary

A concise overview of a document's key points and conclusions targeted to key decision makers.

BUSINESS OR CLIENT PRESENTATIONS

A business or client presentation of your solution or plan is a multi-sensory version of an executive summary. It must contain the same five components listed above to be successful. While in an executive summary, you write in a way that stimulates a visual picture of your proposed effort, a business presentation by its nature is visual. The visual elements create their own impressions regarding consistency, dependability, and competency of the team. They must be very carefully considered and developed to support your approach, not detract from it.

No matter how much time you have to make your presentation, you must capture the attention of your audience in the first few seconds. Establish the need and the broad solution immediately. Then sketch in the details as time—and interest—permits. Make sure to show creative work—slogans, logos, visual tactics—to engage and excite the target audience, but don't continue describing details after interest in them wanes. Get back quickly to the rationale for selecting this plan and the cost of doing so. Also address the cost of not

Tips from the Pros

Overcoming Presentation Anxiety

Lenny Laskowski, President of LJL Seminars, international professional speaker and author of the best-selling book, 10 Days to More Confident Public Speaking, tips you off on how to keep those nerves in check.

While you may not realize it, the majority of speaking anxiety comes from nervousness. I employ a variety of physical and mental techniques to calm nerves.

Physical Techniques

Take a brisk walk before you speak. Physical activity will loosen up your entire body and get your blood circulating. If you are speaking in a large hotel, as I often do, take a walk around the hotel and burn off some nervous energy. Just don't get lost and keep an eye on the time.

Loosen up your arms and hands. While sitting in your seat before you speak, dangle your arms at your sides—letting blood flow to the tips of your fingers. When blood flow is directed away from your skin, fingers, and toes, you often feel a tingling sensation and your skin may begin to look pale and feel cold. Dangling your arms and hands reestablishes blood flow; you will start to feel better and more relaxed. Also while sitting, turn your wrists and shake your fingers to force the blood to flow to your hands and fingers.

Don't sit with your legs crossed. Stand up well in advance of being introduced and walk around so the blood flows in your legs. This will also prevent leg cramping when you first stand.

Scrunch your toes. But be careful not to scrunch so tightly that you get a cramp.

Loosen up your facial muscles. Wiggle your jaw back and forth gently. Yawn (politely, of course).

Use deep breathing exercises.

Mental Techniques

Prepare and rehearse. This is the single most important thing you can do.

Visualize success. Think "success" using visualization techniques. Visualize the audience applauding you when you are done.

Be natural but enthusiastic.

Be personal. Think conversational and include some personal stories during your speech.

Focus on your message and not on your nervousness.

embracing your solution. Then end on a positive note and with the only wise course of action—hiring you.

Principles of Success

Some general principles for success follow.

- Keep the end result in mind at all times. The goal is to gain approval and selection of your plan by the decision makers. Everything you do and say in the presentation must be focused on that goal.

- Focus on establishing a relationship with the key decision maker whether he/she is a client or an executive in your organization.

- Timing is important. Most presentations should be short, concise, and to the point. Long presentations often lose the audience. Set a time limit for each discussion point in the presentation and stick to it. Keep the presentation moving and the ideas flowing. If you sense your audience is losing interest, shift your style to liven up the presentation or, better yet, move on.

- Use logical and customized organization. Use a research-based, analytical approach to problem solving that the client will understand. Focus on opportunities and solutions. Customize the presentation to meet the self-interests and needs of the target audience. Figure 11.1 provides a sample organization for a business presentation, but remember to tailor it to your specific audience. Use examples relevant to the target audience's experience.

- Be prepared. Organize well, use appealing visual aids, and rehearse thoroughly. An audience can always tell when someone is unprepared. Further, your ability to improvise when unexpected problems arise (such as your software not being compatible with the provided technical equipment) is directly related to how well prepared you are. Don't expect to be able to ad lib in an emergency if you haven't thoroughly prepared and practiced.

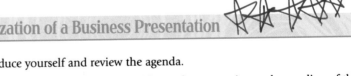

Figure 11.1—Sample Organization of a Business Presentation

© 2008 JupiterImages Corporation.

1. Introduce yourself and review the agenda.

2. Review the opportunities and problems, demonstrating understanding of the potential client's position through research.

3. Present your unique approach for solving the problem.

4. State the objectives and publics/messages necessary to accomplish them.

5. Show some of the creative work. Planning typically has no visual appeal. It must be accompanied by creative work to sell your solution. - ONSCREEN VS. handouts

6. Overview the budget using graphic displays.

7. Provide the rationale for implementing the plan, as well as the inherent difficulties and the cost of not accepting your proposal.

8. Summarize the campaign and make the final pitch.

© iofoto, 2008.

Using Presentation Technology

In today's high-tech environment, expectations for professionalism are also very high. But high-tech presentations have their pitfalls. Computer-designed and driven presentations can be very impressive. But when the technology fails, for whatever reason, the failure reflects on the presenter. While a great presentation can demonstrate the creativity, capability, and innovativeness of a team, a poor presentation can ruin any chance of success.

Technical difficulties are unacceptable. If you are using technology of any kind in a presentation, make sure you know the equipment or computer programs, how to operate them, and how to fix them. Make sure every link and program is compatible. Make sure the presentation area has sufficient power outlets and is wired to support the technology. Arrive early to set up and test the technology. Bring spare cords, bulbs, and other small replacement parts and connectors. Always bring a back up of presentations and have one online. Be prepared well enough to give your presentation without the visuals if necessary.

Recognize also that technology has a tendency to reduce and sometimes eliminate the personal connection between the presenter and the client or executive. The presenter must be conscious of the relationship and work to maintain the personal connection. When possible, use a remote or have someone help you advance slides. Cut the invisible tether that keeps so many people tied to a podium or laptop by moving around, using hand gestures, and pointing out significant information or visuals on the screen.

The presentation is an opportunity to interact with the client or executive and begin to build trust. Technology should support but never drive a presentation. Presentations should always be driven by purpose and content. In today's business climate, a good presentation is your key to opening the door. A bad presentation means your ideas may never see the light of day.

Summary

Executive summaries and business presentations are the key channels of communication for almost every public relations or marketing plan. No matter how revealing the research, no matter how creative and ingenious the strategic plan, no change will occur unless you effectively communicate the plan or solution to the decision makers and demonstrate the criticality of their expending resources on this plan or solution. As with all communication, your target audience must first be persuaded to pay attention to the message and then be persuaded to act on the content. Persuading decision makers to use your solutions requires the same two-step process. You must gain their attention and then their approval.

In our fast-paced world, executive summaries and business presentations are the key to getting the decision makers to pay attention and more deeply examine a proposal. They should be approached with the same care and analysis used in your planning. When done right, these brief overviews will open many doors.

Exercises

1. Take a trip to the nearest library and look for published reports that have executive summaries. They may be reports of research studies or even white papers. Examine a number of executive summaries and evaluate their effectiveness in drawing you into the details in the document.

2. Select any of the plans you have prepared for the exercises in other chapters of this book and create a short presentation that would engage a decision maker and cause them to listen to your ideas. Follow the steps in Figure 11.1 and make sure you have an attention-getting tactic at the beginning of the presentation.

3. Visit other classes within which presentations are being given. Do your own analysis of their effectiveness. What techniques worked well and why? What did not work and what would you have done differently?

References and Additional Readings

Bienvenu, S. (1999). *The presentation skills workshop: Helping people create and deliver great presentations.* New York: AMACOM.

Boylan, B. (2001). *What's your point?: The 3-step method for making effective presentations.* Avon, MA: Adams Media Corporation.

Leech, T. (2004). *How to prepare, stage, and deliver winning presentations.* New York: AMACOM.

Ethics and Professionalism

"A little integrity is better than any career."

—Ralph Waldo Emerson (1803–1882)
American Poet

LEARNING IMPERATIVES

- To understand the values and ethical standards upon which to base decisions and behavior

- To be cognizant of professional codes of ethics and resolve to abide by them

- To understand the characteristics of professionalism and begin to develop behaviors consistent with those characteristics

- To appreciate the contributions of diverse individuals and adopt an attitude of acceptance

Ethics

Personal and professional value systems and standards that underlie decisions and behavior.

It is unfortunate that with increased emphasis on and discussion regarding professional ethics in the last 10 years, we seem to have had a greater number of high profile incidents rather than fewer. We can hope this is a result of a greater level of scrutiny rather than a greater number of questionable actions. As discussed at the beginning of the book, trust in business seems to be rebounding somewhat from the embarrassingly low levels in the 2005 Edelman Trust Barometer. Nevertheless, we have several recent incidents of public relations professionals compensating media professionals (including bloggers) to endorse products or ideas without full disclosure. What these incidents indicate is that some communication professionals still do not understand the disastrous consequences for our profession of corrupting the societal channels of communication. And now mistrust of media, to which the previously mentioned behavior contributes, has sunk lower still. If the major channels for information dissemination in our society are not trusted, how can we possibly expect our messages will be trusted?

Advocacy is a critical function in a free market economy and a free society. Without advocacy, people are unaware of the full range of choices available to them from consumer products to political opinions. Because some organizations have abused the public trust by using manipulative communication and marketing practices and sometimes even deceit, communicators today are often labeled "flacks" or "spin doctors," implying the less than trustworthy practices of advocating questionable causes and twisting truth. Because of past abuses perpetrated by a few, almost all organizations, corporations, and institutions continue to face an uphill battle to gain the trust of their publics.

ETHICS

The ethics and behavior of organizations and individuals have come to the forefront in terms of the expectations of an organization's stakeholders. According to Wilcox, Ault, & Agee:

> Ethics refers to the value system by which a person determines what is right or wrong, fair or unfair, just or unjust. It is expressed through moral behavior in specific situations. An individual's conduct is measured not only against his or her own conscience but also against some norm of acceptability that has been societally, professionally, or organizationally determined (1989, p. 117–118).

As the statement implies, ethical decisions are made at a number of different levels. At the highest level, every society has an implied ethical standard. Nevertheless, societal standards of ethics often deteriorate to become the equivalent of legal standards. With trust at a premium now in our society, the second level of ethical standard-setting is in organizations that have formulated their own ethical codes based on core corporate or organizational values. The goal is to guide employees to comply in programs, procedures, and practices. To be credible, the values and codes must permeate the organization's communication practices.

At the third level, communications and marketing professionals may choose to subscribe to professional codes of behavior like those provided by

Ethical Codes

Written and formalized standards of behavior used as guidelines for decision making.

the American Marketing Association (AMA), the American Advertising Federation (AAF), or the Public Relations Society of America (PRSA). (See Appendix C.) Finally, underlying each of these ethical levels are personal standards of behavior based on individual value systems.

Organizational Ethics

Today's issue for organizations is "transparency." Transparency requires organizations to openly align their behavior and their communication with a set of core values that are societally accepted and important to their key publics. According to Stoker & Rawlins (2004):

> By revealing the organization's motives, the [organization] becomes accountable to the public. Transparency then becomes self-regulating, encouraging organizations to choose only practices they could publicly justify. By being transparent, the organization puts its credibility on the line by aligning its communication with its ethics.

> Gertz (1998) goes a step further by providing two moral rules that must be inviolate. The first is "do not disable." To disable is to diminish a person's ability to choose or act voluntarily. People have a right to the information they need to make reasoned, rational decisions for their own lives. The second rule is "do not deprive of freedom." This rule requires organizations to disclose any information on practices that may affect stakeholders. Gertz includes in this rule any action that would limit someone's ability to act freely, depriving him/her of control over personal actions.

> Gertz applies some additional moral rules to transparency: don't deceive, don't cheat, keep promises, obey laws, and do your duty. Stoker & Rawlins (2004) comment that "these rules directly apply to the communication process. It would be hard to imagine transparency without abiding by these rules. But these are the [minimum] expectations for [communications professionals]."

Codes of Ethics and Professional Standards

Because our effectiveness as professionals is directly dependent upon whether or not we are trusted, professional ethical standards are critical to the strength of our profession. But professional ethical codes are not without problems. By their nature, such codes tend to establish the basest acceptable behavior, bordering on legality rather than morality. Over time, such standards tend to reduce the overall level of ethical practice to that minimally acceptable expectation. To quote James E. Faust in an address given to law students in 2003:

> There is a great risk of justifying what we do individually and professionally on the basis of what is "legal" rather than what is "right. . . ." The philosophy that what is "legal" is also "right" will rob us of what is highest and best in our nature. What conduct is actually "legal" is, in many instances, way below the standards of a civilized society. . . . If [we] accept what is legal as [our] standard of personal or professional conduct, [we] will rob [ourselves] of that which is truly noble in [our] personal dignity and worth.

Further, it is usually quite difficult for a professional organization to enforce a code of ethics. Much has been written about ethical codes and their problems. Nevertheless, professionally it is deemed important for organizations to establish ethical codes for their members. Such codes are seen as crucial for maintaining professional status, respect, and legitimacy. They are also guidelines to entry-level professionals seeking to establish their own ethical standards based on a personal value system. Most professional codes of ethics incorporate stated values that include truth, honesty, fairness, good taste, and decency. Basing behavior on these values will always provide a solid foundation of personal ethics for any communications professional.

Personal Ethics and Decision Making

Our personal ethics are based on our system of values and beliefs. According to Davis Young, you cannot be forced to lose your values; they are only lost if you choose to relinquish them. As was discussed in the chapter on persuasion, values and beliefs are the building blocks for attitudes which direct behavior. Although a very personal determination, our values and ethics are heavily influenced by our culture and background. In American culture, truth, freedom, independence, equity, and personal rights are highly valued and contribute to the formulation of most of our value systems and resultant ethical standards. But another important influence on our value systems is our personal and societal definition of success.

In the late 1980s, Amitai Etzioni, having just completed a book on ethics, prepared to teach the subject to students at Harvard Business School. After a semester of effort, he lamented that he had been unable to convince classes full of MBA candidates "that there is more to life than money, power, fame, and self-interest." Etzioni's experience is disconcerting but not surprising. The situation is no better today. Our society has put such an emphasis on money, power, and fame as primary measures of success that these factors have become the decision-making criteria for generations of professionals. Yet those same professionals, at the ends of their careers (and usually in commencement speeches to graduating college students), regret not having spent enough time with family or serving the community. Even our analysis of self-interests of publics should lead us to the conclusion that money, power, and fame are usually secondary motivators when placed next to important life issues.

Perhaps our personal definitions of success and the pressure to reach the perceived societal definition of success have caused us to neglect those things in life that really matter. Those definitions affect our ethical standards and decisions. It would, therefore, seem important to take another look at our measure of personal success, and reestablish basic values to shape moral and ethical behavior. Ralph Waldo Emerson's definition of success (Figure 12.1) may be a viable starting point.

Consistent with contemporary measures of success, most decisions to behave unethically seem to be based primarily on financial considerations, and secondarily on power considerations. Most professionals find the temptation to behave unethically becomes overwhelming only when money (or the loss of it) is the decision factor. The more there is to lose financially, the greater

Figure 12.1—An Enduring Definition of Success

To laugh often and love much; to win the respect of intelligent persons and the affection of children; to earn the approbation of honest citizens and to endure the betrayal of false friends; to appreciate beauty; to find the best in others; to give of one's self; to leave the world a bit better, whether by a healthy child, a garden patch, or a redeemed social condition; to have played and laughed with enthusiasm and sung with exultation; to know that even one life has breathed easier because you have lived, this is to have succeeded.

— **Ralph Waldo Emerson, 1803–1882**

the ability to rationalize behavior contrary to individual and organizational ethics. When your ability to support and feed your family and keep a roof over it is threatened, you become more open to an unethical alternative.

Once you have compromised, you can expect the demand for compromise to continue. Even changing jobs doesn't necessarily free you. Whatever reputation you establish will follow you to at least some degree for the rest of your professional life. And you will personally have to deal with your own assessment of your character as a person and as a professional. In the communications profession where personal credibility and trustworthiness is an imperative, reputation can mean the difference between success and failure.

All professional codes and standards aside, ethics come down to our personal decisions of appropriate behavior. Six simple rules may help you to protect yourself against situations which will compromise your ethics, and thus your professionalism.

1. **Make your ethical decisions now.** Nancy Reagan's "Just Say No" antidrug campaign was an attempt to convince young people to decide against drug use before they were in a peer pressure situation that would perhaps cause them to succumb. You can make the same kind of decision about ethical conduct. Examine your value system and define your personal and professional ethics now. Examine current case studies of ethical dilemmas and make decisions about what your own conduct will be. It is much easier to stick to ethical decisions you have already made based on personal and professional values than it is to make those decisions in the face of pressure and financial need.

2. **Develop empathy.** Treat others as you would expect to be treated. Don't judge others too harshly, and lend a helping hand. You may be fortunate not to have faced their dilemmas, but it may only be a matter of time. A little empathy and compassion goes a long way and increases the chances of receiving compassion and assistance when you need it.

3. **Take the time to think things through.** Don't be railroaded or rushed into making decisions. When you are pressured to make a quick decision about something and you feel uncertain or confused, take your time. Chances are that if you feel rushed when making an ethical decision, you are being railroaded into doing something unethical and unwise, something you would not do if you had more time to think it through.

4. **Identify behavior as what it really is.** Lying, cheating, and stealing by any other names are still lying, cheating, and stealing. In today's complex business environment, we have an incredible ability to sanitize issues and rationalize behavior by using less poignant terms like "white lies" or "half-truths" or "omission" or "creative storytelling." But deception of any kind is lying; winning by anything but honest and ethical means is cheating; and appropriating anything that does not rightfully belong to you or your employer is stealing. Applying the terms that most people agree are prohibited by both personal and professional standards will help you make ethical decisions in complex or confusing situations.

5. **Recognize that every action and decision has an ethical component.** Ethical dilemmas seldom emerge suddenly. They are the culmination of several seemingly innocuous decisions and actions leading to the point of ethical crisis. Every decision you make has an ethical component even if it is not immediately obvious. Make sure to review the ethical ramifications of actions and decisions along the way. Project where a given decision will lead. Doing so will help you avoid many ethical crises that might otherwise "sneak up" on you.

6. **Establish a freedom fund.** Start today to save some money from each paycheck you receive. Establish a separate savings account and habitually contribute to your freedom fund. As was noted above, most unethical behavior is a result of feeling you simply cannot afford to behave otherwise. You have financial obligations in life and losing your job may mean you will lose your car or your home or that you won't be able to feed your family. If you are asked to do something that violates your personal or a professional code of ethics, you should first try to reason or negotiate not to do it. If you are unable to convince your employer, a freedom fund allows you to quit a job rather than compromise standards and jeopardize your professional reputation. Initially, plan to accumulate the equivalent of three to six months net salary in your freedom fund. As you are promoted to higher professional levels, raise the balance to a year or more of net income. A freedom fund is designed to pay the bills until you find another job. The greater your professional stature, the longer you should expect to look before finding an acceptable position. Plan accordingly and never withdraw money from your freedom fund for anything else. If you do, it won't be there when you need it. In today's environment, chances are that at some point you will need to rely on your freedom fund to preserve your ethical standards.

© 2008 JupiterImages Corporation.

CHARACTERISTICS OF PROFESSIONALISM

Professional reputation is one of the few enduring possessions. Businesses may come and go. Circumstances may, at times, cause difficulties in your career. Your professional success is dependent upon building a good reputation.

Building Relationships

John Paluszek, APR, Fellow PRSA, former PRSA President and former President of Ketchum Public Relations, tips you off on building professional relationships.

A professional builds relationships and gives respect to others. I've found it can be useful to mine the gold within what may appear to be a worn out cliché. For example, "walk a mile in another person's shoes."

Several years ago, we applied this advice in an issues management assignment for the chemical industry by managing an "alternative dispute resolution" or mediation between industry leaders and the heads of several NGO critics. After a few facilitated sessions in Washington, DC (agenda and ground rules set in advance), a compromise was reached which precluded time- and resource-consuming battles in the media and in Congress. But the comments of participants on each side—in candid, informal assessments after the meetings—were both revealing and rewarding.

Industry leaders observed, "You know, those folks [NGO participants] are extremely bright and have some interesting suggestions; it may take a while to implement, but they are certainly worth considering."

NGO activists concluded, "I now see that these company chiefs don't have horns; they have to balance responsibilities to shareholders, stakeholders, and society."

When people—even those with diametrically opposing viewpoints—meet and work together face-to-face, respecting one another, understanding is often the result.

Obviously, ethical behavior is one of the most important attributes of a solid professional. But it is not the only attribute. In fact, lists of characteristics and attributes necessary for professional survival abound. Four key categories of attributes deserve attention.

Personal and Professional Development

A professional should never stop learning. Formal and informal means of education are continually available. Strengthen your skills and keep up with changes and innovations, particularly in the area of technology. Read profusely both in and out of the field. One of the reasons behind the broad liberal arts curriculum in communication programs is the need for communicators and business professionals to be familiar with other areas of learning. The skills needed to communicate come from communication curriculum. Background in what you will be communicating comes from other fields of knowledge.

Obtain membership in at least one professional association and actively pursue the educational opportunities offered. Read the newspaper and the

DigitalStock.

professional journals. Read the important new books that everyone is reading. Read national magazines that broaden your knowledge of current events and world information. You will be interacting with people in personal, professional, and social situations. It is imperative that you be able to converse about current events, new discoveries, important studies and research, politics, sports, entertainment, and other topics. Knowing your profession thoroughly will not alone impress the decision makers you need to influence to gain approval for projects or just to keep your job.

Learn from your colleagues and fellow professionals. Be actively involved in professional organizations that provide networking opportunities. Be willing to serve in those organizations and diligently do good work. Call professionals you meet to gain information and advice, and be available to mentor. Send them appropriate notes of congratulations, thanks, and encouragement. Send out lots of holiday cards. Keep your network vital and alive by developing relationships that demonstrate your care and respect for others.

Finally, don't be afraid to ask questions. Have confidence in yourself, your knowledge, and your ability but remain humble and teachable. Overconfidence often masks incompetence. Don't be afraid to admit you have more to learn.

Work Habits and Job Performance

Know your own strengths and weaknesses and own up to your mistakes. Otherwise, you'll never overcome your challenges. Prioritize tasks, allocate time, and work within constraints. Don't be concerned with the number of hours worked, but with the results and successes. Be goal-oriented, not just task-oriented. Pay attention to detail and always deliver work on time. Work hard and be absolutely dependable.

If you want to be promoted, do your job well and then help do the job of the person you would like to replace. Help that person whenever possible. When people are promoted, they often have a hand in selecting a replacement. Make yourself the obvious choice.

Personal Conduct

Always act in a professional manner and dress professionally. Always be on time. Be aware of what goes on around you. Observe procedures and power structures (formal and informal) and work within them. Always be ethical and never allow yourself to be persuaded to compromise your personal standards. The respect of others is directly proportional to your respect for yourself and your respect for them. Work toward a balance in your life. Don't live to work or you'll be too stressed to maintain other vital relationships in life. If all you have in life is your job, you might be good at what you do, but you'll be very dull. Cultivate other interests and relationships. Be a generous contributor to charitable causes and serve in your community.

Human Relations

Courtesy is fast becoming a lost art in our culture. A few years ago, Ann Landers provided a concise perspective in one of her columns:

> When you get right down to it, good manners are nothing more than being thoughtful and considerate of others. They are the principal lubricant of the human machinery we use when we interact with others.

Be personable and likeable. Learn to work well with people, treating them as equals. Work with and respect administrative assistants and other staffers. They can help you succeed or cause you to fail. Develop relationships that win loyalty and dedication. Know people's names (and the proper spelling) and use them. Be a mentor to newcomers.

Keep a sense of humor and of perspective. Don't hold grudges and stay out of office politics for at least the first year in any organization. It will take that long to figure out the informal power and communications structure. Never allow yourself to believe the job couldn't be done without you. Remember that cooperative effort is the key to success. Always be grateful and show that gratitude openly and often. Give others credit freely for their contributions.

EMBRACING DIVERSITY

In today's world, both ethics and professionalism demand that we embrace diversity. Because issues of diversity in our society have come to the fore as trendy and politically correct, detractors may scorn their importance. More damaging though are those who have taken up the cause because it is trendy, rather than because it is morally right and a critically important part of the essence of our humanity.

Often, we wrongly equate diversity with equal employment opportunity and hiring quotas, failing to recognize that diversity celebrates the differences in all people, uniting them for better solutions and a brighter future. Harnessing diversity in our organizations and communities means creating an environment in which all individuals, regardless of difference, can work toward reaching their personal potential while serving the common good. Diversity

Diversity

Appreciating differences in culture, gender, race, background and experience.

does not focus just on race or gender. It addresses the contributions all individuals have to make because of their differences, not in spite of them. Nelson Mandela, in his 1994 inaugural speech, quoted a poem by Marianne Williamson on individual ability and contribution:

> Our deepest fear is not that we are inadequate. Our deepest fear is that we are powerful beyond measure. It is our light, not our darkness, that most frightens us. We ask ourselves, who am I to be brilliant, gorgeous, talented and fabulous? Actually, who are you not to be? You are a child of God. Your playing small doesn't serve the world. There's nothing enlightened about shrinking so that other people won't feel insecure around you. We were born to make manifest the glory of God that is within us. It's not just in some of us; it's in everyone. And as we let our own light shine, we unconsciously give other people permission to do the same. As we are liberated from our own fear, our presence automatically liberates others.

Diversity demands we examine privilege in our lives and accept the responsibility that comes with that privilege. It requires that we set aside "tolerance" in preference for acceptance. It requires that we not identify one right way, one mainstream to which all others must conform, but that we recognize myriad viable paths to a solution. It means we must set aside ethnocentrism and learn to appreciate the variety of our world and its inhabitants.

Guidelines to Embracing Diversity

In the workplace, issues of diversity become even more critical. In today's environment, employers seek not only trained and skilled individuals; they are looking for versatility, flexibility, and skill in operating in diverse environments. They require not only job skills, but skills in communication and human relations. Preparing for the workforce, especially as a communicator, means preparing for work in diverse environments with individuals who are different in many ways: culture, race, gender, religion, sexual orientation, physical ability, age, national origin, and socioeconomic status. Some guidelines to developing characteristics to embrace diversity follow.

- **Understand yourself and your history.** The first step to embracing diversity is to understand yourself and the part played in your life by culture. Culture largely determines behavior. When we accept something as correct, right, or proper, we have often made a cultural judgment. Understand also the privileges and opportunities you have been afforded that have contributed to the person you are now. Recognize that with those privileges come responsibilities and own up to those responsibilities. Also identify situations in which you were disadvantaged and how they have contributed to who you are. Rather than feeling self-pity, use those circumstances to develop empathy for others. We have all experienced both privilege and disadvantage to some degree. Reaching out to join cooperatively in the elimination of disadvantages of any kind is a positive way to deal with our own disadvantages.

- **Shed the guilt and stop the blame.** One of the biggest barriers to embracing diversity is guilt. Guilt is manifested in defensive postures. "It's not my fault," is heard all too often when we deal with issues of diversity. Learn to recognize a statement of fact without feeling blamed. It is a fact that certain groups in our society have been disadvantaged in ways that have been difficult to overcome. Supporting their efforts is not an admission of guilt. It is an attempt to prevent further pain and suffering by helping them overcome disadvantages, regardless of their cause. On the other hand, do not become engaged in blaming behaviors. It does no good to blame people and drive them into a defensive posture. Blame and guilt are divisive, not unifying or productive.

- **Minimize ethnocentrism.** Although ethnocentrism is typically manifested between national cultures, it is present within nations as well. Ethnocentrism, or identifying our own particular culture and circumstance as the ideal to which all others should strive, is like wearing blinders. Different doesn't mean wrong or less effective. It just means different. Just as there is not just one right answer in creatively solving problems, there is not just one "right" culture. Appreciate your own culture but recognize it is not better, just different than others.

- **Avoid stereotypes.** Stereotyping is sometimes a useful tool in understanding publics, but when we talk about diversity it is almost always harmful. Don't assume stereotypical characteristics about people with whom you have not worked or become acquainted. Also avoid the tendency to classify people as valuable members of a team just because of their membership in a particular group that may be a target public. All trained communicators should be able to marshal the resources and research to target any public.

- **Appreciate different ways of doing things.** Learn not only that there is more than one right answer or way to accomplish something but also that different ways of doing something may have advantages not evident at first glance. Appreciate that using different approaches may enhance the creativity of the whole team. And recognize that sometimes a different approach has a contribution to make that standard methods could not. Western medicine is a typical example of ethnocentrism and stereotype which has hindered the widespread use of less traumatic treatments that work. Eastern-trained healers who work with the nervous system, the body's electrical impulses, and pressure points have been successful time and again at curing ailments Western medicine pronounced incurable.

- **Recognize professionalism and ability.** Stereotypes often prevent us from recognizing the skills and competence of individuals. Professional communications and marketing skills are not genetic. If we begin to look at colleagues as fellow professionals instead of classifying them by their differences, we will find we have more in common than we thought.

- **Learn to develop relationships with individuals.** Begin to see people as individuals: living, breathing, and pursuing a quality of life similar to that which you pursue. Friendships begin when people take the time to get to know one another as human beings. Ask questions if you are uncertain of how to behave. Whereas "Blacks" used to be appropriate terminology, African-American is now widely used and preferred. The broad term "Native American" has been replaced in favor of specific tribal affiliations. Similarly, using only the term "Hispanic," can exclude Puerto Ricans, Mexicans, and Mexican-Americans, to name only a few. Ask people how they define themselves and then show respect for the individual by adopting that definition in your interactions with them. It is the same personal respect you would wish to be accorded.

In the marketing and communications professions, more often than not, we work in teams. Seldom is a solution developed or implemented by one person in isolation from others. Learning to harness diversity means learning to let differences work for you, allowing diversity to enhance solutions and performance. In today's world, those who excel professionally will be those who have learned to appreciate and embrace diversity.

Summary

It is only logical to conclude our examination of strategic communications planning with a discussion of professionalism and ethical practice. Without these elements, no communications effort will succeed over the long term. Successful communication is based on trust, and trust is built by exhibiting professional and ethical behavior. Ethics are based on individual and group value systems (ethical codes) governing acceptable behavior. Value systems must place a premium not only on ethical behavior but also on diversity. True professionals exhibit a sincere commitment to an environment in which all may reach their potential while contributing to the overall goals.

Exercises

1. Do some thinking about your own personal value system and how it will drive your ethical choices in the professional world. Develop your own definition of success and identify the ethical standards it implies.

2. Open a savings account designated as your freedom fund.

3. Initiate a serious discussion with one or two other colleagues or friends about diversity. Explore your similarities and your differences. Speak honestly about your privilege or how you have been advantaged as well as your disadvantages.

References and Additional Readings

Etzioni, A. (1989, September 18). Money, power and fame. *Newsweek* 10.

Faust, J. E. (2003, February 28). "Be healers." Address given to the J. Reuben Clark Law School at Brigham Young University, Provo, Utah.

Gertz, B. (1998). *Morality: Its nature and justification*. New York: Oxford.

Howard, C. & Mathews, W. (1994). *On deadline: Managing media relations* (2nd ed.). Prospect Heights, IL.: Waveland Press.

Stoker, K., & Rawlins, B. (2004). "Light and air hurt no one: The moral and practical imperative for transparency." Paper presented at the International Public Relations Research Conference, Miami, FL.

Tannen, D. (1994, October 10). Gender games. *People,* 71–74.

Wilcox, D. L., Ault, P. H., & Agee, W. K. (1989). *Public relations: Strategies and tactics* (2nd ed.). New York: Harper and Row.

Young, D. (1987, November 8–11). "Confronting the ethical issues that confront you." Address given at the 40th Annual PRSA National Conference in Los Angeles.

Appendix A

Teaching Case:
The Case of the Warehouse Welfare Health Care

A description of the case problem is given here along with each completed step of the matrix. Through this teaching case you will learn how to build a complete campaign for any marketing or communications opportunity or problem as you compare each step of the matrix with the example illustrated in this case.

CASE DESCRIPTION

Navajo Flats and its suburbs is a mid-sized community nestled in a valley among the peaks of the Mystic Mountains in northern Arizona. With approximately 400,000 residents, Navajo Flats' economy is based on a variety of industries; the largest among them are four food packing and packaging plants owned by major corporations, a golf cart manufacturer, and several large and mid-sized technology companies. Smaller companies supplement and support the economic base and provide the range of services necessary in a community this size including health care, financial services, and other kinds of retail and service businesses. The valley is also home to a large private university and two state community colleges as well as a number of other technical schools supporting the high-tech and medical industries.

These robust businesses coexist with varying degrees of civility with the remnants of family farming and ranching operations that have shrunk with the demand for land for housing and industry but still retain much of the outlying land in the valley and other smaller mountain valleys nearby. Much of the produce from the farms is sold locally in retail stores or to the food processing operations in the packing and packaging plants. Some of the meat from the ranches is also sold locally, but most is shipped to other markets. The farming and ranching draw migrant workers and Navajo Flats' immigrant community has grown significantly over the years.

One of the pressing needs in Navajo Flats is health care for underprivileged children, low-income families, and the migrant community. These populations do not have insurance and cannot pay for health care. While the local health care facilities do provide as much charity care as possible, it is insufficient for the growing need. Local health care providers, local churches, and social service nonprofits recognize the need for a free clinic staffed by volunteers (retired medical people who want to give back to the community) to serve this population. And opportunity is knocking.

The local Wal-Mart has vacated its big box store on the west side of town in favor of a new Super Center the company has constructed on the other side of town. The local Community Action Services (CAS), the nonprofit that operates the food bank and housing and employment services for those in need, has sufficient reserves and loans to buy the vacated building at a concessionary rate offered by Wal-Mart. CAS will use 70% of the facility as a warehouse and processing center for the food bank and related services, but it will need to lease the remaining 30% of the space to service the loans and maintain the facility.

Working with CAS, the local United Way has leveraged partnerships in the community—health care providers and churches—to operate and maintain a free medical clinic in the remaining 30% of the warehouse facility, including the lease, a full-time administrator and assistant, and the necessary insurance coverage on volunteer medical personnel. Some of the equipment and furnishings will be donated by local health care providers as they upgrade and replace equipment, and an annual contribution from the United Way will provide renewable medical supplies. Local builders have volunteered their construction crews. But the partnership lacks the estimated $500,000 that is required for materials to build out the space and initially equip it as a free clinic. It has been determined that, for the goal of a free medical clinic to be realized, the clinic partnership will need to raise $500,000 from the community.

SAMPLE CAMPAIGN

Matrix: Research
Step One—Background

(For the purposes of this teaching case, the background is abbreviated. Your investigation of the issues and the market may need to be much more extensive depending upon the challenge. Figure 4.1 in Chapter 4 is a guideline to follow for the information you may need to resolve a problem.)

The case description provides an overview of the Navajo Flats community, but much more information is required. Our research shows that Navajo Flats has a very active nonprofit social service sector that is already well supported by community members. The local United Way runs successful workplace campaigns in all the major companies in town and in about 50% of companies with 500 or fewer employees. The average employee participation in workplace campaigns is 65%. Corporate donations are also substantial. Further, CAS and other local nonprofits are led by boards of directors drawn from respected business, civic, and religious leaders in the community. Navajo Flats is a community that contributes both time and money to good causes. Nevertheless, local nonprofits are anxious that the money to be raised does not deplete the annual giving to their organizations. Approximately 90 nonprofit agencies provide for the social service needs in this community; services like improving literacy, drug rehabilitation, hospice, disaster relief, job training, and related needs. These agencies depend upon stable annual donations to meet current community needs.

The economic base of Navajo Flats is somewhat diverse. As mentioned previously, it includes four food packing and packaging plants owned by major corporations, a golf cart manufacturer, and several large and mid-sized technology companies. The economy is also supported by several smaller companies (250–500 employees) that have spun off or been inspired by the anchor businesses. Several small, high-tech companies do well in this environment and employ anywhere from 10 to 100 people each. The packaging plants and the golf cart manufacturer both count other businesses in the community as suppliers to their production. And, of course, the community hosts the retail and service businesses that build up to support any community of this size. Some, like several of the banks and a health care company, have grown quite large and expanded to other markets in the region, maintaining headquarters in Navajo Flats. The large private university, two state community colleges, and the technical schools provide part- and full-time employees for the high-tech and medical companies. Of course, typical businesses have grown to support the student population. The post-high school student population is estimated at about 50,000 full- and part-time students.

Because of the diversity of industry, the workforce is equally diverse. The high-tech, financial services, and health care industries employ mostly well-educated white-collar workers. The packing and packaging plants and golf cart manufacturer employ blue-collar labor (including students as part-time workers), some of which is unionized. There is also a substantial migrant population—both legal and illegal immigrants—built up initially to support the farming and ranching operations but now extending to other service industries in town requiring manual labor. It is estimated that 15% of the population of the greater Navajo Flats area is Hispanic.

The health care community in Navajo Flats consists of two major hospitals each owned by separate nonprofit health care corporations. Southwest Health Care (SWHC) is headquartered locally and has spread to other communities in the region. The other provider does not have local roots, but is a strong competitor to SWHC. Both have networks of local clinics and doctors, but SWHC is the provider that has partnered with the local United Way, the churches, and CAS on this project. With roots in this community, it has typically been more community-involved, but both corporations provide some charity care at their facilities. Dr. Bill Tucker, retired from SWHC, and his wife Eleanor Tucker, a retired SWHC nurse, are leading the team of retired health care workers who have volunteered to staff the clinic. The Tuckers are well respected members of the community who are known by many civic and community leaders because of their active support of social service causes over the years.

Those most affected by the rising cost of health care are blue-collar families or hourly workers and immigrants. Within that underserved population is approximately 15,000 children who potentially have no access to health care. Students are also affected by unaffordable health care. When people have no insurance coverage, they have few options when faced with the astronomical cost of the simplest of medical procedures and medications. They simply go without. The consequences are usually more complicated health care issues, the spread of illness and disease, an increase in demand on other social services, and exacerbation of other social problems. The lack of affordable health care has a ripple effect on a community.

Navajo Flats is served by two television stations and several radio stations with a variety of formats from talk to pop and country music. There is a daily metro newspaper and a few localized weeklies focused on local high school and college sports, local business, and arts and crafts. The migrant community is served by a Spanish-language radio station and a weekly newspaper.

SWOT Analysis

Strengths
Generous community
Supportive community leaders
Strong economic base
Viable project/trusted partners

Weaknesses
Already giving substantially
Limited experience with the issue
Low awareness of the need

Opportunities
Engage people not engaged before
Unite community
Relieve suffering

Threats
Six-month deadline
Depletion of support to other efforts

Profiles of Potential Publics

Partnership Boards: These are the members of the boards of directors or advisory councils for the organizations involved in the free clinic partnership. The United Way, CAS, and SWHC all have boards of directors that meet monthly to direct the affairs of those organizations. The involvement of local churches is coordinated through the Interfaith Council of Navajo Flats (ICNF), which includes a leader (either the religious leader or an influential member) from each of the participating churches. All of these individuals are well respected within their circles of influence and operation. They are looked up to by their professional colleagues, friends, neighbors, and fellow citizens. They are visible community servants within their spheres. Most are in their board positions because they have achieved professional success either because of expertise in a particular area or sufficient success, affluence, and influence to be invited to participate. By their nature, they are generous donors to community causes, both in time and money. They recognize that the invitation to serve on boards of organizations like these comes with an expectation of continued generous donation and a responsibility to use their position to sway others in support of the organization. Fully two-thirds are male, 70% are married with families, and 80% are regular church-goers. Median annual income is in excess of $125,000. They are all very busy with many commitments professionally, socially, and in the community. They are willing to lend their names to the cause but have little time to dedicate above their current board commitments.

Probably most importantly, these individuals have been involved in the negotiations for the establishment of the free clinic. They are intimately acquainted with the issues, efforts, and commitments that have finally brought the clinic to the brink of realization. They recognize the need and have hammered out the solution. They have ownership in the effort and passion for the cause. We have established channels of personal communication with each board member.

Current relationship: Exceptionally positive. These board members not only support this effort, they have been involved in bringing it to fruition and are passionate about its success.

Influentials: Peers on the boards, board chairs, partnership executives, colleagues, religious leaders, and families.

Self-interests: Tend to be more altruistic because of their community commitment. Conserving time and energy for their professional responsibilities is crucial. Peer esteem and their opinion leadership is important to them.

Corporate Executives: The local business community has a handful of major corporations, each with 2,500 to 6,000 employees. Dozens of companies, predominantly high-tech, have between 1,000 and 2,500 employees. The executives of the large corporations are mostly imported to the valley and have been here for an average of about four years. Most of the companies in the technology sector are local entrepreneurial start-ups that have done well in the Navajo Flats community, particularly drawing on employees who are products of the excellent educational institutions. Hundreds of smaller companies also do business in the valley. Corporate executives recognize the health care problem in Navajo Flats, particularly among blue-collar workers and the migrant population. For a few of them, the problem is their own, as they rely upon those very populations for labor. The entrepreneurs among the corporate executives are less likely to believe it is an issue that concerns them. Nevertheless, a good portion of the mid- to large-size companies are partners with the local United Way and can be counted upon for support. Most executives see their community involvement as a significant element in their success as individuals and as companies. Only 25% of them are female. Their demographics are very like those of the members of the partnership boards, because those boards draw significantly from this public.

Current relationship: We have worked closely with many of these executives to address community problems in the past. Many are members of the partnership boards and most will be supportive with some kind of donation, even if small. They know us and trust us to know what is good for the community.

Influentials: Peers, partnership board members, United Way, and social service leaders in the community.

Self-interests: Their companies' reputations as community supporters, the success of their companies, their employees, the welfare of the community.

Employees of Local Business: This is a broad and diverse group ranging from white-collar salaried managers to blue-collar hourly workers. Their demographics would mirror the aggregate census, rather than segments. They would have to be further segmented either by some workforce demographics or by the kinds of employers. A significant number of this public already gives annually to local causes, many through workplace campaigns. The blue-collar workers are in a position to see the effects of the lack of affordable health care, whereas for the white-collar workers, it is just another social issue. The channels to reach this public are through their workplace, but the threat is that they are more likely than other publics to shift their annual giving to this cause rather than giving additional money. This would result in the annual support of local social service organizations being threatened.

Current relationship: Varied relationships from none at all to a strong relationship with those who donate or serve annually with the local social service agencies. Some would empathize with the issue, others are distant enough from it that they would probably not be easy to commit.

Influentials: Peers, coworkers, employers, families.

Self-interests: Making a living, supporting self and families, quality of life, peer acceptance, job advancement.

Blue-collar Workers: Approximately 75,000 people in the workforce locally are blue-collar workers. They range in age from 16 to 65 and work for hourly wages. Annual income ranges from $18,000 a year to $60,000 for the more skilled and experienced workers. Division of male and female is equal, but a higher percentage is unmarried (60%). The majority of the Hispanic population falls in this category. About 65% of this public belong to unions that negotiate wages and benefits for them. The older they are, the more likely they are to be union members and working for one of the major corporations in town. About 35% of those in this public do not intend to work for hourly wages for their entire lives. They are taking advantage of educational opportunities for advancement or job training to improve their employment situation. Many attend local colleges and technical schools. This public tends to be more giving and empathetic than the white-collar worker because they are personally acquainted with people who need assistance of one kind or another. Many already give time and money through their workplaces to support local causes.

Current relationship: Very positive. They support social causes and understand the need for health care. Nevertheless, many already give to local agencies and we don't want to upset that relationship.

Influentials: Peers, families, friends and neighbors, unions.

Self-interests: Surviving, adequately supporting family and getting education to get a better job, helping one another.

Retirees and Senior Citizens: These individuals are at least 55 years of age, most between 65 and 75. Most have had successful careers which have given them the financial security to retire. About 25% live less affluently on social security, sometimes supplemented by a small pension. Nearly 90% are of local origin, or retired from employment locally. They are familiar with the culture and issues of Navajo Flats. Many have been involved in charitable organizations or causes locally both as donors and as volunteers. About 30% require some kind of care beyond family, either through home health care or in care centers or retirement communities. While many have limited ability to give, some are quite affluent and many of those already give generously. About half are married but the other half is either unmarried or widowed. Nearly 65% have children and grandchildren living locally.

Current relationship: Most in this group know of our partnership agencies and trust them. They would be supportive of the free clinic as a compassionate and caring service in the community.

Influentials: Spouse and family, doctors/health care workers, long-time friends, and former coworkers.

Self-interests: Although probably the most altruistic, especially if self-supporting, members in this group also have concern for their long-term ability to support themselves financially, particularly with the rising cost of health care. While some may have the capacity to give, they would be better targeted as community leaders than as retirees.

Small Business Leaders: Hundreds of business leaders in Navajo Flats fall into this category. Almost all are entrepreneurs who have started their own business. Some businesses have stayed small with a few employees, others have grown to companies of anywhere from 50 to 1,000 employees. A very small number of these leaders have hired from among the Hispanic community, but most have hired students or trained professionals. These individuals have initiative and an ability to confront problems head on and solve them. Many are members of the professional community as doctors, lawyers, accountants, or other professionals. Many are members of professional associations or of the local Chamber of Commerce or civic clubs. Some are leaders in the community but most are somewhat isolated from the community service mainstream unless they have taken the initiative to become involved. Nevertheless, it is a public that local nonprofits would like to get involved in the community because they are opinion leaders with the power to motivate their friends and neighbors, and with the ability to support community efforts. They range in age from about 30 to 65. About 65% are male. Among this group, women and those who are over 50 tend to be those most community involved. About 73% of this public is married with families.

Current relationship: Unless they are involved in community efforts already, this public has low awareness of the issue or the agencies involved in the partnership. They would be aware of SWHC and possibly of the Interfaith Council but would not have a strong affinity to help or support the partnership or the project unless they are among those few in this public who are community involved.

Influentials: Peers, customers, families.

Self-interests: Business success, profitability, financial security, family welfare.

Local Area Professionals: These individuals are in professions typified by private practice, like doctors, dentists, attorneys, and accountants. Many are members of business and professional associations in Navajo Flats. They are typically prosperous, with annual incomes in excess of $200,000. Most are approximately 35 to 55 years old and 70% are male. Nearly 90% are married and raising families in Navajo Flats. Hence, they are active in the local schools, sports and cultural activities. All are somewhat entrepreneurial, some as small business owners. They are economically and politically conservative, but because of their entrepreneurial spirit, would enthusiastically support this new venture. Self-reliance is a core value for this public but they are also aware of an obligation for community service and caring for the less fortunate, although many do not currently act on that awareness. They are tuned into local media and follow the news both print and broadcast. Combined memberships of the local Bar Association, the Dental Association, the Medical

Association, Chamber of Commerce, and other such professional and business organizations is approximately 30,000, although there are closer to 40,000 area professionals because not all the associations are required memberships. Many community leaders and social service board members are included in this group of professionals. Because of the nature of United Way donation through the workplace and the nature of their employment in private practice rather than large companies, the members of this public who donate to local social service causes do not do so through traditional channels. In other words, most cannot say "I gave at the office."

Current relationship: A number of the members of this public are already giving and serving in the community, although many are not involved because the isolated nature of their small practices allows them to escape the traditional workplace giving involvement of larger companies. They are aware of pressing community issues, the agencies involved in the partnership, and will likely support our effort philosophically. We just need to change that support into a financial contribution.

Influentials: Peers, fellow professionals, business and civic leaders, spouses.

Self-interests: Professional reputation and success, clients, ability to support family, lifestyle, fitness, and appearance.

Health Care Workers: About 15,000 people are employed in health care in the Navajo Flats community, from doctors, nurses, and specialists to physical therapists and nursing assistants. They are at the hospitals, clinics, in doctor's offices, and working with home health care agencies. Many are in positions to recognize the critical need and the importance of this initiative in the community. Many work long hours in short-staffed situations. Incomes of nurses, assistants, and therapists range from $35,000 a year to $85,000, with doctors and specialists typically earning in excess of $200,000 annually. The supporting staff is typically younger, with an average age of 29, while the average age of doctors is 46. Nearly 60% are married with families. They are strong participants in giving campaigns for local agencies, and will also volunteer time to support local health initiatives. They could be opinion leaders on this issue because they understand it well and are in what would be considered compassionate professions.

Current relationship: Strong. They understand the need and are typically giving and supportive of community health care efforts for the underprivileged.

Influentials: Peers, leaders of the social service agencies.

Self-interests: Strong altruistic motivation on this issue, patients, family.

College Students: The educational institutions in the valley enroll approximately 50,000 full- and part-time students with an average age of 22. About 50% are from Navajo Flats and the surrounding communities (within 100 miles). Another 40% come from elsewhere in Arizona, and 10% are from outside the state, most from the Southwestern states. Nearly 90% of students work at least part time. Schedules range from 10 to 40 hours per week at hourly jobs with an average wage of $8.50 an hour. Between school and work, students have very busy schedules, but they also tend to be activists, particularly on social issues. They are a tremendous source of volunteers in the community, but they have limited resources for giving. They have great energy and would stage fundraising events, but such events targeted at students typically yield more raised awareness and passion than money.

Current relationship: Students aren't particularly aware of the partnership or of the issue, but would be passionate supporters if informed.

Influentials: Peers, professors, parents.

Self-interests: Strong altruism and compassion, social good, education, social life, friends.

Hispanic Community: The Hispanic community in Navajo Flats is 60,000 strong, with 30,000 of those people in the workforce. Most are unskilled, hourly workers and some are illegal immigrants with phony social security numbers or who work for cash only. Most work either for the food packing plants or the golf cart manufacturer, or as manual laborers for landscapers, builders, or other such employers. Many of the women work in the fast food industry. Upwards of 70% are in a family unit of some kind, but others have left their families in their home countries. Most are religious, but few attend church because of cultural differences. The community is close knit and isolated from the mainstream in Navajo Flats. This public tends to be one that is served by the free clinic rather than one capable of contributing financially to it. Leaders within the Hispanic community include successful businessmen in Navajo Flats, primarily professionals in sole practice or entrepreneurs with small companies and few employees. These are few in number, but are opinion leaders for this public.

Current relationship: This public is aware of CAS because many have accessed its services in the past. They understand the problem, because they live it, but they are unaware of any planning for the free clinic.

Influentials: Hispanic community leaders, peers, family.

Self-interests: Survival, welfare of their families.

Community Leadership Givers: We can count on this public to support this project. They already give heavily to causes in the community and are typically in financial positions to be generous. They might be willing to make a commitment for a one-time gift of $1,000 (or perhaps more) to support this clinic. They are typically members of boards of directors for local nonprofits and formal opinion leaders in visible positions of authority in government or as leaders of community organizations. The United Way has directories of most of the nonprofit social service agencies' boards and a fairly complete list of other opinion leaders in the community. The integrated list contains about 2,500 names of these potential leadership givers. About half of these leaders are typical upper- middle-class or upper-class members of the Navajo Flats community working as professionals in private practice or in management positions in local corporations. (Most of these would be included in the membership of local professional associations.) The other half represents the wealthier segment of the Navajo Flats community, with assets well in excess of a million dollars. They are local philanthropists and benefactors, all with favorite causes. They are both male and female, almost all are married, but with grown children. They are heavily involved in the local social, political, and cultural scene. They are also well informed, both from mass media and from personal contacts who keep them abreast of important news and events.

This group of philanthropists is well connected with one another. They all know each other well as they have together served the Navajo Flats community and each other for decades. It might be relatively easy to tap one or two of these benefactors to fully fund the free clinic, but the free clinic partnership would prefer that the financial support for the effort be a bit more broad-based so that the free clinic will be seen as a cooperative community venture, and not the pet project of one of the philanthropists alone. Nevertheless, support from among this group will be key to motivating the support of the rest of our community leaders and community members.

Current relationship: The members of this public are already giving and serving in the community. They are aware of pressing community issues, the agencies involved in the partnership and will likely support our effort. Whether they allow us to publicize their contributions will depend upon the effect on their other philanthropic activities.

Influentials: Peers, other community leaders, employees.

Self-interests: These individuals do have an altruistic attitude toward the community. While they are motivated by personal and business success and the ability to support their families, they are also compassionate towards the needs of the community and feel a responsibility to use their positions for the benefit of the members of the community. They like their status and enjoy the appreciation and honors others give them for their service, but they also recognize needs and use their position to help fill those needs. Finally, they are generous with their money, but their time is highly valued. We need to make it easy for them to help us.

Current Donors: Because of the very active nonprofit community and the giving and volunteer nature of the Navajo Flats community, a large number of community members currently give to one cause or another. Many companies feature annual United Way campaigns and their employees are generous supporters. The local United Way raises in excess of $8 million annually which is distributed among the local social service agencies that qualify. Many who already give will likely give another one-time donation to support the free clinic, but we need to make sure that we ask in such a way that they will give in addition to what they already give rather than diverting their current donations.

The United Way has a reliable profile of their current donors. They are employees of local corporations. Most are between 35 and 65 years of age. The older they are, the more they donate annually. Most are members of families with at least two children. About 25% of those families are in single-parent homes. The typical income of the majority of donors is between $32,000 and $60,000 annually. A lower percentage of members of other income groups are annual donors to their companies' United Way campaigns but probably give independently and more privately.

Current relationship: Very positive relationship with these individuals. They tend to appreciate the efforts of the nonprofits. But many feel they already do their part.

Influentials: Peers, family, community leaders, employers.

Self-interests: Some altruism here, they want to live in a healthy community and care for their neighbors. They are concerned about the welfare of their families. They like being among those who give.

Members of Local Churches: Approximately 75% of the adults in Navajo Flats consider themselves religious, but only 50% attend a church service at least once a year and 35% say they attend services regularly. Nevertheless, 60% identify themselves with a particular church and know their spiritual leader by name. Nearly 85% of those who attend services do so as a family unit. Even among those who attend infrequently, most have children who are involved to some degree in youth groups affiliated with their church. There is a high correlation between regular church attendance and giving to and volunteering with community nonprofit organizations. This is one of the publics that the partnership will rely upon for volunteers to staff the free clinic. Most are in the lower- to upper-middle class income range.

Current relationship: Most of the churches are members of the Interfaith Council, but most of the members don't know that. The lay members are somewhat aware of the issue, but unaware of the effort to establish the free clinic.

Influentials: Church leaders, fellow members, spouses.

Self-interests: Some altruism, social good, status in their social circles, family.

Matrix: Research
Step Two—Situation Analysis

The community of Navajo Flats has a rare opportunity to fill a critical need for the less fortunate among them. Providing health care for this underserved population will eliminate other costly problems that stem from lack of access to medical treatment. Statistics show that lack of adequate health care is directly related to the demand for other social services such as welfare and aid to dependent children. Further, it contributes to stress in families that can lead to domestic violence and even to rising crime rates. Community members in Navajo Flats are already very generous with money and time in support of local social service agencies and retired doctors, nurses, and technicians have volunteered their time and expertise to staff the clinic. CAS will be an ideal landlord for the clinic, but must fill the space and begin collecting on the lease relatively quickly in order to afford the building. We have a six-month window of opportunity to raise the $500,000 necessary to open the free clinic. The money must come from donations over and above what the community is already giving to support social services. If we are unable to raise the money and open the clinic, the need for health care among the migrant population, blue-collar families, and students will become more acute, exacerbating other social problems. Rallying community support to raise money for the clinic will also help people feel some ownership in helping to provide for their less fortunate neighbors.

Matrix: Research
Step Three—Core Problem/Opportunity

Through the United Way partnership, establish the free medical clinic serving those members of the Navajo Flats community who would otherwise have no access to health care, by raising the $500,000 needed to build out the facility within six months.

Matrix: Action Planning
Step Four—Goal and Objectives

Goal

The United Way partnership's goal is to raise $500,000 from the community by the end of August to build out the space offered by CAS, without affecting the current level of support to other social service agencies.

Objectives

1. Raise awareness of the opportunity to 80% among key publics: to 20% within two months (by April 30th), to 60% within three months (by May 31st) and to 80% within five months (by July 31st).
2. Obtain $150,000 in new leadership gifts ($1,000 or more) within two months (April 30th).
3. Obtain $250,000 in new corporate sponsorships within four months (June 30th).
4. Obtain the remaining $100,000 within six months (August 31st).

Matrix: Action Planning
Step Five—Key Publics and Messages and
Step Six—Strategies and Tactics

Four publics have been chosen for this campaign. Because of the limited time to raise $500,000, we have selected those with the greatest inclination and capacity to give. *Members of the boards of directors of the free clinic partnership* will be crucial not only in leadership giving, but in opinion leadership to persuade other community leaders to give. *Community leadership givers*, those who routinely support community efforts, will be fairly easily persuaded for a one-time donation and will set an example for their peers who are local area professionals. Many of the *local area professionals* are in independent practice and typically are not targeted for regular giving and could be persuaded for a one-time gift. Finally, *corporate executives* will be important for the corporate sponsorships which will not only provide a needed service for many of their blue-collar employees, but will spotlight their companies as community citizens fulfilling their corporate social responsibility.

Partnership Boards

The cooperation and visible involvement of these community leaders will be key to the success of our campaign. These leaders not only have the capacity to give a leadership gift ($1,000 or more), but more importantly, they are known and respected in the Navajo Flats community and will be highly influential in securing the support and contributions of other members of the community. They are truly committed to the community, and they value their status as community leaders. In most cases, we can count on their support both as leadership givers and as an intervening public, but we will need to make it easy and non-time-intensive for them to be involved. They already know about the free clinic, they have been involved in the negotiations to bring it about. But we must now convince them to become personally involved in the fundraising and to use their influence one-on-one and through mass media to raise the $500,000. The United Way board has 20 members, the CAS board has 15, the SWHC board has 24 members, and the Interfaith Council has 31 members for a total of 90 of these respected community leaders to personally ask other community leaders for their support.

Primary and Secondary Messages

Primary message: Because you are personally recognized and your name is known for good within this community, your visible support of this effort will be key to its success.

Secondary messages:

- To raise $500,000 in the next six months will require larger than average donations. In typical fundraising campaigns, we receive small donations ($25 to $200) from many generous citizens in Navajo Flats. But we will not be able to raise half a million dollars in six months from $25 donations. We will need to enlist the support of those able to give larger one-time donations in the range of $500 to $2,500.
- To accomplish this task, we will need to receive leadership donations ($1,000 or more). The publics in this community who are able to give that kind of donation are the business and civic leaders (many of whom are your friends and colleagues) and the members of the professional community (such as doctors, dentists, attorneys, and accountants). These individuals are in an income range that would make it possible to give this kind of a one-time donation without difficulty.
- These potential donors will respond best to a personal approach for a one-time gift from someone they know and respect. You are more likely to get a positive response because they know you.
- A final public we will need to target to raise this much money quickly is corporate executives. Corporate donations will need to be a part of the effort if we are to succeed. You also know these individuals and have some influence on them. These executives will support the clinic because you support it and they trust your judgment.

Primary message: Commit to make the phone calls and personal visits/presentations. Our staff will work with you to identify five of your colleagues to contact and two corporate executives to visit with us.

Secondary messages:

- These professionals and executives are most likely to respond favorably to an appeal from a friend and colleague. They know you. They know you know this community. They respect your judgment and advice. They are likely to support causes in which you are involved.
- We know you are extremely busy so our staff will do all the legwork. We will do all we can to make this easy and painless for you. We will provide

all the information you need to make the calls and will organize the visits and design and create the presentations and collateral material. All you have to do is show up and pitch the project to your professional and corporate executive colleagues.

Primary message: Commit to your own leadership donation of $1,000 or more.

Secondary messages:

- Your own donation will give you leverage when you ask your business and professional colleagues in this community to join you in supporting the free clinic.
- This one-time donation is a relatively small commitment that will pay big dividends for the community. There will never be a follow-up request because of your efforts and the efforts of everyone else on the partnership boards to create a self-sustaining entity that fills a critical community need.
- You demonstrate your personal integrity in monetarily supporting a project you have worked to launch for the good of this community.
- You reinforce your position as a respected and esteemed leader in this community with the ability to find real solutions to the most troublesome problems.
- Unless you direct otherwise, your support will be recognized as part of the Circle of Caring display in the free clinic and in associated publicity and media coverage.

Strategies and Tactics

Strategy one: Secure the participation of these board members in the presentations, personal visits, and phone calls to colleagues through a presentation by the chair of each clinic partnership board to respective board members that also provides all necessary information, resources and support to make their involvement easy without taking a lot of their time.

Tactics:

- Ten-minute presentation by the board chair at the March board meeting of each organization (United Way, CAS, SWHC and ICNF).
- A written invitation for each of these board members to give at some level to make it easier for them to ask others to give.
- Information on the Circle of Caring recognition.
- Campaign event outline.
- Resource packet that includes: Half-page flyer listing in bold each task we are asking them to perform and the desired completion date, one-page instruction sheet for each task providing all necessary information and suggested approaches to accomplishing the task, proposal leaflet, fact sheet on the free clinic and on the partnership, 24/7 contact information for all individuals leading the partnership and the partnership staffers, and donation card.

- Print copy of Web portal for online information and giving.
- Information packet about the free clinic partnership's 5K race and how their organizations can get involved to support the event. The packet will contain information on how to organize a team and participate in the 5K run/bike/walk that includes a fact sheet on the event with all particulars including entrance fees and deadlines, a fact sheet on health care in the community and the proposed free clinic, templates for flyers and posters and other collateral to promote the run within their own companies, template of story for company newsletter, template of an e-mail to employees, templates for t-shirts or arm/wrist bands for the run, employee pass-along cards promoting the cause and the event with the Web address for online donation, team-building benefits, entrance applications and other necessary information, and a CD of all templates and collateral in electronic format.
- Follow-up e-mails reminding board members of the importance of the tasks and the deadlines.

Strategy two: Reinforce personal commitments to help raise the money through staff communications from the respective boards.

Tactics:

- Personally written thank you from each board's chair for the member's commitment and effort to support the free clinic.
- Circle of Caring paperweight delivered to the office with a note of appreciation and reminder of tasks to be completed.
- Personal thank you note from the director of one of the nonprofits involved in the partnership (United Way, CAS, SWHC, or ICNF).
- Report of campaign's progress and reminders at each monthly meeting of each board.
- Monthly e-mails reporting on campaign progress and highlighting what board members are doing.
- Phone calls from partnership directors to board members not making progress offering personal or staff assistance in helping them complete their tasks.
- Electronic packet of resources to encourage their organization's participation in the 5K run/bike/walk and a reminder to organize early.
- Advance invitation to the free clinic's grand opening Circle of Caring Celebration.

Community Leadership Givers

We can count on this public to support this project. They already give generously to causes in the community, but are typically in financial positions to be generous and would likely accept a commitment for a one-time gift of $1,000 or more to support this clinic, particularly if asked personally by a partnership board member. They are aware of pressing issues in the community and trust the agencies involved in the partnership. They are committed to the community and value their status and recognition as generous supporters of community causes. They may allow us to publicize their contributions to encourage their peers and others to give as well. They are very busy, so we need to make it easy for them to support this cause. The United Way has a list of about 2,500 people in this category.

Primary and Secondary Messages

Primary message: The United Way, Southwest Health Care, Community Action Services, and the Interfaith Council have joined in a partnership to take advantage of an opportunity to establish a free health clinic to serve our area's low-income and uninsured citizens. We need your help as a leader in this community in a one-time effort to raise $500,000 within six months to open the clinic.

Secondary messages:

- One of the critical social issues in our community is affordable health care. While many have access and insurance, we have an underserved population (including 15,000 children) that has no access and a need too large to be met by the generous charity care provided by local health care facilities.

- Community Action Services (CAS), the local nonprofit that operates the food bank and housing and employment services for those in need, has an opportunity to purchase the vacated Wal-Mart building at a concessionary rate. CAS will use 70% of the facility as a warehouse and processing center for the food bank and related services, but it will need to lease the remaining 30% of the space to service the loans and maintain the facility. Working with CAS, the local United Way has leveraged partnerships in the community—health care providers and churches—to operate and maintain a free medical clinic in the remaining 30% of the warehouse facility, including the lease, a full-time administrator and assistant, and the necessary insurance coverage on volunteer medical personnel. Some of the equipment and furnishings will be donated by local health care providers as they upgrade and replace equipment, and an annual contribution from the United Way will provide renewable medical supplies. Local builders have volunteered their construction crews.

- The partnership lacks the estimated $500,000 that is required for materials to build out the space and initially equip it as a free clinic. It has been determined that, for the goal of a free medical clinic to be realized, the clinic partnership will need to raise $500,000 from the community.

- The partnership is comprised of entities you already support and trust: the United Way, SWHC, CAS, and local churches. The leaders and members of their boards of directors are your friends and colleagues. You, like they, are a leader in this community involved in ensuring the quality of life for all our residents and businesses.

- Local retired health care workers and your friends Dr. Bill Tucker and nurse Eleanor Tucker, are leading the team of retired health care professionals who will volunteer their time to staff the clinic.

- The need for health care among the migrant community, blue-collar families and students is acute. The lack of affordable health care means many simply go without treatment and medication. Potentially 15,000 children in our community currently have no access to health care. When people do not receive necessary medical care, other social problems are compounded.

- For example, Estancia is the seven-year-old daughter of Guillermo and Maria Fuentes. Guillermo originally came to our community to work in the produce fields and sent his earnings home to his wife and family in Mexico. Through diligence and hard work, Guillermo eventually brought his wife and children to Navajo Flats. Now Guillermo and Maria work in one of the packaging plants for minimum wage. Their children attend public school and are good students, because Guillermo and Maria know the importance of education. But Estancia recently developed respiratory problems that affect her ability to do as well in school as her siblings have. She is often ill, as the lack of treatment of her asthma makes her susceptible to constant colds and infections. Doctors say her health problems are manageable, with proper treatment and medication. But Guillermo and Maria have no insurance, and while their frugality enables them to adequately support their family, they simply cannot afford the cost of asthma treatments and medication. Every time Estancia is too sick to go to school, one of her parents has to stay home from work and doesn't get paid. That's a burden we all end up bearing. Estancia continues to suffer with her condition, which affects her not only physically, but threatens her future success. Your support of this partnership will secure Estancia's future, and help many more of our community's children grow up healthy and be successful.

- Because of your stature within our community, your visible support of this partnership is crucial to our success.

Primary message: In order to take advantage of this phenomenal opportunity to provide care, we need your leadership gift of $1,000 or more.

Secondary messages:

- Your gift will earn you a place in the clinic's Circle of Caring, a visible display in the lobby of the clinic highlighting those corporations and individuals whose leadership contributions made the clinic possible.

- Your gift will be an example to others in the community who will follow your lead in giving to support the free clinic. Knowing of your gift, they too will give.

- Your participation in this effort reinforces your civic leadership in Navajo Flats in addressing the needs of community members.

- Receiving your leadership gift by April 30th will allow us to leverage your support with other community members.

Strategies and Tactics

Strategy one: Solicit leadership contributions from local business and civic leaders, particularly those serving on boards of directors or as officers in the local social service agencies, through personal contact by partnership board members.

Tactics:

- Each partnership board member will call and ask five people whom he/she knows on the list of community leadership givers. (Coordinated by the United Way staff to assure no duplication.) The board member will tell them he/she is putting some information in the mail and ask them to consider supporting the free medical clinic as a leadership giver. Some partnership board members may prefer to host a lunch for their assigned asks so their appeal will be in person.
- Package mailed (or personally given) to each potential donor includes the leaflet proposal for the free clinic, the Circle of Caring brochure, and the donation card with return envelope. The package will also contain a pass-along card with statistical information on the health care need in the community, the free clinic, and a Web site address for more information or online giving.
- The board member will send a follow-up e-mail (template provided by the partnership staff) requesting support or thanking for support. E-mail will also contain hot link to the Web portal for online information or giving.

Strategy two: Express gratitude and give recognition to all who contribute through community opinion leaders.

Tactics:

- Thank you card written and signed by a well known United Way Board member or the Tuckers sent to all who contribute as soon as they contribute. Enclose an updated Circle of Caring brochure with their names included.
- Invitation to the grand opening of the free clinic.
- Circle of Caring display in clinic lobby with engraved nameplates of leadership givers, both companies and individuals.
- Final Circle of Caring brochures distributed to all at the grand opening.
- Recognition at the grand opening by those conducting the ceremony.
- Opportunities for media sound bites and interviews at the grand opening.
- A full-page ad in each community newspaper replicating the Circle of Caring display with thanks from the partnership to individually recognized contributors.
- Thank you flyer at 5K run/bike/walk listing all contributors.

Local Area Professionals

These members of the business and professional associations in Navajo Flats are those we need to convert to leadership givers. They are prosperous, but many are not engaged in community service or giving because they are independent and somewhat isolated from charitable organizations that target larger companies and their employees. Through the local Bar Association, the Dental Association, the Medical Association, Chamber of Commerce, and other such professional and business organizations, we can potentially reach 30,000 professionals and persuade them to become involved in their community by supporting the free health clinic as a leadership giver and/or as a participant in the 5K run/bike/walk. They will be influenced to give by community leaders and by their fellow professionals. Their motivations for giving will be less altruistic. We need to help them see the benefit of community involvement to their professional stature and success, and that their one-time gift is a fairly effortless way to be involved. The appeal of the 5K run/bike/walk will be both the visibility of their support to their peers and their employees, as well as an appeal to their fitness, a concern for many of those in this public.

Primary and Secondary Messages

Primary message: Many of your fellow citizens in Navajo Flats are in critical need of health care and are without insurance and without financial means to access it. Join us in helping them.

Secondary messages:

- Join your friends and colleagues who are leading professionals in Navajo Flats who are uniting to support this free clinic as a solution to needs in the community. Your one-time leadership gift will identify you to colleagues and clients as a caring member of the Navajo Flats community.

- As many as 15,000 children in our community are without the health care they need to succeed in school and become contributing members of our community.

- Community Action Services (CAS), the local nonprofit that operates the food bank and housing and employment services for those in need, has an opportunity to purchase the vacated Wal-Mart building at a concessionary rate. CAS will use 70% of the facility as a warehouse and processing center for the food bank and related services, but it will need to lease the remaining 30% of the space to service the loans and maintain the facility. Working with CAS, the local United Way has leveraged partnerships in the community—health care providers and churches—to operate and maintain a free medical clinic in the remaining 30% of the warehouse facility, including the lease, a full-time administrator and assistant, and the necessary insurance coverage on volunteer medical personnel. Some of the equipment and furnishings will be donated by local health care providers as they upgrade and replace equipment, and an annual contribution from the United Way will provide renewable medical supplies. Local builders have volunteered their construction crews.

- The partnership lacks the estimated $500,000 that is required for materials to build out the space and initially equip it as a free clinic. It has been determined that, for the goal of a free medical clinic to be realized, the clinic partnership will need to raise $500,000 from the community.

- The partnership is comprised of trusted local entities strongly supported by the community: the United Way, SWHC, CAS, and local churches. The leaders and members of their boards of directors are your friends and colleagues, leaders in this community involved in ensuring the quality of life for all our residents and businesses. They welcome you to join their circle of influence in the community.

- Local retired health care workers and your friends Dr. Bill Tucker and nurse Eleanor Tucker are leading the team of retired health care professionals who will volunteer their time to staff the clinic.

- The need for health care among the migrant community, blue-collar families and students is acute. The lack of affordable health care means many simply go without treatment and medication. Potentially 15,000 children in our community currently have no access to health care. When people do not receive necessary medical care, other social problems are compounded.

- For example, Estancia is the seven-year-old daughter of Guillermo and Maria Fuentes. Guillermo originally came to our community to work in the produce fields and sent his earnings home to his wife and family in Mexico. Through diligence and hard work, Guillermo eventually brought his wife and children to Navajo Flats. Now Guillermo and Maria work in one of the packaging plants for minimum wage. Their children attend public school and are good students, because Guillermo and Maria know the importance of education. But Estancia recently developed respiratory problems that affect her ability to do as well in school as her siblings have. She is often ill, as the lack of treatment of her asthma makes her susceptible to constant colds and infections. Doctors say her health problems are manageable, with proper treatment and medication. But Guillermo and Maria have no insurance, and while their frugality enables them to adequately support their family, they simply cannot afford the cost of asthma treatments and medication. Every time Estancia is too sick to go to school, one of her parents has to stay home from work and doesn't get paid. That's a burden we all end up bearing. Estancia continues to suffer with her condition, which affects her not only physically, but threatens her future success. Your support of this partnership will secure Estancia's future, and help many more of our community's children grow up healthy and be successful.

Primary message: As a leader in this community we are looking to you for a one-time leadership gift to help your less fortunate friends and neighbors.

Secondary messages:

- Your one-time leadership gift of $1,000 or more will earn you a place in the clinic's Circle of Caring, a visible display in the lobby of the clinic highlighting those corporations and individuals whose leadership contributions made the clinic possible. With your permission, your support will also be acknowledged in associated publicity and media coverage.

- Your gift will be an example to your fellow professionals who will follow your lead in giving to support the free clinic. Through planned recognition, your clients and peers will know of your generosity. Knowing of your gift, they too will give.

- Your participation in this effort reinforces your civic leadership in Navajo Flats in addressing the needs of community members.
- Receiving your leadership gift by April 30th will allow us to leverage your support with other community members.

Primary message: Participate in the 5K run/bike/walk to further reinforce your commitment to the welfare of your fellow citizens in Navajo Flats.

Secondary messages:

- To raise awareness of the clinic and the community support of this effort, a 5K run/bike/walk will be held on Saturday, May 20th, beginning at Liberty Park.
- We encourage you to participate, and to bring your colleagues and coworkers. We will provide a packet of information on organizing an office team to participate. The involvement of your office staff is good visibility for your professional practice.
- Office teams involved in this community benefit will increase camaraderie and unity among your coworkers. They will view you as a caring community leader.
- Leadership givers will be recognized at the event in collateral material and signage.

Strategies and Tactics

Strategy one: Seek support of the free clinic and leadership contributions among local area professionals through presentations to members of local professional associations, business, and professional organizations like Chamber of Commerce and local service clubs and civic organizations like Lions and Rotary.

Tactics:

- PowerPoint presentation by partnership board members who are also members of the association to which they are presenting.
- Information packet for each professional at the presentation with proposal leaflet, Circle of Caring brochure describing the program, pass-along card with statistics on health care and the free clinic and information on how to give, and a donation card and return envelope with information on contributing by phone or online.
- Copy (for each professional) of an article in a related trade or professional journal about the business and reputation benefits of investing in your local community.
- Print copy of Web portal for online information and giving.

Strategy two: Reinforce the asks at the presentations and provide the information to professionals not in attendance at a presentation through the established communication channels of business, professional, service, and civic membership organizations.

Tactics:

- Story in the organization's newsletter on the opportunity to be involved.
- Letter from the president of the professional/civic organization enclosing the leaflet, Circle of Caring brochure, and donation card and envelope.
- E-mail copy of the trade or professional journal article on the benefits of investing in your local community.
- Video e-mails of partnership board members encouraging professionals to invest in the free clinic to support the community (TV PSAs sent electronically).
- E-mail reminder and health care statistics with facts on free clinic. Include a hotlink to the Web portal for online information or giving.
- Posting on organization's member Web site.

Strategy three: Enlist the support and contributions of local area professionals through targeted mass media.

Tactics:

- Pitch the story of the clinic and current professional community support to the TV/radio news with press kit.
- TV PSAs during news and prime time with recognizable partnership board members enlisting the support of the professional community and promoting the 5K run/bike/walk.
- Drive-time radio PSAs on the Circle of Caring using partnership board members as voiceovers and featuring local professionals who have contributed.
- Press release to the business section of the local newspapers.
- Facility tour (as build-out begins) featured on Sunday afternoon's local business and professional hour on television.
- Pitch to local financial columnist on local professionals investing in the community.

Strategy four: Engage professionals and motivate donation through a 5K run/bike/walk.

Tactics:

- Invitation from professional association to personally participate or to organize an office team to participate in the 5K run/bike/walk.
- Reinforce the invitations with TV announcements of the event and Web site for more information and registration.
- Pass-along cards in all local gyms, athletic clubs, bike shops, and similar locations promoting the cause and the event.
- Announcements of the event on the Web sites of the above shops.
- Event registration Web site with organizing information and collateral templates. Include access to an electronic information packet on organizing a team including a fact sheet on the event with all particulars including

entrance fees and deadlines, a fact sheet on health care in the community and the proposed free clinic, templates for flyers and posters and other collateral to promote the run within their own companies, template of story for company newsletter, template of an e-mail to employees, templates for t-shirts or arm/wrist bands for the run, employee pass-along cards promoting the cause and the event with the Web address for online donation, team-building benefits, entrance applications, and other necessary information.

Strategy five: Thank and recognize professionals who have contributed and encourage others to step up to contribute and be recognized through mass media.

Tactics:

- Media coverage of 5K run/bike/walk with opportunities for vignettes of local professionals supporting the cause.
- Race signage and collateral material for participants thanking and recognizing those community leaders and professionals who have contributed to the free clinic.
- Drive-time radio PSAs on the Circle of Caring using partnership board members as voiceovers and featuring local professionals who have contributed.
- Full-page in localized newspapers replicating the Circle of Caring display with thanks from the partnership to individually recognized contributors.
- Pitched series of feature stories (TV, radio, and newspaper) on local area professionals who are investing in the community by supporting the free clinic.

Corporate Executives

The CEOs (or local executives) of major corporations with operations in Navajo Flats and the CEOs of the mid-size companies (1,000 or more employees) are typically supportive of community initiatives, particularly those supported by the United Way of Navajo Flats. They know and have done business with many of the partnership board members. Most are in a position to recognize the health care issues because some of their own employees or the families of their employees are affected. These executives see their community involvement as playing a significant role in maintaining corporate reputation and employee morale. Some have even been involved in the planning as members of the partnership boards. We need to make sure they see a tangible reward for their corporate support of this initiative which will undoubtedly be popular among their employees. They may also give a personal leadership gift, but our primary focus with this public is a larger corporate gift.

Primary and Secondary Messages

Primary message: We appreciate your continual community support and need your help on a one-time opportunity to provide health care to underserved people in Navajo Flats.

Secondary messages:

- Your one-time corporate gift and personal leadership gift will give members of the community, some of whom may be your own employees, access to health care they otherwise could not afford. Your company will be recognized as part of an exclusive group of corporate contributors.

- Your corporate gift will earn you a place in the clinic's Circle of Caring, a visible display in the lobby of the clinic highlighting those corporations and individuals whose leadership contributions made the clinic possible. With your permission, your support will also be acknowledged in associated publicity and media coverage.

- One of the critical social issues in our community is affordable health care. We have an underserved population, including as many as 15,000 children, in our community who are without the health care they need to succeed in school and work and to become contributing members of our community.

- Community Action Services (CAS), the local nonprofit that operates the food bank and housing and employment services for those in need, has an opportunity to purchase the vacated Wal-Mart building at a concessionary rate. CAS will use 70% of the facility as a warehouse and processing center for the food bank and related services, but it will need to lease the remaining 30% of the space to service the loans and maintain the facility. Working with CAS, the local United Way has leveraged partnerships in the community—health care providers and churches—to operate and maintain a free medical clinic in the remaining 30% of the warehouse facility, including the lease, a full-time administrator and assistant, and the necessary insurance coverage on volunteer medical personnel. Some of the equipment and furnishings will be donated by local health care providers as they upgrade and replace equipment, and an annual contribution from the United Way will provide renewable medical supplies. Local builders have volunteered their construction crews.

- The partnership lacks the estimated $500,000 that is required for materials to build out the space and initially equip it as a free clinic. It has been determined that, for the goal of a free medical clinic to be realized, the clinic partnership will need to raise $500,000 from the community.

- The partnership is comprised of trusted local entities strongly supported by the community: the United Way, SWHC, CAS, and local churches. The leaders and members of their boards of directors are your friends and colleagues, leaders in this community involved in ensuring the quality of life for all our residents and businesses. They appreciate all you have done in the past and welcome your involvement and support of this crucial initiative.

- Local retired health care workers Dr. Bill Tucker and nurse Eleanor Tucker, are leading the team of retired health care professionals who will volunteer their time to staff the clinic.

- The need for health care among the migrant community, blue-collar families and students is acute. The lack of affordable health care means many simply go without treatment and medication. Potentially 15,000 children in our community currently have no access to health care. When people do not receive necessary medical care, other social problems are compounded.

- Your gift will be an example to your fellow professionals who will follow your lead in giving to support the free clinic. Through planned recognition, your peers and your employees will know of your generosity and respect your support of the Navajo Flats community.

- Your participation in this effort reinforces your civic leadership in Navajo Flats in addressing the needs of community members.

- Receiving your leadership gift by June 30th will allow us to leverage your support with other corporate leaders.

Primary message: Involve your employees in your corporate support through corporate teams in the 5K run/bike/walk.

Secondary messages:

- To raise awareness of the clinic and the community support of this effort, a 5K run/bike/walk will be held on Saturday, May 20th, beginning at Liberty Park.

- We encourage you to participate and to host a corporate team. If you designate a corporate point of contact, we will provide a packet of information on organizing a corporate team to participate. Your employees will appreciate being involved in your corporate support of this effort and their involvement will bring visibility to your corporation as socially responsible and a good citizen in this community.

- Involving your employees as a team in this community cause will increase camaraderie and unity among your employees, and reinforce their pride in their employer. They will view you and your company as a caring community leader.

- Leadership and corporate givers will be recognized at the event in collateral material and signage.

Strategies and Tactics

Strategy one: Motivate a corporate gift through a personal visit from a director of one of the partnership organizations and a couple of board members.

Tactics:

- Set appointments with CEOs and corporate executives to ask for a corporate gift. The visit should include a director from one of the partnership organizations and one or two board members from partnership organizations who have an established relationship with the CEO or executive being visited.

- Provide a fact sheet detailing the local health care problem and the resulting social costs. Provide statistics specific to that company's workforce as appropriate.

- Provide the free clinic proposal leaflet at the meeting.
- Include a pass-along card with statistics on health care and the free clinic.
- Provide a Circle of Caring brochure and fact sheet detailing the public recognitions to be given donors through events (grand opening and the 5K run/bike/walk) and through mass media.
- One member of the visit team should follow up with a phone call to those not making an immediate commitment.

Strategy two: Motivate participation of corporate teams in the 5K run/bike/walk through personal contact and standardized collateral to make team organization easy.

Tactics:

- At the above corporate visits, provide a 5K run/bike/walk organizing packet as detailed in tactics above.
- Provide a fact sheet of benefits and publicity planned.
- Partnership organization's staff make phone calls to appropriate points of contacts within local corporations to request they host at least one team of employees in the event.
- Send electronic organizing packets to all interested corporations.
- Provide the organizing packet and template download from the event Web site.
- E-mail the television PSAs on the 5K run/bike/walk to corporate points of contact.

Strategy three: Reinforce the gift commitment through public recognition and thanks.

Tactics:

- Thank you card written and signed by a well known United Way Board member or the Tuckers sent to all who contribute as soon as they contribute. Enclose an updated Circle of Caring brochure with their corporation recognized.
- Invitation for executives to the grand opening of the free clinic.
- Circle of Caring display in clinic lobby with engraved nameplates of leadership givers, both companies and individuals.
- Final Circle of Caring brochures distributed to all at the grand opening.
- Recognition at the grand opening by those conducting the ceremony.
- Media coverage of 5K run/bike/walk with opportunities for interviews and sound bites from corporate participants.
- Race signage and collateral material for participants thanking and recognizing those community leaders, professionals, and corporations who have contributed to the free clinic.

- Drive-time radio PSAs on the Circle of Caring using partnership board members as voiceovers and featuring local corporations who have made donations.
- Full-page in localized newspapers replicating the Circle of Caring display with thanks from the partnership to individually recognized contributors.
- News releases to the business section of newspaper and to broadcast news directors on the corporate support of the free clinic.
- Video series following the renovation of the clinic and the start of operation, recognizing those corporations and philanthropists responsible for the negotiations to get it set up and the donations to fund the renovation.

Sample Campaign

Matrix: Action Planning
Step Seven—Calendar

Key Public	Community Leadership Givers	March Wk 1	Wk 2	Wk 3	Wk 4	April Wk 1	Wk 2	Wk 3	Wk 4	May Wk 1	Wk 2	Wk 3
Strategy	**Gratitude/recognition.**											
Tactics	Written thanks with C of C brochures				x—							—x
	Invitation to C of C Celebration											
	C of C Celebration/clinic opening:											
	Final C of C brochures											
	Verbal recognition as sponsor											
	Engraved nameplate C of C											
	C of C paperweight											
	Media interviews of donors											
	C of C banners											
	Fresh flowers											
	Refreshments											
	Venue set-up											
	Full-page C of C thanks in papers											
	Thank you flyer with names at 5K											x
Key Public	**Local Area Professionals**											
Strategy	**Get gifts through professional assoc/civic clubs.**											
Tactics	PowerPoint presentations								x—			
	Info packet:								x—			
	Leaflet proposal											
	C of C brochure											
	Donation card and envelope											
	Pass-along stats and clinic card											
	Copy of journal article								x—			
	Print copy of Web portal								x—			
Strategy	**Reinforce through mass media.**											
Tactics	Pitch stories to news directors											
	Press kit:											
	Release											
	Fact Sheet											
	Leaflet proposal											
	C of C brochure											
	Pass-along card											
	Campaign event outline											
	TV PSAs on 5K production								x			
	Placement								x—			—x
	Drive time radio C of C PSAs prod								x			
	Placement										x—	
	Release to business section											
	Facility tours for media											
	Pitch financial columnist											
Key Public	**Corporate Executives**											
Strategy	**Motivate corporate 5K team through personal contact.**											
Tactics	Packet to organize 5K team						x					
	Fact sheet on benefits and publicity						x					
	Phone calls offering help							x—		—x		
	Electronic 5K organizing packets							x				
	5K packet on Web site					x—				—x		
	E-mail TV PSAs on 5K						x					

Note: This calendar is abbreviated for space. It serves only as an illustration. Calendars must include all strategies and tactics for every public.

		June				July				August				September			
	Wk 4	Wk 1	Wk 2	Wk 3	Wk 4	Wk 1	Wk 2	Wk 3	Wk 4	Wk 1	Wk 2	Wk 3	Wk 4	Wk 1	Wk 2	Wk 3	Wk 4
														x			
														x			
																	x
																	x
																	x
																	x
																	x
																	x
																	x
																	x
														x			
									x								
									x								
									x								
									x								
	x				x				x				x				x
	x				x				x				x				x
											x						
			x										x				
														x	x		
					x												

Sample Campaign

Matrix: Action Planning
Step Eight—Budget

Key Public	Members of Partnership Boards	Detail	Per Item Cost	Total Projected	Sponsored Credit	Actual Projected
Strategy	Secure participation through board presentation.					
Tactics	PowerPoint presentations	Prepared by UW staff	$0.00	$0.00	$0.00	$0.00
	Written invitation to give	90@.10/ea Each partner sponsors	$0.10	$9.00	$9.00	$0.00
	C of C recognition brochure	90 2-color @ .35/ea Printer @ 20% off	$0.35	$31.50	$6.30	$25.20
	Campaign event outline	90 @ .02/ea	$0.02	$1.80	$0.00	$1.80
	Resource packet:	90 covers @ .10/ea	$0.10	$9.00	$0.00	$9.00
	1/2 page flyer on tasks	90 @ .01/ea	$0.01	$0.90	$0.00	$0.90
	1-page instruction on each task	90 @ .02/ea	$0.02	$1.80	$0.00	$1.80
	Leaflet proposal for free clinic	No color/trifold 90 @ .25/ea	$0.25	$22.50	$0.00	$22.50
	Fact sheet on clinic/partnership	90 @ .02/ea	$0.02	$1.80	$0.00	$1.80
	Contact sheet on all staff/chairs	90 @ .02/ea	$0.02	$1.80	$0.00	$1.80
	Donation card/envelope	90 (3 per cardstock @ .10/ea) + env.	$0.08	$7.20	$0.00	$7.20
	Print copy of Web portal	90 @ .02/ea	$0.02	$1.80	$0.00	$1.80
	Resource packet to organize 5K:	90 covers @ .25/ea (5K fee covers)	$0.25	$22.50	$22.50	$0.00
	Fact sheet on event	90 @ .02/ea (5K fee covers)	$0.02	$1.80	$1.80	$0.00
	Fact sheet on clinic	90 @ .02/ea (5K fee covers)	$0.02	$1.80	$1.80	$0.00
	Templates for flyers	3 styles 270 @ .02/ea (5K fee covers)	$0.06	$5.40	$5.40	$0.00
	Templates for posters	3 styles 270 @ .25/ea (5K fee covers)	$0.75	$67.50	$67.50	$0.00
	Template for newsletter story	90 @ .02/ea (5K fee covers)	$0.02	$1.80	$1.80	$0.00
	Template of employee e-mail	90 @ .02/ea (5K fee covers)	$0.02	$1.80	$1.80	$0.00
	Logos for t-shirt, arm/wrist bands	90 @ .02/ea (5K fee covers)	$0.02	$1.80	$1.80	$0.00
	Pass-along cards on clinic and 5K	90 (10 per cardstock @ .10/ea) 5K fee	$0.01	$0.90	$0.90	$0.00
	Fact sheet/team building benefits	90 @ .02/ea (5K fee covers)	$0.02	$1.80	$1.80	$0.00
	Apps and new registration forms	90 @ .02/ea (5K fee covers)	$0.02	$1.80	$1.80	$0.00
	CD of all template materials	90 @ .25/ea (5K fee covers)	$0.25	$67.50	$67.50	$0.00
	E-mail reminders of tasks	90 @ .02/ea	$0.02	$1.80	$0.00	$1.80
		Strategy Subtotal	$2.47	$267.30	$191.70	$75.60
Strategy	Reinforce commitments through board comms channels.					
Tactics	Board thank you notes	90 @ .10/ea Each partner sponsors	$0.10	$9.00	$9.00	$0.00
	C of C paperweight with tasks:					
	Paperweight	90 @$15/ea (Local supplier 30%)	$15.00	$1,350.00	$405.00	$945.00
	1/4 sheet task list	90 (4 per slickstock @ .20/ea)	$0.05	$4.50	$0.00	$4.50
	Nonprofit director thank you note	90 @ .10/ea + .41 to mail (nonprofits)	$0.51	$45.90	$45.90	$0.00
	Progress report at board mtg	PowerPoint—no cost	$0.00	$0.00	$0.00	$0.00
	E-mailed progress reports	No cost	$0.00	$0.00	$0.00	$0.00
	Director phone calls	No cost	$0.00	$0.00	$0.00	$0.00
	Electronic resource packet on 5K	No cost	$0.00	$0.00	$0.00	$0.00
	Invitation to C of C and opening	90 @ .25/ea + .41 to mail	$0.66	$59.40	$0.00	$59.40
		Strategy Subtotal	$16.32	$1,468.80	$459.00	$1,008.90
		Public Subtotal	$18.79	$1,736.10	$651.60	$1,084.50
Key Public	Community Leadership Givers					
Strategy	Gratitude/recognition.					
Tactics	Written thanks with	250 @ .10/ea + .41 Asker mails	$0.51	$127.50	$127.50	$0.00
	C of C brochure	300 @ .35/ea Printer 20% off	$0.35	$105.00	$21.00	$84.00
	Invitation to C of C Celebration	600 @ .25/ea + .41 to mail	$0.66	$396.00	$0.00	$396.00
	C of C Celebration/clinic opening:					
	Final C of C brochures	750 @ .35/ea Printer 20% off	$0.35	$262.50	$52.50	$210.00
	Verbal recognition as sponsor	No cost	$0.00	$0.00	$0.00	$0.00
	Engraved nameplate C of C	250 @ $5/ea	$5.00	$1,250.00	$0.00	$1,250.00
	C of C paperweight	250 @ $15/ea Supplier 30% off	$15.00	$3,750.00	$1,125.00	$2,625.00

Note: This budget is abbreviated for space. It serves only as an illustration. Budgets must include all strategies and tactics for every public.

		Detail	Per Item Cost	Total Projected	Sponsored Credit	Actual Projected
Key Public	**Community Leadership Givers**					
	Media interviews of donors	No cost	$0.00	$0.00	$0.00	$0.00
	C of C banners	1 outdoor/1 indoor @ 150/4' x 6' ea	$150.00	$300.00	$0.00	$300.00
	Fresh flowers	3 sprays at $100/ea Florist comped	$100.00	$300.00	$300.00	$0.00
	Refreshments	400 @ $3/ea Local bakery comped	$3.00	$1,200.00	$1,200.00	$0.00
	Venue set-up	No cost/UW and CAS	$0.00	$0.00	$0.00	$0.00
	Full-page C of C thanks in papers	Daily @ $900/3 Weeklies @ $500/free	$900.00	$2,400.00	$1,500.00	$900.00
	Thank you flyer with names at 5K	500 @ .02/ea (5K fee covers)	$0.02	$10.00	$10.00	$0.00
		Strategy Subtotal	**$1,174.89**	**$10,101.00**	**$4,336.00**	**$5,765.00**
		Public Subtotal	**$1,174.89**	**$10,101.00**	**$4,336.00**	**$5,765.00**
Key Public	**Local Area Professionals**					
Strategy	**Get gifts through professional assoc/civic clubs.**					
Tactics	PowerPoint presentations	Prepared by UW staff	$0.00	$0.00	$0.00	$0.00
	Info packet:	500 @ .79 per packet (above)	$0.79	$395.00	$40.00	$355.00
	Leaflet proposal					
	C of C brochure	Printer 20% off (.07/ea)				
	Donation card and envelope					
	Pass-along stats and clinic card	5K fee covers (.01/ea)				
	Copy of journal article	500 @ .10/ea (club prints)	$0.10	$50.00	$50.00	$0.00
	Print copy of Web portal	500 @ .02/ea	$0.02	$10.00	$0.00	$10.00
		Strategy Subtotal	**$0.91**	**$455.00**	**$90.00**	**$365.00**
Strategy	**Reinforce through mass media.**					
Tactics	Pitch clinic story to news directors					
	Press kit:	5 covers @ .50/ea	$0.50	$2.50	$0.00	$2.50
	Release	5 @ .02/ea	$0.02	$0.10	$0.00	$0.10
	Fact Sheet	5 @ .02/ea	$0.02	$0.10	$0.00	$0.10
	Leaflet proposal	5 @ .25/ea	$0.25	$1.25	$0.00	$1.25
	C of C brochure	5 @ .35/ea Printer 20% off	$0.35	$1.75	$0.35	$1.40
	Pass-along card	5 @ .01/ea (5K fee covers)	$0.01	$0.05	$0.05	$0.00
	Campaign event outline	5 @ .02/ea	$0.02	$0.10	$0.00	$0.10
	TV PSAs production	1 30-sec @ $20K/comped prod.	$20,000.00	$20,000.00	$20,000.00	$0.00
	Placement	10/wk 4 wks $400/ea 2 sta/comped	$400.00	$16,000.00	$16,000.00	$0.00
	Drive time radio PSAs production	5 30-sec @$150/ea comped prod.	$150.00	$750.00	$750.00	$0.00
	Placement	10/wk 12 wks $100/av 2 sta/comped	$100.00	$24,000.00	$24,000.00	$0.00
	Release to business section	5 @ .02	$0.02	$0.10	$0.00	$0.10
	Facility tours for media	No cost	$0.00	$0.00	$0.00	$0.00
	Pitch financial columnist	No cost	$0.00	$0.00	$0.00	$0.00
		Strategy Subtotal	**$20,651.19**	**$60,755.95**	**$60,750.40**	**$5.55**
		Public Subtotal	**$20,652.10**	**$61,210.95**	**$60,840.40**	**$370.55**
Key Public	**Corporate Executives**					
Strategy	**Motivate corporate 5K team through personal contact.**					
Tactics	Packet to organize 5K team	40 visits @ $1.48/ea (5K fee covers)	$1.48	$59.20	$59.20	$0.00
	Fact sheet on benefits and publicity	40 @ .02	$0.02	$0.80	$0.00	$0.80
	Phone calls offering help	No cost	$0.00	$0.00	$0.00	$0.00
	Electronic 5K organizing packets	As many as needed—no cost	$0.00	$0.00	$0.00	$0.00
	5K packet on Web site	No cost	$0.00	$0.00	$0.00	$0.00
	E-mail TV PSAs on 5K	No cost (produced for area pros)	$0.00	$0.00	$0.00	$0.00
		Strategy Subtotal	**$1.48**	**$59.20**	**$59.20**	**$0.00**
		Public Subtotal	**$1.48**	**$59.20**	**$59.20**	**$0.00**
		CAMPAIGN TOTAL	**$21,848.75**	**$73,694.25**	**$65,946.20**	**$7,748.05**

Sample Campaign

Matrix: Communication
Step Nine—Communication Confirmation

Key Public	Self-interests	Primary Messages	Influentials
Members of Partnership Boards	Opinion leadership/peer esteem, funding clinic for community, not spending a lot of time to do it.	1. Because of your community leadership, your visible support is key to our success. 2. Commit to make contacts. Staff will provide all materials and coordinate visits. 3. Commit to a leadership gift of $1,000 or more as an example and leverage.	Peers on boards, board chairs, professional colleagues.
Community Leadership Givers	Community status and respect, sincere care for community's welfare.	1. As community leader, you know the health care needs. Support the free clinic partnership. 2. We welcome your leadership gift of $1,000 or more.	Peers, other community leaders, employees, family members.
Local Area Professionals	Professional reputation, financial success.	1. Many Devon neighbors in need of health care. They need your help. 2. Show your leadership with a one-time gift. 3. Participate in 5K benefit to show your commitment to community.	Peers, business and civic leaders, fellow professionals.

Note: The Communication Confirmation Table (CCT) confirms the logic of the plan by converting it into short statements for each public in tabular form. This CCT is abbreviated for space. It serves only as an illustration. CCTs must include the complete planning for every public.

Objectives	Strategies	Tactics
1. Raise awareness to 80%. 2. Raise $150K in leadership gifts. 3. Raise $250K in corporate gifts. 4. Raise $100K in other gifts.	1. Secure participation through presentation by respective board chair and make involvement easy. 2. Reinforce commitments through their respective boards established communication channels.	10-min. pres. at next board mtg. with collateral: written invitation for them to personally give, info on C of C recognition, campaign event outline, resource packet, flyer and instruction sheet on required tasks, proposal leaflet, info on clinic and staff contacts, print copy of Web portal. Resource packet to organize 5K team. Follow-up e-mails on tasks and deadlines. Personal thank you from board chair. C of C paperweight with task reminders delivered to office. Personal thank you from director of one of the involved nonprofits. Campaign progress report at monthly board mtg. E-mailed progress reports. Phone calls from directors to those not making progress. Electronic resource packet on 5K team organization. Advance invitation to C of C celebration and clinic opening.
1. Raise awareness to 80%. 2. Raise $150K in leadership gifts.	1. Solicit leadership gifts through personal contact of partnership board members. 3. Gratitude and recognition through community opin. ldrs.	Each board member asks five leaders on leadership givers list. Info packet with leaflet proposal, C of C brochure, donation card and envelope, pass-along card with stats and case for clinic, and Web site address to give. Follow-up e-mail from board members thanking or reminding. Written thanks with updated C of C brochure. Invitation to C of C Celebration and clinic opening. Engraved C of C nameplates at opening. Final C of C brochures at opening. Recognition at opening by dignitary speaking. Media interviews at opening. Full-page C of C w/names in all local papers. Thank you flyer w/names at 5K.
1. Raise awareness to 80%. 2. Raise $150K in leadership gifts. 4. Raise $100K in other gifts.	1. Seek support and contributions through pres. to local professional associations and civic/service clubs. 2. Reinforce mtg. asks and ask those not attending through established comms channels of each organization. 3. Enlist support through targeted mass media.	Pres. at mtg. by partnership board member also a member of the association presenting to. Info packet w/proposal leaflet, C of C brochure, pass-along card with stats and info on free clinic and how to give, donation card/return envelope. Copy of article in professional journal about career benefits from investing in community. Print copy of Web portal. Story in organization's newsletter. Letter from pres. of the org. w/proposal leaflet, C of C brochure, and donation card/envelope. E-mail copy of professional journal article. Video e-mails of partnership board members encouraging gift. E-mail reminder and stats on clinic w/hotlink to Web portal for online giving. Post notice on organization's Web site. Pitch story of clinic and current professional community support to news directors w/press kit. TV PSAs during news and prime time featuring partnership board members encouraging local area professionals to give and do 5K. Drive time radio PSAs on C of C featuring professionals who give. Release to business section of all local weeklies and daily paper. Facility tour pitched to Sunday TV business program. Pitch local financial columnists on professionals investing in community.

Matrix: Evaluation
Step Ten—Evaluation Criteria and Tools

Objective 1

Criteria

Awareness of the opportunity rose to 80% among key publics by March 31st.

Tools

Partnership board staff members will determine the total target public by combining the 2,500 community leaders from the United Way list and the number of professional and civic association members (approximately 30,000) to arrive at the total campaign target population. They will then keep track of presentations and mass media coverage to estimate whether 80% were exposed to the message (because of limited time and money, exposure is the only measure to be used although it doesn't measure message penetration).

Objective 2

Criteria

Collection of $150,000 in new leadership gifts by April 30th.

Tools

Records kept of donations from leadership appeals.

Objective 3

Criteria

Collection of $250,000 in new corporate sponsorships by June 30th.

Tools

Records kept of corporate donations.

Objective 4

Criteria

Collection of the remaining $100,000 by August 31st.

Tools

Records kept of revenue from 5K run/bike/walk and all other general donations.

Appendix B

Copy Outlines

COPY OUTLINE—Backgrounder/Brief History

Key public (audience):

Secondary publics (audiences), if any:

Action desired from public(s):

How that action ties to the key public's self-interest:

Issue:

Primary messages: usually 2–3, short statements/selling points to be conveyed
Secondary messages: bulleted supporting data, facts, cases, testimonials, etc.

1. Primary Message:

    Secondary: •
    •
    •

2. Primary Message:

    Secondary: •
    •
    •

3. Primary Message:

    Secondary: •
    •
    •

Third-party influentials and how they will be used (testimonials, quotes, etc.):

Proposed backgrounder/brief history title:

Proposed photos/art (if any):

Method and timing of distribution (Internet, mail, fax, etc.):

Follow-up (if any):

Timeline/deadline:

COPY OUTLINE—Billboard/Poster

Key public (audience):

Secondary publics (audiences), if any:

Action desired from public(s):

    How that action ties to the key public's self-interest:

Overriding Message:

Primary messages: usually 2–3, short statements/selling points to be conveyed
    Secondary messages: bulleted supporting data, facts, cases, testimonials,
    etc.

    1.   Primary Message:

        Secondary: •
                  •
                  •

    2.   Primary Message:

        Secondary: •
                  •
                  •

    3.   Primary Message:

        Secondary: •
                  •
                  •

Third-party influentials and how they will be used (testimonials, quotes, etc.):

Slogan or tagline:

Proposed art:

Size of billboard or poster:

Location(s) of billboard/posters:

Method and timing of distribution:

Print quantity and number of colors (poster):

Timeline/deadline:

COPY OUTLINE—BLOG

Key public (audience):

Secondary publics (audiences), if any:

Action desired from public(s):

How that action ties to the key public's self-interest:

Overriding message and tone:

Proposed title:

Primary messages: usually 2–3, short statements/selling points to be conveyed
Secondary messages: bulleted supporting data, facts, cases, testimonials, etc.

1. Primary Message:

    Secondary: •
                •
                •

2. Primary Message:

    Secondary: •
                •
                •

3. Primary Message:

    Secondary: •
                •
                •

Third-party influentials and how they will be used (testimonials, quotes, etc.):

Content manager:

Comment manager:

Blog software (third-party such as blogger.com or hosting your own using WordPress):

Graphic theme (build your own or download a free theme):

URL:

Timeline/deadline:

COPY OUTLINE—BROCHURE

Key public (audience):

Secondary publics (audiences), if any:

Action desired from public(s):

    How that action ties to the key public's self-interest:

Primary messages: usually 2–3, short statements/selling points to be conveyed
    Secondary messages: bulleted supporting data, facts, cases, testimonials, etc.

    1. Primary Message:

        Secondary: •
                   •
                   •

    2. Primary Message:

        Secondary: •
                   •
                   •

    3. Primary Message:

        Secondary: •
                   •
                   •

Third-party influentials and how they will be used (testimonials, quotes, etc.):

Proposed cover title and cover copy:

Proposed cover photos/art (if any):

Method and timing of distribution (self-mailer, point of purchase display, etc.):

Brochure size and paper (weight, finish, etc.):

Print quantity and number of colors:

Other art to be used (other than cover):

Timeline/deadline:

COPY OUTLINE—Direct Mail Piece

Key public (audience):

Secondary publics (audiences), if any:

Action desired from public(s):

   How that action ties to the key public's self-interest:

Overriding message and tone:

Proposed p.s.:

Primary messages: usually 2–3, short statements/selling points to be conveyed
   Secondary messages: bulleted supporting data, facts, cases, testimonials,
   etc.

   1. Primary Message:

      Secondary: •
                  •
                  •

   2. Primary Message:

      Secondary: •
                  •
                  •

   3. Primary Message:

      Secondary: •
                  •
                  •

Third-party influentials and how they will be used (testimonials, quotes, etc.):

Proposed cover title and cover copy:

Proposed cover photos/figures/art (if any):

Source of mailing list:

Mailer size and paper (weight, finish, etc.):

Print quantity and number of colors:

Other art to be used (other than cover):

Timeline/deadline:

COPY OUTLINE—FACT SHEET

Key public (audience):

Secondary publics (audiences), if any:

Action desired from public(s):

    How that action ties to the key public's self-interest:

Overriding Message:

Primary messages: usually 2–5, short statements/selling points to be conveyed
    Secondary messages: bulleted supporting data, facts, cases, testimonials,
    etc.

    1. Primary Message:

        Secondary: •
                  •
                  •

    2. Primary Message:

        Secondary: •
                  •
                  •

    3. Primary Message:

        Secondary: •
                  •
                  •

Third-party influentials and how they will be used (testimonials, quotes, etc.):

Proposed figures/art (if any):

Method and timing of distribution (Internet, media kits, w/letter, etc.):

Follow-up (if any):

Finished size and paper (weight, finish, etc.):

Print quantity and number of colors:

Timeline/deadline:

COPY OUTLINE—FEATURE STORY

Key public (audience):

Secondary publics (audiences), if any:

Action desired from public(s):

    How that action ties to the key public's self-interest:

Proposed theme:

Proposed headline:

Proposed lead:

Primary messages: usually 2–5, short statements/selling points to be conveyed
    Secondary messages: bulleted supporting data, facts, cases, testimonials, etc.

    1. Primary Message:

       Secondary: •
                  •
                  •

    2. Primary Message:

       Secondary: •
                  •
                  •

    3. Primary Message:

       Secondary: •
                  •
                  •

Third-party influentials and how they will be used (testimonials, quotes, etc.):

Proposed photos/art (if any):

Desired length (number of words or pages):

Method and timing of distribution (E-mail, fax, etc.):

Specific media to receive story:

Follow-up with media:

Timeline/deadline:

COPY OUTLINE—Letter to the Editor

Key public (audience):

Secondary publics (audiences), if any:

Action desired from public(s):

    How that action ties to the key public's self-interest:

News reference (previous story and date it appeared or current issue):

Primary messages: usually 2–3, short statements/selling points to be conveyed
    Secondary messages: bulleted supporting data, facts, cases, testimonials, etc.

1. Primary Message:

    Secondary: •
                •
                •

2. Primary Message:

    Secondary: •
                •
                •

3. Primary Message:

    Secondary: •
                •
                •

Third-party influentials and how they will be used (testimonials, quotes, etc.):

Proposed length (newspaper's suggested word count):

Method of distribution (editor's name and address):

Timeline/deadline:

Note: Use a typical letter format complete with your signature.

COPY OUTLINE—MEDIA KIT

Key public (audience):

Secondary publics (audiences), if any:

Action desired from public(s):

How that action ties to the key public's self-interest:

Third-party influentials and how they will be used (testimonials, quotes, etc.):

Special event or reason to send the kit:

Proposed contents (fact sheet, executive bios, backgrounders, photos, etc.) and how they appeal to the key public's self-interests (each communications piece should have its own copy outline).

a.

b.

c.

d.

e.

Proposed packaging (folder, box, envelope, etc.):

Packaging art (logo, photo, etc.):

Method and timing of distribution (sent with story, handed out at event, etc.):

Print quantity:

Specific media to receive kit:

Follow-up with media (if any):

Timeline/deadline:

COPY OUTLINE—Newsletter

Key public (audience):

Secondary publics (audiences), if any:

Action desired from public(s):

　　How that action ties to the primary public's self-interest:

Third-party influentials and how they will be used (testimonials, quotes, etc.):

Overall tone:

Masthead text and art:

Proposed lead story:

Proposed lead story art:

Regular features or sections (special columns, reports, and letters) and how they appeal to the key public's self-interests (each feature and news story should have its own copy outline).

　　a.

　　b.

　　c.

　　d.

Other stories or articles (again, each should have its own copy outline):

Other photos/art:

Method and timing of distribution (self-mailer, Internet, handed delivered, etc.):

Finished size, number of pages, and paper (weight, finish, etc.):

Print quantity and number of colors:

Timeline/deadline:

COPY OUTLINE—NEWS PITCH

Key public (audience):

Secondary publics (audiences), if any:

Action desired from public(s):

    How that action ties to the key public's self-interest:

News hook:

Story headline:

Story lead:

Primary messages: usually 2–3, short statements/selling points to be conveyed
    Secondary messages: bulleted supporting data, facts, cases, testimonials, etc.

    1.   Primary Message:

        Secondary: •
                   •
                   •

    2.   Primary Message:

        Secondary: •
                   •
                   •

    3.   Primary Message:

        Secondary: •
                   •
                   •

Third-party influentials and how they will be used (testimonials, quotes, etc.):

Proposed photos/figures/art to accompany story (if any):

Method and timing of distribution (E-mail, fax, etc.):

Specific media to receive pitch:

Follow-up with media (if any):

Timeline/deadline:

COPY OUTLINE—NEWS RELEASE

Key public (audience):

Secondary publics (audiences), if any:

Action desired from public(s):

    How that action ties to the key public's self-interest:

News hook:

Proposed headline:

Proposed lead:

Primary messages: usually 2–3, short statements/selling points to be conveyed
    Secondary messages: bulleted supporting data, facts, cases, testimonials,
    etc.

    1. Primary Message:

        Secondary: •
                 •
                 •

    2. Primary Message:

        Secondary: •
                 •
                 •

    3. Primary Message:

        Secondary: •
                 •
                 •

Third-party influentials and how they will be used (testimonials, quotes, etc.):

Proposed photos/figures/art (if any):

Method and timing of distribution (E-mail, fax, etc.):

Specific media to receive release:

Follow-up with media (if any):

Timeline/deadline:

COPY OUTLINE—Op-Ed Piece

Key public (audience):

Secondary publics (audiences), if any:

Action desired from public(s):

How that action ties to the key public's self-interest:

Overriding message and tone:

Primary messages: usually 2–3, short statements/selling points to be conveyed
Secondary messages: bulleted supporting data, facts, cases, testimonials, etc.

1. Primary Message:

    Secondary: •
                •
                •

2. Primary Message:

    Secondary: •
                •
                •

3. Primary Message:

    Secondary: •
                •
                •

Third-party influentials and how they will be used (testimonials, quotes, etc.):

Proposed headline:

Proposed lead:

Method distribution (E-mail, fax, mail, etc.):

Specific media to receive piece:

Follow-up with media (if any):

Timeline/deadline:

COPY OUTLINE—Podcast

Key public (audience):

Secondary publics (audiences), if any:

Action desired from public(s):

　　How that action ties to the key public's self-interest:

List of participants:

Proposed length:

Overriding message/theme and tone:

Proposed title or title of series:

Scripted intro (if any):

Primary messages: usually 2–3, short statements/selling points to be conveyed
　　Secondary messages: bulleted supporting data, facts, cases, testimonials, etc.

　　1.　Primary Message:

　　　　Secondary:　•
　　　　　　　　　　•
　　　　　　　　　　•

　　2.　Primary Message:

　　　　Secondary:　•
　　　　　　　　　　•
　　　　　　　　　　•

　　3.　Primary Message:

　　　　Secondary:　•
　　　　　　　　　　•
　　　　　　　　　　•

Third-party influentials and how they will be used (testimonials, quotes, etc.):

Source media:

Special post-production needs (sound editing, music track, sound effects, etc.)

Timeline/deadline:

COPY OUTLINE—PRINT ADVERTISEMENT

Key public (audience):

Secondary publics (audiences), if any:

Action desired from public(s):

   How that action ties to the key public's self-interest:

Overriding message and tone:

Primary messages: usually 2–3, short statements/selling points to be conveyed
   Secondary messages: bulleted supporting data, facts, cases, testimonials,
   etc.

   1.   Primary Message:

        Secondary: •
                    •
                    •

   2.   Primary Message:

        Secondary: •
                    •
                    •

   3.   Primary Message:

        Secondary: •
                    •
                    •

Third-party influentials and how they will be used (testimonials, quotes, etc.):

Proposed ad art:

Slogan or tagline (if any):

Target publication(s):

Ad size, format, and number of colors:

Timeline/deadline:

COPY OUTLINE—PUBLIC SERVICE ANNOUNCEMENT (PSA)

Key public (audience):

Secondary publics (audiences), if any:

Action desired from public(s):

    How that action ties to the key public's self-interest:

Overriding message and tone:

Format (jingle, single voice, dialogue, etc.):

Primary messages: usually 2–3, short statements/selling points to be conveyed
    Secondary messages: bulleted supporting data, facts, cases, testimonials, etc.

    1.   Primary Message:

       Secondary: •
                •
                •

    2.   Primary Message:

       Secondary: •
                •
                •

    3.   Primary Message:

       Secondary: •
                •
                •

Third-party influentials and how they will be used (testimonials, quotes, etc.):

Production format and length (script, recording, 30 sec., 60 sec., etc.):

Production quantity:

Specific media to receive spot:

Follow-up with media (if any):

Timeline/deadline:

COPY OUTLINE—Radio Advertisement

Key public (audience):

Secondary publics (audiences), if any:

Action desired from public(s):

How that action ties to the key public's self-interest:

Overriding message and tone:

Format (jingle, single voice, dialogue, etc.):

Primary messages: usually 2–3, short statements/selling points to be conveyed
Secondary messages: bulleted supporting data, facts, cases, testimonials, etc.

1. Primary Message:

    Secondary: •

                •

                •

2. Primary Message:

    Secondary: •

                •

                •

3. Primary Message:

    Secondary: •

                •

                •

Third-party influentials and how they will be used (testimonials, quotes, etc.):

Production format and length (script, recording, 30 sec., 60 sec., etc.):

Slogan or tagline if any:

Production quantity:

Target stations:

Timeline/deadline:

COPY OUTLINE—SPECIAL EVENT

Key public (audience):

Secondary publics (audiences), if any:

Action desired from public(s):

    How that action ties to the key public's self-interest:

Event date and time:

Event location:

Overriding message/theme and tone (including title or slogan):

Keynote speaker(s):

Primary messages: usually 2–3, short statements/selling points to be conveyed
    Secondary messages: bulleted supporting data, facts, cases, testimonials, etc.

    1. Primary Message:

        Secondary: •
                    •
                    •

    2. Primary Message:

        Secondary: •
                    •
                    •

    3. Primary Message:

        Secondary: •
                    •
                    •

Third-party influentials and how they will be used (testimonials, quotes, etc.):

Decorations/signage (center pieces, easels, banners, etc.):

Invitation list (general, media, other special guests, etc.):

Collateral materials and means of distribution (invitations, programs, multi-media, etc.):

Event management checklist (create your own or use an existing checklist):

Timeline/deadline:

COPY OUTLINE—Speech/Presentation

Key public (audience):

Secondary publics (audiences), if any:

Action desired from public(s):

> How that action ties to the key public's self-interest:

Presenter(s):

Event:

Length:

Location:

Overriding message/theme and tone:

Proposed title:

Opening attention getting device (story, joke, statistics, picture, video clip, etc.):

Conclusion or summary:

Primary messages: usually 2–3, short statements/selling points to be conveyed
Secondary messages: bulleted supporting data, facts, cases, testimonials, etc.

1. Primary Message:

   Secondary: •
   •
   •

2. Primary Message:

   Secondary: •
   •
   •

3. Primary Message:

   Secondary: •
   •
   •

Third-party influentials and how they will be used (testimonials, quotes, etc.):

Visuals to be used:

Timeline/deadline:

COPY OUTLINE—TELEVISION ADVERTISEMENT

Key public (audience):

Secondary publics (audiences), if any:

Action desired from public(s):

    How that action ties to the key public's self-interest:

Overriding message and tone:

Format (jingle, voice over, situation, etc.):

Primary messages: usually 2–3, short statements/selling points to be conveyed
    Secondary messages: bulleted supporting data, facts, cases, testimonials,
    etc.

1. Primary Message:

    Secondary: •
                  •
                  •

2. Primary Message:

    Secondary: •
                  •
                  •

3. Primary Message:

    Secondary: •
                  •
                  •

Third-party influentials and how they will be used (testimonials, quotes, etc.):

Proposed visuals:

Production length (30 sec., 60 sec., etc.):

Slogan or tagline (if any):

Production quantity:

Target stations:

Timeline/deadline:

COPY OUTLINE—Video/DVD

Key public (audience):

Secondary publics (audiences), if any:

Action desired from public(s):

How that action ties to the key public's self-interest:

Overriding message/theme and tone:

Primary messages: usually 2–5, short statements/selling points to be conveyed
Secondary messages: bulleted supporting data, facts, cases, testimonials, etc.

1. Primary Message:

    Secondary: •
                •
                •

2. Primary Message:

    Secondary: •
                •
                •

3. Primary Message:

    Secondary: •
                •
                •

Third-party influentials and how they will be used (testimonials, quotes, etc.):

Proposed title and cover copy:

Proposed photos/art for the case (if any):

Proposed length:

Method and timing of distribution (Internet streaming, mailed to homes, shown at venue, etc.):

Production quantity and format:

Timeline/deadline:

COPY OUTLINE—VIDEO NEWS RELEASE (VNR)

Key public (audience):

Secondary publics (audiences), if any:

Action desired from public(s):

    How that action ties to the key public's self-interest:

Overriding message and tone:

Proposed headline:

Proposed lead:

Primary messages: usually 2–3, short statements/selling points to be conveyed
    Secondary messages: bulleted supporting data, facts, cases, testimonials, etc.

    1. Primary Message:

        Secondary: •
                  •
                  •

    2. Primary Message:

        Secondary: •
                  •
                  •

    3. Primary Message:

        Secondary: •
                  •
                  •

Third-party influentials and how they will be used (testimonials, quotes, etc.):

Proposed visuals:

Desired length (number of seconds, minutes):

Method and timing of distribution (satellite, mail):

Specific media to receive story:

Follow-up with media:

Timeline/deadline:

COPY OUTLINE—Web Site

Key public (audience):

Secondary publics (audiences), if any:

Action desired from public(s):

How that action ties to the key public's self-interest:

Overriding message and tone:

Design elements (logos, pictures, colors, etc.):

Primary messages for the home page:

1. Primary Message:

2. Primary Message:

3. Primary Message:

Primary navigation categories and subcategories (and self-interest appeal):

A.
   a.
   b.
   c.

B.
   a.
   b.
   c.

C.
   a.
   b.
   c.

D.
   a.
   b.
   c.

List databases that will need to be connected (electronic sources):

Planned publicity to drive traffic to URL:

Timeline/deadline:

Appendix C

Professional Codes of Ethics

CODE OF ETHICS—PUBLIC RELATIONS SOCIETY OF AMERICA (PRSA)

PREAMBLE

**Public Relations Society of America
Member Code of Ethics 2000**

- Professional Values
- Principles of Conduct
- Commitment and Compliance

This Code applies to the Public Relations Society of America (PRSA) members. The Code is designed to be a useful guide for PRSA members as they carry out their ethical responsibilities. This document is designed to anticipate and accommodate, by precedent, ethical challenges that may arise. The scenarios outlined in the Code provision are actual examples of misconduct. More will be added as experience with the Code occurs.

The PRSA is committed to ethical practices. The level of public trust PRSA members seek, as we serve the public good, means we have taken on a special obligation to operate ethically.

The value of member reputation depends upon the ethical conduct of everyone affiliated with the PRSA. Each of us sets an example for each other—as well as other professionals—by our pursuit of excellence with powerful standards of performance, professionalism, and ethical conduct.

Emphasis on enforcement of the Code has been eliminated. But, the PRSA Board of Directors retains the right to bar from membership or expel from the Society any individual who has been or is sanctioned by a government agency or convicted in a court of law of an action that is in violation of this Code.

Ethical practice is the most important obligation of a PRSA member. We view the Member Code of Ethics as a model for other professions, organizations, and professionals.

PRSA MEMBER STATEMENT OF PROFESSIONAL VALUES

This statement presents the core values of PRSA members more broadly, of the public relations profession. These values provide the foundation for the

Member Code of Ethics and industry standard for the professional practice of public These values are the fundamental beliefs that guide our and decision-making process. We believe our professional are vital to the integrity of the profession as a whole.

Advocacy

- We serve the public interest by acting as responsible advocates for those we represent.
- We provide a voice in the marketplace of ideas, facts, and viewpoints to aid informed public debate.

Honesty

- We adhere to the highest standards of accuracy and truth in advancing the interests of those we represent and in communicating with the public.

Expertise

- We acquire and responsibly use specialized knowledge and experience.
- We advance the profession through continued professional development, research, and education.
- We build mutual understanding, credibility, and relationships among a wide array of institutions and audiences.

Independence

- We provide objective counsel to those we represent.
- We are accountable for our actions.

Loyalty

- We are faithful to those we represent, while honoring our obligation to serve the public interest.

Fairness

- We deal fairly with clients, employers, competitors, peers, vendors, the media, and the general public.
- We respect all opinions and support the right of free expression.

PRSA CODE PROVISIONS
FREE FLOW OF INFORMATION

Core Principle

- Protecting and advancing the free flow of accurate and truthful information is essential to serving the public interest and contributing to informed decision-making in a democratic society.

Intent

- To maintain the integrity of relationships with the media, government officials, and the public.
- To aid informed decision-making.

Guidelines

A member shall:

- Preserve the integrity of the process of communication.
- Be honest and accurate in all communications.
- Act promptly to correct erroneous communications for which the practitioner is responsible.
- Preserve the free flow of unprejudiced information when giving or receiving gifts by ensuring that gifts are nominal, legal, and infrequent.

Examples of Improper Conduct Under This Provision

- A member representing a ski manufacturer gives a pair of expensive racing skis to a sports magazine columnist to influence the columnist to write favorable articles about the product.
- A member entertains a government official beyond legal limits and/or in violation of government reporting requirements.

COMPETITION

Core Principle

- Promoting healthy and fair competition among professionals preserves an ethical climate while fostering a robust business environment.

Intent

- To promote respect and fair competition among public relations professionals.
- To serve the public interest by providing the widest choice of practitioner options.

Guidelines

A member shall:

- Follow ethical hiring practices designed to respect free and open competition without deliberately undermining a competitor.
- Preserve intellectual property rights in the marketplace.

Examples of Improper Conduct Under This Provision

- A member employed by a "client organization" shares helpful information with a counseling firm that is competing with others for the organization's business.
- A member spreads malicious and unfounded rumors about a competitor in order to alienate the competitor's clients and employees in a ploy to recruit people and business.

DISCLOSURE OF INFORMATION

Core Principle

- Open communication fosters informed decision-making in a democratic society.

Intent

- To build trust with the public by revealing all information needed for responsible decision making.

Guidelines

A member shall:

- Be honest and accurate in all communications.
- Act promptly to correct erroneous communications for which the member is responsible.
- Investigate the truthfulness and accuracy of information released on behalf of those represented.
- Reveal the sponsors for causes and interests represented.
- Disclose financial interest (such as stock ownership) in a client's organization.
- Avoid deceptive practices.

Examples of Improper Conduct Under This Provision

- Front groups: A member implements "grass roots" campaigns or letter-writing campaigns to legislators on behalf of undisclosed interest groups.
- Lying by omission: A practitioner for a corporation knowingly fails to release financial information, giving a misleading impression of the corporation's performance.
- A member discovers inaccurate information disseminated via a Web site or media kit and does not correct the information.
- A member deceives the public by employing people to pose as volunteers to speak at public hearings and participate in "grass roots" campaigns.

SAFEGUARDING CONFIDENCES

Core Principle

- Client trust requires appropriate protection of confidential and private information.

Intent

- To protect the privacy rights of clients, organizations, and individuals by safeguarding confidential information.

Guidelines

A member shall:

- Safeguard the confidences and privacy rights of present, former, and prospective clients and employees.
- Protect privileged, confidential, or insider information gained from a client or organization.
- Immediately advise an appropriate authority if a member discovers that confidential information is being divulged by an employee of a client company or organization.

Examples of Improper Conduct Under This Provision

- A member changes jobs, takes confidential information, and uses that information in the new position to the detriment of the former employer.
- A member intentionally leaks proprietary information to the detriment of some other party.

CONFLICTS OF INTEREST

Core Principle

- Avoiding real, potential, or perceived conflicts of interest builds the trust of clients, employers, and the publics.

Intent

- To earn trust and mutual respect with clients or employers.
- To build trust with the public by avoiding or ending situations that put one's personal or professional interests in conflict with society's interests.

Guidelines

A member shall:

- Act in the best interests of the client or employer, even subordinating the member's personal interests.

- Avoid actions and circumstances that may appear to compromise good business judgment or create a conflict between personal and professional interests.
- Disclose promptly any existing or potential conflict of interest to affected clients or organizations.
- Encourage clients and customers to determine if a conflict exists after notifying all affected parties.

Examples of Improper Conduct Under This Provision

- The member fails to disclose that he or she has a strong financial interest in a client's chief competitor.
- The member represents a "competitor company" or a "conflicting interest" without informing a prospective client.

ENHANCING THE PROFESSION

Core Principle

- Public relations professionals work constantly to strengthen the public's trust in the profession.

Intent

- To build respect and credibility with the public for the profession of public relations.
- To improve, adapt, and expand professional practices.

Guidelines

A member shall:

- Acknowledge that there is an obligation to protect and enhance the profession.
- Keep informed and educated about practices in the profession to ensure ethical conduct.
- Actively pursue personal professional development.
- Decline representation of clients or organizations that urge or require actions contrary to this Code.
- Accurately define what public relations activities can accomplish.
- Counsel subordinates in proper ethical decision-making.
- Require that subordinates adhere to the ethical requirements of the Code.
- Report ethical violations, whether committed by PRSA members or not, to the appropriate authority.

Examples of Improper Conduct Under This Provision

- A PRSA member declares publicly that a product the client sells is safe, without disclosing evidence to the contrary.
- A member initially assigns some questionable client work to a nonmember practitioner to avoid the ethical obligation of PRSA membership.

RESOURCES

Rules and Guidelines

The following PRSA documents, available in *The Blue Book*, provide detailed rules and guidelines to help guide your professional behavior:

- PRSA Bylaws
- PRSA Administrative Rules
- Member Code of Ethics

If, after reviewing them, you still have a question or issue, contact PRSA headquarters as noted below.

QUESTIONS

The PRSA is here to help. Whether you have a serious concern or simply need clarification, contact Judy Voss at judy.voss@prsa.org.

PRSA Member Code of Ethics Pledge

I pledge:

To conduct myself professionally, with truth, accuracy,
fairness and responsibility to the public;
to improve my individual competence and advance the
knowledge and proficiency of the profession through
continuing research and education;
and to adhere to the articles of the Member Code
of Ethics 2000 for the practice of public relations as adopted
by the governing Assembly of the
Public Relations Society of America.

I understand and accept that there is a consequence for
misconduct, up to and including membership revocation.

And, I understand that those who have been or are sanctioned by a
government agency or convicted in a court of law of an action that
is in violation of this Code may be barred from membership or
expelled from the Society.

_____

Signature

_____

Date

CODE OF ETHICS—AMERICAN MARKETING ASSOCIATION (AMA)

Members of the American Marketing Association are committed to ethical professional conduct. They have joined together in subscribing to this Code of Ethics embracing the following topics:

Responsibilities of the Marketer

Marketers must accept responsibility for the consequences of their activities and make every effort to ensure that their decisions, recommendations, and actions function to identify, serve, and satisfy all relevant publics: customers, organizations, and society.

Marketers' Professional Conduct must be guided by:

1. The basic rule of professional ethics: not knowingly to do harm;
2. The adherence to all applicable laws and regulations;
3. The accurate representation of their education, training, and experience; and
4. The active support, practice, and promotion of this Code of Ethics.

Honesty and Fairness

Marketers shall uphold and advance the integrity, honor, and dignity of the profession by:

1. Being honest in serving consumers, clients, employees, suppliers, distributors, and the public;
2. Not knowingly participating in conflict of interest without prior notice to all parties involved; and
3. Establishing equitable fee schedules including the payment or receipt of usual, customary, and/or legal compensation for marketing exchanges.

Rights and Duties of Parties in the Marketing Exchange Process

Participants in the marketing exchange process should be able to expect that:

1. Products and services offered are safe and fit for their intended uses;
2. Communications about offered products and services are not deceptive;
3. All parties intend to discharge their obligations, financial and otherwise, in good faith; and
4. Appropriate internal methods exist for equitable adjustment and/or redress of grievances concerning purchases.

It is understood that the above would include, but is not limited to, the following responsibilities of the marketer:

In the area of product development and management:

- Disclosure of all substantial risks associated with product or service usage;
- Identification of any product component substitution that might materially change the product or impact on the buyer's purchase decision;
- Identification of extra cost-added features.

In the area of promotions:

- Avoidance of false and misleading advertising;
- Rejection of high-pressure manipulations, or misleading sales tactics;
- Avoidance of sales promotions that use deception or manipulation.

In the area of distribution:

- Not manipulating the availability of a product for the purpose of exploitation;
- Not using coercion in the marketing channel;
- Not exerting undue influence over the reseller's choice to handle a product.

In the area of pricing:

- Not engaging in price fixing;
- Not practicing predatory pricing;
- Disclosing the full price associated with any purchase.

In the area of marketing research:

- Prohibiting selling or fundraising under the guise of conducting research;
- Maintaining research integrity by avoiding misrepresentation and omission of pertinent research data;
- Treating outside clients and suppliers fairly.

Organizational Relationships

Marketers should be aware of how their behavior may influence or impact the behavior of others in organizational relationships. They should not demand, encourage, or apply coercion to obtain unethical behavior in their relationships with others, such as employees, suppliers, or customers.

1. Apply confidentiality and anonymity in professional relationships with regard to privileged information;
2. Meet their obligations and responsibilities in contracts and mutual agreements in a timely manner;
3. Avoid taking the work of others, in whole, or in part, and representing this work as their own or directly benefiting from it without compensation or consent of the originator or owner; and

4. Avoid manipulation to take advantage of situations to maximize personal welfare in a way that unfairly deprives or damages the organization of others.

Any AMA member found to be in violation of any provision of this Code of Ethics may have his or her Association membership suspended or revoked.

American Marketing Association Code of Ethics for Marketing on the Internet

Preamble

The Internet, including online computer communications, has become increasingly important to marketers' activities, as they provide exchanges and access to markets worldwide. The ability to interact with stakeholders has created new marketing opportunities and risks that are not currently specifically addressed in the American Marketing Association Code of Ethics. The American Marketing Association Code of Ethics for Internet marketing provides additional guidance and direction for ethical responsibility in this dynamic area of marketing. The American Marketing Association is committed to ethical professional conduct and has adopted these principles for using the Internet, including online marketing activities utilizing network computers.

General Responsibilities

Internet marketers must assess the risks and take responsibility for the consequences of their activities. Internet marketers' professional conduct must be guided by:

1. Support of professional ethics to avoid harm by protecting the rights of privacy, ownership, and access.
2. Adherence to all applicable laws and regulations with no use of Internet marketing that would be illegal if conducted by mail, telephone, fax, or other media.
3. Awareness of changes in regulations related to Internet marketing.
4. Effective communication to organizational members on risks and policies related to Internet marketing, when appropriate.
5. Organizational commitment to ethical Internet practices communicated to employees, customers, and relevant stakeholders.

Privacy

Information collected from customers should be confidential and used only for expressed purposes. All data, especially confidential customer data, should be safeguarded against unauthorized access. The expressed wishes of others should be respected with regard to the receipt of unsolicited E-mail messages.

Ownership

Information obtained from the Internet sources should be properly authorized and documented. Information ownership should be safeguarded and respected. Marketers should respect the integrity and ownership of computer and network systems.

Access

Marketers should treat access to accounts, passwords, and other information as confidential, and only examine or disclose content when authorized by a responsible party. The integrity of others' information systems should be respected with regard to placement of information, advertising, or messages.

ADVERTISING ETHICS AND PRINCIPLES—
AMERICAN ADVERTISING FEDERATION (AAF)

Truth

Advertising shall tell the truth, and shall reveal significant facts, the omission of which would mislead the public.

Substantiation

Advertising claims shall be substantiated by evidence in possession of the advertiser and advertising agency, prior to making such claims.

Comparisons

Advertising shall refrain from making false, misleading, or unsubstantiated statements or claims about a competitor or his/her products or services.

Bait Advertising

Advertising shall not offer products or services for sale unless such offer constitutes a bona fide effort to sell the advertising products or services and is not a device to switch consumers to other goods or services, usually higher priced.

Guarantees and Warranties

Advertising of guarantees and warranties shall be explicit, with sufficient information to apprise consumers of their principal terms and limitations or, when space or time restrictions preclude such disclosures, the advertisement should clearly reveal where the full text of the guarantee or warranty can be examined before purchase.

Price Claims

Advertising shall avoid price claims which are false or misleading, or saving claims which do not offer provable savings.

Testimonials

Advertising containing testimonials shall be limited to those of competent witnesses who are reflecting a real and honest opinion or experience.

Taste and Decency

Advertising shall be free of statements, illustrations, or implications which are offensive to good taste or public decency.

* Adopted by the American Advertising Federation Board of Directors, March 2, 1984, San Antonio.

Glossary

Analytical Process   A process in which action in each step is determined by the information acquired and decisions made in previous steps.

Attitudes   Collections of beliefs organized around an issue or event that predispose behavior.

B

Beliefs   Inferences we make about ourselves and the world around us.

Brainstorming   A structured group creative exercise to generate as many ideas as possible in a specified amount of time.

C

Channel   The conduit or medium through which messages are sent to a specific public to accomplish a specific purpose.

Communication Confirmation Table   A visual tool used to validate the logic of a communications plan.

Confidence Level   The percentage of certainty that the results of a survey would be the same if replicated.

Cooperative Communities   Relationship-based interaction among all members of a community to achieve individual and collective goals.

Copy Outline   An analytical tool that extends strategic planning to creation of effective tactics.

Creativity   The process of looking outside ourselves and our routine to discover new ideas and innovative solutions.

Crisis Management   The process of anticipating and preparing to mediate problems that could affect an organization's environment and profitability.

D

Demographic Data   Information used to segment publics according to tangible characteristics such as age, gender, and socioeconomic status.

Disinformation   Information that is intentionally inaccurate or misleading.

Diversity   Appreciating differences in culture, gender, race, background, and experience.

E

Ethical Codes   Written and formalized standards of behavior used as guidelines for decision making.

Ethics   Personal and professional value systems and standards that underlie decisions and behavior.

Evaluation Criteria   Standards set to measure success.

Evaluation Tools   Methods used to gather data needed to assess whether or not evaluation criteria were met.

Executive Summary   A concise overview of a document's key points and conclusions targeted to key decision makers.

F

Focus Group   Moderator-led discussions with fewer than 15 participants providing in-depth information on attitudes and behaviors.

Formal Research   Data gathering structured according to accepted rules of research.

Frame of Reference   The collection of experiences, knowledge, culture, and environment that forms our perceptual screen.

G

Goal   The result or desired outcome that solves a problem, takes advantage of an opportunity, or meets a challenge.

I

Influential   A formal or informal opinion leader that can serve as an intervening public to carry the message to your public or can influence your public to act.

Informal Research　Data gathering that does not follow specific rules.

Interactivity　The degree to which the tactic provides interaction between the sender of the message and the receiver.

Intervening Public　An individual or public used as a message channel to reach and influence a key public.

Issue Management　A long-term approach to identifying and resolving issues before they become problems or crises.

K

Key Public/Audience　Segmented groups of people whose support and cooperation are essential to the long-term survival of an organization or the short-term accomplishment of its objectives.

M

Misinformation　Information that is unintentionally inaccurate or misleading.

N

Nonprobability Sampling　Survey of whoever is available.

Nonsampling Error　A mistake made in selecting the sample and designing and implementing the questionnaire.

O

Objective　Specific, measurable statements of what needs to be accomplished to reach the goal.

Opinion Leader　A trusted individual to whom one turns for advice because of his/her greater knowledge or experience regarding the issue at hand.

P

Panel Study　Respondents who have agreed to be surveyed repeatedly to track opinion and attitude change over time.

Partnership　A mutually beneficial short- or long-term cooperative relationship to reach common goals.

Personal Drop-off　Personally delivering a survey for later pick-up or mailing.

Persuasion　Disseminating information to appeal for a change in attitudes, opinions, and/or behavior.

Planning　The process of using research to chart the step-by-step course to solve a problem, take advantage of an opportunity, or meet a challenge.

Primary Messages　Sound bite statements that encompass what you need the public to do and an appeal to the public's self-interest to act.

Primary Research　Firsthand information gathered specifically for your current purpose.

Probability Sampling　Every individual in the population has an equal chance of being selected.

Professionalism　Characteristics and behavior befitting a professional.

Psychographic Data　Information used to segment publics according to values, attitudes, and lifestyles.

Public Opinion　What most people in a particular public express about an issue that affects them.

Public Relations　An organization's efforts to establish and maintain mutually beneficial relationships in order to communicate and cooperate with the publics upon whom long-term success depends.

Purposive Sampling　Identifying and surveying opinion leaders to determine attitudes and behaviors.

Q

Qualitative Research　Focuses on individual cases or groups that are not statistically representative of a given population.

Quantitative Research　Gathers statistical data for analysis

R

Relationship Building　A return to the roots of human communication and persuasion that focuses on personal trust and mutual cooperation.

Research　Gathering information to clarify an issue and solve a problem.

Research-based　When decision making in the planning and implementation process is based on the acquisition, interpretation, and application of relevant facts.

S

Sampling Error   Measured as margin of error, it indicates the possible percentage variation of the sample data from the whole population.

Secondary Messages   Bulleted details that include facts, testimonials, examples, and all other information or persuasive arguments that support a primary message.

Secondary Research   Information previously assimilated for other purposes that can be adapted to your needs.

Segmentation   Defining and separating publics by demographics and psychographics to ensure more effective communication.

Selective Perception   The inherent human function of selecting from the millions of daily stimuli only those messages one chooses to perceive.

Selective Retention   The inherent human function of selecting from the hundreds of stimuli perceived only those messages one chooses to retain.

Self-interest   The fundamental motivation for an individual's behavior.

Strategic Communications Planning   An approach to communications planning that focuses actions on the accomplishment of organizational goals.

Strategic Function   One that contributes significantly to the accomplishment of an organization's mission and goals.

Strategic Management   The process of evaluating all proposed action by focusing on organizational goals, usually defined in short-term contributions to the bottom line.

Strategies   Public-specific approaches specifying the channel to send the messages to achieve objectives.

Stratified Sampling   Selecting the sample to ensure proportionate representation of segments within the universe.

Slogan or Theme   Short, catchy phrase that integrates primary messages and appeals to the broad interests of many key publics.

T

Tactics   Strategy-specific communication products that carry the message to key publics.

Tag Line   A short summarizing theme that appears at the end of a slogan or advertisement.

Triggering Event   An event that transforms readiness to act into actual behavior.

Trust   An emotional judgment of one's credibility and performance on issues of importance.

V

Values   Core beliefs or beliefs central to an individual's cognitive system.

Index